THE
INTERNATIONAL
DESIGN
YEARBOOK

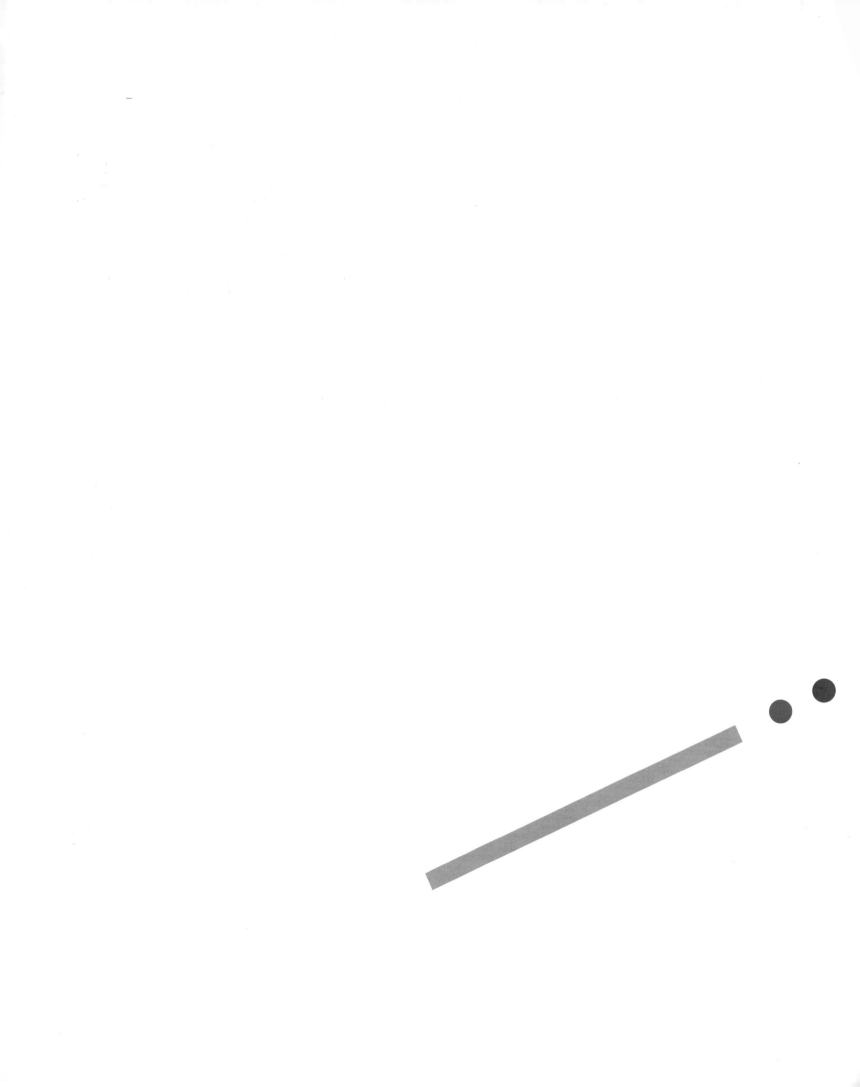

THE
INTERNATIONAL
DESIGN
YEARBOOK

1992

Editor
Andrée Putman

General Editor
Rick Poynor

Assistant Editor
Jennifer Hudson

THAMES AND HUDSON

First published in Great Britain in 1992
by Thames and Hudson Ltd, London

This book was produced by
John Calmann and King Ltd, London

Based on an original idea by
Stuart Durant

Designed by Michael Phillips
Typeset by Wyvern Typesetting, Bristol
Origination by Toppan, Singapore
Printed in Italy

Andrée Putman would like to thank Rick Poynor, Jennifer Hudson
and the staff at John Calmann and King who were involved in the
preparation of this book, especially Jane Havell. The publishers and
both the Editors would like to thank the designers and manufacturers
who submitted work for inclusion; Junko Popham for her help in
collecting the Japanese contributions; Kenneth M. Butti of Electronic
Book Publishing in Tokyo, and the following photographers and
copyright holders for the use of their material:

Arrici & Bernardi 4.4; Satoshi Asakawa 1.11, 12; Aldo Ballo 1.3;
Ed Barber 4.7, 8; Chris Barnes 5.18; Gaston Bergeret 1.27; Tom Bernsten 5. 27;
John Bessler 1.53; Jon Betthauser 5.57; Patric Blake 5.53;
M. Boudinet 1.111, 5.63, 65; Andrew Brown 3.47, 48; Patricia Canino page 7;
Michael Chan 5.20, 21, 22, 23; Penelope Chauvilot 1.26; Joseph Coscia Jr 1.43;
Corrado Crisciani 3.9; Nick Crowe 5.24; Philip Davis 5.75;
Jan-Kees de Jager 5.10, 11, 12, 13; Design Studio TAD 5.91;
Alain Dovifat 1.7, 61, 62, 4.11; Frédéric Dumas 3.30; Rick English 5.30;
Fachinetti 2.22; Siggi Fischer 2.39; Mitsumasa Fujitsuka 5.15;
Gottschall Foto Design 1.13, 2.40; Léon Gulikers 3.14, 15, 19; Ian Haigh 3.22;
Hans Hansen 1.74, 132, 2.15, 45; James Haworth 1.6;
Marcus Hilton 1.87, 89, 94, 95, 3.20; J. Hoflehner 5.37;
J. Hoflehner & G. Zugmann 5.38; Hector Ibanez 4.19; Hiroyasu Ito 5.89;
Marcus Jans 1.86; Elliot Kaufman 1.31; Izu Kenro 5.49; Andy Knight 1.100;
Karin Knoblich 1.101, 102, 103; Koji Koboyashi 5.8, 9; Soich Kondo 5.19;
Harri Korhonen 1.68; Dan Kramer 3.1, 2, 3; Per Kruss 5.41;
Carlo Lavatori 1.105; Athos Lecce 3.4; Till Leeser 2.30;
Frederik Liberath 4.15, 16, 17; Jonathan Marks 5.29; Michael McDonald 1.38;
Masaru Mera 5.14; Nacasa & Partners 1.5, 5.74; Takeshi Nakasa 4.25;
Guido A. Niest 3.8; Odeon Studio 3.42; Lluis Padrissa 2.35;
Sascha Panknin 1.114, 115; Peter Paterson 1.28; Christof Piepenstock 1.47;
Pjotr 3.31; Professional Photo 1.32; Jaroslav Prokop 1.36; John Rigby 3.36;
Gilles Rousset 3.27; Benvenuto Saba 1.135, 136, 137, 138; Abby Sadin 1.134;
Rudy Schmutz 1.71; Roberto Sellitto 1.3; Akira Shimizu 2.3;
Kishin Shinayama 1.1; Siepke & Riemenschneider 4.3; Rick Skacan 1.73, 5.25;
Alberto Smuragua 3.28; Ib Sørensen 5.92; Studio Azzurro 2.17, 18;
Studio Bettina Rheims 4.9, 10; Studio Lippa 3.41; Studio Marcone 4.20;
Studiovisus 1.81; C. Suarez 2.19; L. Sully Jaulms 1.65, 66, 5.47;
Luciano Svegliado 2.6; Don Sweney 3.40; Hisanori Taguchi 5.39;
Isao Takahashi 3.5; Yoshio Takase 1.117; Toshiba Corporation 5.58;
Emilio Tremolada 2.25, 29; Hiroshi Tsukada 5.90; Hiroshi Tsukinoki 1.97, 5.26;
Nick Turner 2.11, 5.17; Tom Vack 1.51, 57, 58, 2.1, 2;
David van den Branden & Dan Machnik 5.88; Tucker Viemeister 3.29;
Deidi von Schaewen pages 8, 9; Woka 2.27; Michael Wurzbach 2.41, 42;
Mel Yates 5.36; Tetsuo Yuasa 1.25; Andrea Zani 1.129, 2.7, 8, 9;
Zimmermann 1.9.

As I worked on this edition of *The International Design Yearbook* I began to have misgivings about taking on such a project when my thoughts on the subject were becoming much less positive than before. When I came to express my doubts to young designers and artists, however, I realised I was not alone in my views. They seemed to be thinking along similar lines, and told me that the things I wanted to say needed to be said.

Design has turned into a tool of fame; designers have become world stars and gurus. A kettle for boiling your water in the morning cannot simply be designed in the old, anonymous way—the kettle's owner wants to know about the designer's lifestyle, what he or she looks like, how much money he or she makes, what he or she wears. Fashion, hype and meaningless trends have invaded the design worlds, and chairs now date more quickly than hemlines. High Tech, for example, became a trend and trends by definition are always short-lived; High Tech died of self-sabotage. Yet the idea behind it—the glorification of the industrial environment—was fine. New York painters invented High Tech out of necessity—they wanted huge, beautiful, industrial spaces, sparsely furnished, in which to work and live. Now I have been told about a businessman who *re*designed a Park Avenue apartment into a 'loft' space, adding pipes to the ceiling! Designers themselves have fallen into that trap. What gets into the news is constant change, the creation of new trends. What is so painful about this fashion cycle is the way in which ideas are at first scorned, then adored, then misused and finally rejected, whatever their value. I believe design is the material aspect of a message or a feeling; it is a way of expression, not a trend or a product of consumption.

Personally, I am interested in things which have a continuity, a fundamental strength in themselves which allows them not to fall into limbo. In the same showroom where I introduce people like Eileen Gray (who pushed Le Corbusier to design furniture), Mallet Stevens and Pierre Chareau, I also produce the work of young designers such as Sylvain Dubuisson, Paul Mathieu, Michael Ray and Patrick Naggar, the New York-based Egyptian architect. Nobody has ever asked when any of these designers was born, if they were dead, if they were young. Is it important to know whether a chair has been designed recently? Clients do not come to me with the intention of ignoring re-editions; nobody says, 'I want only the brand new, the real thing, the sign of today.' This is what I want to prove in my own collections.

Recently, I was with a young designer who lived on a boat. He had absolutely no money. He went to the Swedish furniture chain Ikea for many things, but he modified each piece, giving to the objects his personal perception, his vision of their existence in his own world. He was an 'artisan designer'. It seemed to me so important, this freedom to go back to basics, to be truly individual. If he is successful, I am afraid he will be designated just a 'designer'. Handcraft has little prestige now, although it is how the design activity started. Often, artisans fear humiliation in front of designers, because unless designers are unusually sympathetic they treat artisans like tools. Despite this, there are still many young people who want to be artisans,

Andrée Putman

craftspeople, woodworkers. It is the parents, rather than their children, who object to the idea of apprenticeship: it reminds them of poverty! In this way, the values of the 1980s have certainly started to imprison us. Design consumers have appeared, design stars are born. In some circles, design has become a kind of addiction.

In my case, encouragement to start my own company came from a few interior design jobs I had done in a rather clandestine way for friends. I did not take myself too seriously. I started with a kind of doubt; I needed a frame, a calmer way of looking at things, and it opened a field. It revealed an obsession in my work for continuity, permanence, eternity. These are the elements that I have always looked for in the pieces that have impressed me most in my life: the Katsura garden in Tokyo, Chinese art, Egyptian art, Matisse. A house in Saint Tropez which I designed in 1962 (for a friend who later became French Minister of Culture) remained for years as a place that did not age, something so simple and so classic that for a small group of people this quality of 'agelessness' became my hallmark. People said later, 'After ten years it looks as if it had been done yesterday. You should go on!' And so I did.

The name 'Ecart' means out of the main stream; marginal; apart; on the side. Its mirrored image, its anagram, reads 'Trace', which speaks for itself. In my re-editions I realised that my choice was dictated by pieces that would never date. I like restraint, reticence in details, so that an effect almost disappears. I do not mind if it takes, as I was once told, three days to see a detail in my work. This quality does not come across particularly well in photographs, but I like effects that are very simple, almost 'anti-design', something with a mystery which reveals itself only slowly.

For many years I have been criticising French self-satisfaction, the nostalgia for Versailles, the love of power and status signs. Everything I liked was regarded as inappropriate, even disgraceful—especially in art. This is why I so much dislike the conventional and dictatorial notion of good taste. In my opinion, real good taste is the conjunction of personality, self-confidence, the ability to discriminate and creation of a style—your own style, not an adopted one. The usual idea of good taste is a kind of imposture; it ruins spontaneity. Good taste is a bore because it does not really exist, except as a dark cloud obscuring one's personal judgement with the fear of what other people will think. Fear of choosing something in 'bad taste' inhibits people's approach to design. Will it match this? Will it work next to that? are questions that you hear constantly.

Entrance to the men's salon at the hairdressers CARITA, Paris, 1988.

I remain optimistic, however, because I see examples of people who have forced themselves out of such constraints. I often come back to the example of artists: almost any artist's home is interesting, because the lack of inhibition makes for the liveliest possible interior and use of objects. Design has not only to do with beauty: it has to do with wit and charm, the humour or playfulness that animates an idea. I own a number of objects which appeared, when I acquired them, to be simply ugly. But I found myself liking them because they contain great charm and feeling. This is not a designer's attitude, I admit, but it is an attitude that allows me to have enormous fun and imagine all kinds of stories about furniture and objects. For example, I have a model of the Eiffel Tower, which unexpectedly contains a clock. To me it is fascinating, partly because I endow it with all sorts of things that have nothing to do with it, and partly because of the way in which it is displayed.

It is bourgeois and boring to believe that everything considered as 'design' has to be expensive. There is a moral beauty in objects like the Shaker furniture, which are related to a whole philosophy and a way of living; they retain their power and attraction even today. I want to convince people that almost anything can be beautiful, that it is possible to mix costly pieces with junk. It is almost an ethical principle. People should become more aware of what they put in their homes, because an interior is a kind of conversation, a form of self-description. Projects of my own, such as Morgan's Hotel in New York, might appear to represent the conventional idea of good taste, but this is only because they have achieved acceptance. Morgan's integrated new ideas of hotel hospitality: it broke every rule. It ignored all the standard ways of ensuring success; there was not even a name on the door. This approach extended to the staff, their appearance and the way they behaved. Too much politeness is unbearable; nobody wants that any more and, if they do, they will not find it at Morgan's. These things were such an assault on conventional notions of hotel manners that at one time they might have seemed to be in 'bad taste'!

Living room in a suite at the HOTEL IM WASSERTURM, Cologne, 1990.

My approach to design is built upon a few simple ideas. It does not have the unbelievably articulate thinking of, say, Mario Bellini. Most essential is the notion of seeing design as something unsystematic. I believe design kills itself by being too serious and thus conformist. It is quite important for me to address each design issue in a free, liberated and playful manner. I hope it is more humane and less intellectual than some other designers. When I enter a place I try to remain open-minded to let its spirit speak to me. One example is the CAPC Museum in Bordeaux, which had been used as a storage house for spices from the Antilles, India and elsewhere. The odour and the light, not to mention the spaces, were overwhelming, and stimulated me to dream of exotic places far away. This inspiration was translated into my design for the restaurant napkins which, instead of being a solid colour (standard design response), were made of batik patterns (I could almost imagine having discovered them in a wooden crate tucked away in the recesses of the building, remnants from a time long past).

Humour is also important: sometimes I like to tease those who enter the spaces I create. In the hotel Le Lac in Japan, I tried to make fun of the traditional, European, manner of using a bathroom. I made the sink free-standing and put it in front of a full-height picture window. Instead of being an enclosed space in which to bathe, the bathroom opens up into the hotel room. Funnily enough, this treatment, almost against the good sense of hotel design, turned out to underline the importance of the bath in Japanese culture. Such contradictions are for me the fuel for design, as are accidents and restrictions, because of the way they push you. They force you to create. Difficulty is challenge, it helps you to surpass yourself. For instance, the lack of daylight in the Wasserturm hotel helped me use something I had not touched for a long time: colour.

It is my belief that designers should remain out of the 'star system', fame and public view. They should search for new directions that are more sincere, because without sincerity nothing can be achieved. The designers of the Bauhaus were, above all, committed.

Guest room and bath at the HOTEL LE LAC, near Tokyo, 1990.

They were visionaries, optimists, dreamers; they had a remarkable obsession with human needs and how life could be organised for the better. Surely it is no accident that now, at the beginning of the nineties, one result of the huge changes in eastern Europe is that the Bauhaus is being reborn in Dessau, with the precise intention that its original ideals should be revived. Now, groups of architects and designers from all over the world are arriving to study there, to design new social housing and to create a humane architecture for ordinary people and not, as some architects did, to build Versailles for the poor.

The future will see a more eclectic approach to design. Offices will be installed in homes and more personality will be given to offices. Design will be less narcissistic, less intimidating, less invasive. It will be perceived, instead, as a sign of an individual's sensitivity, as a self-portrait, as a form of intellectual delicacy. In a troubled world, homes will increasingly be used as refuges, as places of consolation. Individuality is emerging very strongly; people seem to need to express themselves and to assert their differences. In Europe, we have rediscovered spirituality almost with relief, a new sense of curiosity and an increased awareness of the world. In the eighties, everything had to be fast and to make money. It was the triumph of the image: 'I have an image, therefore I exist.' It was fashionable to be in a hurry, to telephone from a car, to fax from home. By the end of the decade, however, there was a flood of baroque or very nostalgic forms. I find it quite odd, this type of inconsistency: it is replete with hypocrisy.

I am hopeful that today there is an ever-growing number of individuals who, in their daily life, express simplicity and a return to basics—even though a glance at many homes reveals interiors decked out in the style of French chateaux. Fortunately, in the midst of this, we do have certain reassurances. Softness has reappeared. Silence, light, transparency, the balance between things pure and abstract, showing nature and health—they are all on the increase. The 'social worldliness' phenomenon has modified our attitude; culture has become an 'Esperanto'. I notice a certain movement towards a discretion in design, towards cleaning up and wiping out the excesses of the eighties. Designers should rely more on themselves, reflecting their own personality in their work. A good resolution could be to neglect aesthetic terrorism and return to this discretion, without falling into the 'déjà vu'. Innovation should not only be seen in the form of things. As Baudelaire remarked:

'Modernity applies to the manner but not the time.'

The seventh edition of *The International Design Yearbook* has been assembled at a time when design is by general consensus at a watershed. Pundits were pronouncing the 'design decade' over almost as soon as the clock struck midnight on 31 December 1989. But the real evidence that the bubble had finally burst was to come the following year as Britain and America went into recession. Design empires that were once the envy of colleagues around the world began to lay off staff by the dozen (and, in some cases, hundred); one or two broke up in spectacular crashes. Conran, Fitch, Michael Peters—even the most charmed names were rocked by a downturn in client spending and a growing feeling that design did not, contrary to the more optimistic assertions of the eighties, have all the answers. A British television quiz in which designers like Nigel Coates and Philippe Starck attempted to identify famous chairs and company logos for the doubtful benefit of the population at large struck a curiously misplaced note, as though someone had failed to tell the producers that the party was over, the music had come to an end, and most of the guests had gone home.

These are gloomy words with which to begin an introduction to the best designs of the last two years, but they reflect a change of mood and—for some designers—a change of heart that cannot be overlooked. Guest editor Andrée Putman makes exactly this point in her foreword. Design in the eighties became self-obsessed; it seemed to believe that it was an end in itself, and in the process lost contact with the other areas of culture and society that sustain it, shape it and give it meaning. Recognising this danger, the best designers have always looked outside design for inspiration and ideas. Putman herself studied musical composition with Nadia Boulanger and she makes no secret of finding other areas of culture, particularly painting and the visual arts, far more stimulating than design. Yet design, though it should hardly need repeating, *is* a cultural activity, as well as a commercial one—different from, but on a par with the other arts. One of the most depressing signs of design's fallen status in Britain is the way that newspapers rushed to introduce regular design columns, only to drop them when it was no longer the buzzword of the hour, or they published design stories under the neutral heading of 'style'—a sure sign that the editors, despite a decade of design, had failed to grasp what the subject was about. What chance the public?

So where does design go from here? In advertising-starved magazines that once wrote so feverishly about the latest shop opening, restaurant, or hand-sculpted one-off posing as art, there is bracing talk of new agendas and the emergence of a new, less extravagant aesthetic. After a decade in which design identified itself openly and enthusiastically with the consumerist causes of fashion, luxury, lifestyle and packaging, attention is switching—in theory at least, if not yet very often in practice—to design for social need and the public good. It is too early, however, to say where this sudden penitent embrace of social responsibility and 'green' values will lead, or whether many designers will be able to sustain the logic of such a position, however sincerely held, in the chill wind of commercial reality. To do so would mean

Rick Poynor

reconciling themselves to smaller budgets, less glamorous projects and greatly reduced revenues. It would mean leaner offices and a much higher level of individual commitment. It would require a self-sacrificing reorientation of design as a profession that seems, in the late twentieth century, highly unlikely to occur.

What is more likely is that designers will learn new ways to present their services to clients and society. If the word 'design' has temporarily become an embarrassment, or lost its allure, then perhaps it could be changed for something less familiar and more seductive. Design consultants, particularly those with clients in Japan, are starting to use terms like 'cultural engineering' to suggest the complex role that design has to play in the way that corporations present themselves to the world. Naoki Sakai of Water Studio in Tokyo prefers to call himself a 'conceptor'. The conceptor does not wait for the manufacturer's marketing department to tell him what to design: he dreams up the product, on the basis of his understanding of the tastes, desires and emotions of the consumer, then talks the manufacturer into making it. The design work begins only when the client has been thoroughly persuaded of the validity of the 'concept'—almost invariably nostalgic in nature. Manufactured in limited editions and sold by advance order, Water Studio's retro-concepts include the Olympus *Ecru* and *O-product* cameras (*International Design Yearbook 1990/91*), the Suzuki *SW-1* motorbike and the *Pao* car for Nissan.

'Our work specifically involves remembering and researching the past,' says Sakai, 'investigating and observing the present, and dreaming about what might be, should be, could be. We have drawn up a complete map of people's desires—and now we can think about how to design those desires' (*Blueprint* No. 79, July/August 1991). In reality, of course, this is desire-creation in the time-honoured advertising sense, though given a technological boost by the techniques of just-in-time production. By playing on the consumer's desire for exclusivity, boredom with mass production and the standard ubiquitous model is defeated, and demand is provoked.

The extent to which such an approach could be applied in the west remains to be seen. While demand for Water Studio's concepts has been high, Japanese consumers accustomed to instant gratification have not reacted well to delays in supply. But the conceptor's conviction that the consumer longs to be different from the mass, though fraught with contradiction (these are editions of 20,000, after all), certainly coincides with Andrée Putman's observation that individuality has become a central issue in design. Putman's argument is precisely that design, however much it tries to tie up our desires with its concepts, cannot answer *all* our needs. Although she has designed apartments for other people, specifying all the furniture as a matter of course, she has come to feel that it is wrong for designers to attempt to impose their taste, and their system for living, on the domestic circumstances of their clients (the public spaces she continues to design are of necessity more structured). Designers can supply many of the tools that make for a rewarding life, but the way in which they are combined in the home should be a matter for the individual to decide—a point implicitly made by Achille Castiglioni's infinitely adjustable shelf unit for Zanotta (page 83).

Such thoughts lead Andrée Putman to value a certain reticence in design. Examined overall, this is a quieter collection than any of its predecessors. Partly this reflects the kind of designs being produced. This is not a time for manifestos. There is less unchecked experiment. Furniture manufacturers are more cautious about producing wild and unsaleable designs, no matter how much impact they might make on the catwalks of Milan. Milan itself was postponed after 29 years in the autumn, from September 1990 to the following April, a telling indicator of the uncertainty which, in mid-1991, pervades the furniture business at all levels. This was a year in which even Ron Arad turned in a collection of accessible upholstered pieces (for Moroso) alongside his more uncompromising and expensive metal designs. Isolated pieces such as Nigel Coates's extravagant *Delfino* wardrobe and shelving system and, as always, the entire outlandish output of Bořek Šípek, stood out for daring to go against the pinched, recessionary mood of the fair. In product design, too, there are fewer surprises. The day of the post-modern refrigerator appears, for the time being at least, to be over. The deconstructed radios that the advance guard of the early eighties seemed to herald *en masse* have not materialized a decade later, although the products category as a whole looks strong.

While restraint might be one characteristic of the designs of the early nineties, it is a quality further emphasised in the editing of this *Yearbook*. Andrée Putman was not as rigorous as some past editors in excluding designs simply because they have yet to make it (or have no chance whatsoever of making it) into mass production. She *was* rigorous in excluding the convoluted, tortuous, pretentious and banal. Sometimes this meant over-emphatic one-off 'art' furniture and objects; sometimes it meant mass or batch production pieces that were pointlessly contrived in conception, needlessly complex in construction, or just clumsily resolved. The furniture, lighting, tableware, textiles and products Andrée Putman favours are united by the economy and elegance with which they resolve the problems they set out to address. They are rarely unassuming, yet with a handful of dramatic exceptions—Šípek, Arad, Starck, Gavoille—they avoid the loud, declamatory gestures and over-determined presence we have come to expect from experimental design in the last decade. Their reticent virtues are most aptly summed up by the British designer Jasper Morrison, creator of a remarkable range of simple plywood cupboards for Cappellini, whose only drawback is their inordinate cost. But Jasper Morrison pieces at Ikea prices: now that really would be a revolution in taste.

FURNITU

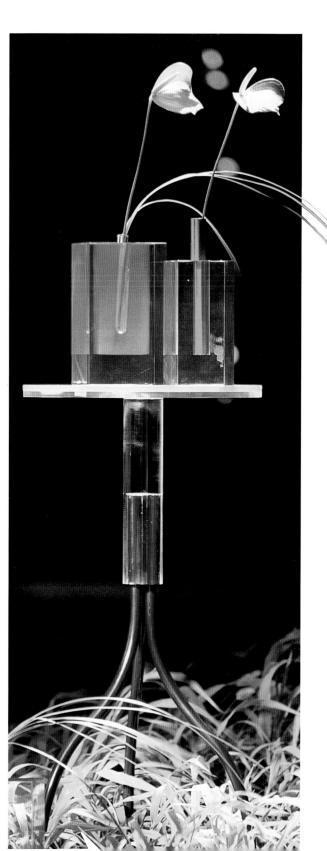

The decision of the organisers of the Milan Furniture Fair to move the Salone from its customary date in September to April of the following year sent shock waves through the international furniture community. If the most prestigious and keenly attended event of the furniture calendar was in difficulty, as this unprecedented manoeuvre suggested, then it was clear that the euphoria that had marked successive Milans since the beginning of the eighties, and the seismic arrival of Memphis, would now be replaced by a mood of caution.

At the thirtieth Salone in 1991, art, flamboyance and the furniture of extremes were the exceptions rather than the rule. Only a few designers could compare with the poetic brilliance of Shiro Kuramata (left), who died in 1991. In a climate of recession, companies are less inclined to manufacture pieces they have little hope of selling simply for the sake of the publicity they might generate and the glory they reflect on other, less experimental designs. In recent years, furniture has often been likened to fashion, with Milan as the ultimate catwalk. The dubious logic of this superficially attractive resemblance is now more obvious than ever, since only the most affluent could afford to change a sofa every season, and only the most design-obsessed would want to. Major companies such as Cassina are resisting the pressure to supply a continuous stream of novelties. The emphasis now is on designs that will last.

Andrée Putman catches something of this swing back to first principles in her selection. The virtues she favours are traditional: refinement of line, quality of finish, delicacy rather than daring, restraint as opposed to excess. 'I think we should discourage that kind of furniture because it's hurting design,' she says of those pieces that aspire too clumsily to be art. It is important, she says, that furniture should not be seen to be trying too hard. Its wit, like Kuramata's, should be effortless and uncontrived.

1 FURNITURE

Previous spread

1 SHIRO KURAMATA
STOOL
ACRYLIC, FEATHER
H 53.8cm (21⅛in) W 33cm (13in) D 39.8cm
(15⅝in)
MANUFACTURER: SHIRO KURAMATA, JAPAN

2 SHIRO KURAMATA
VASES
ACRYLIC STRUCTURE, TEST-TUBE VASE
Page 14: H 26cm (10¼in) W 27cm (10½in)
D 8cm (3⅛in)
Page 15, left: H 19cm (7½in) W 11cm (4⅜in)
D 11cm (4⅜in)
Right: H 16.5cm (6½in) W 8cm (3⅛in) D 8cm
(3⅛in)
MANUFACTURER: SHIRO KURAMATA, JAPAN

4

3

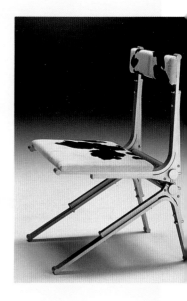

5

This spread

3 MARIO BOTTA
CHAIR, *BOTTA 91*
STEEL TUBE FRAME PAINTED BLACK, LEATHER
BACK AND SEAT
H 83cm (32⅝in) W 52cm (20½in) D 53cm
(20⅞in)
MANUFACTURER: ALIAS, ITALY

4 PAOLO RIZZATTO
SWIVEL CHAIR AND TABLE, *TREE*
DIE-CAST ALUMINIUM, OPEN-PORE LACQUERED
BEECH, CHERRYWOOD, BAND-PLAITED VIENNESE
STRAW
Chair: H 80cm (31½in) W 59cm (23in)
D 59cm (23in)
Table: H 60–75cm (23½–29½in) Di 60cm (23½in)
MANUFACTURER: ALIAS, ITALY

5 SHIN TAKAMATSU
CHAIR, *RACHEL*
ALUMINIUM, HIDE
H 81cm (31⅞in) W 50cm (19⅝in) D 56cm (22in)
MANUFACTURER: OKAMURA CORPORATION,
JAPAN

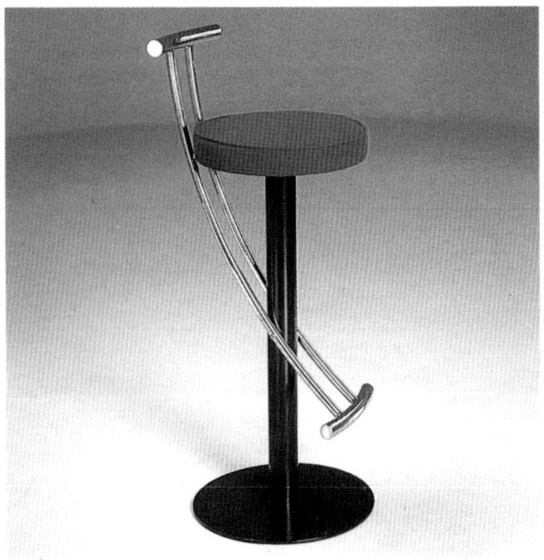

6

7

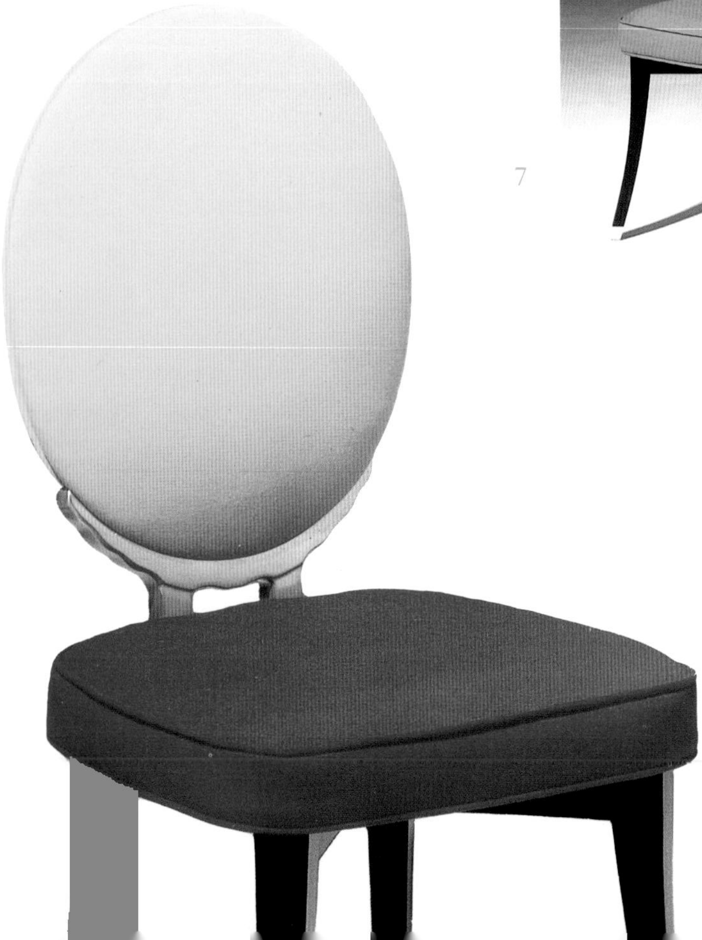

6 Paul Chamberlain and Peter Christian
Stool, *Oyster*
Mild steel, upholstered seat
H 96cm (37⅞in) W 40cm (15¾in) D 43cm (16⅞in)
Manufacturer: Primo Furniture, UK

7 Jean-Charles de Castelbajac
Chair, *My Funny Valentine*
Okoumé multi-plywood
H 92cm (36⅛in) W 43cm (16⅞in) D 51cm (20⅛in)
Manufacturer: Ligne Roset, France

8 Daniel Weil and Gerard Taylor
Children's furniture
Beech, lacquered beech
Punch and Judy show: H 118cm (46½in) W 45.5cm (17⅞in) D 5.5cm (2⅛in)
Cabinet: H 119cm (46⅞in) W 48cm (18⅞in) D 45.5cm (17⅞in)
Toy box: H 16cm (6½in) W 47.5cm (18¾in) D 45.5cm (17⅞in)
Wardrobe: H 135cm (53⅛in) W 48cm (18⅞in) D 46cm (18⅛in)
Bookshelf: H 115cm (45¼in) W 48cm (18⅞in) D 23cm (9in)
Chair: H 50cm (19⅝in) Di 32cm (12½in)
Table: H 67cm (26⅜in) W 63cm (24⅞in) D 53cm (20⅞in)
Manufacturer: Anthologie Quartett, Germany

9 Florian Borkenhagen
Screen, *Marché Aligre*
Fruit-box wood, sanded glass, steel
One-off
H 200cm (78¾in) W 180cm (70⅝in) D 2cm (¾in)
Manufacturer: Florian Borkenhagen, Italy

8

9

10

1 FURNITURE

10 CARLO BARTOLI
DINNER TABLE, *INDIA*
GRANITE
H 72cm (28¾in) W 160cm (63in) D 130cm
(51⅛in)
MANUFACTURER: ARTELANO, ITALY

11 FUMIO ENOMOTO
ARMCHAIR
STEEL PIPE, WOOD, PLYWOOD
Limited batch production
H 78cm (30¾in) W 53cm (20⅞in) D 51cm
(20⅛in)
MANUFACTURER: ISHIMARU, JAPAN

12 FUMIO ENOMOTO
TABLE
GLASS, STEEL
Limited batch production
H 72cm (28¾in) Di 80cm (31½in)
MANUFACTURER: ISHIMARU, JAPAN

13 TAKENOBU IGARASHI
STOOL, *ZAO*
ALUMINIUM, CAST IRON
H 45cm (17¾in) Di 34cm (13¾in)
MANUFACTURER: CLASSICON, GERMANY

11

12

13

14

Bořek Šípek is one of design's consummate showmen. On Driade's stand at the Milan Furniture Fair, slave-boys in loin-cloths dragged pieces from his new collection back and forth. At his showroom opening in the city, figures in goggles and capes moved through clouds of billowing smoke, while his fans waited on the pavement outside to get in. If there is one quality that unites Šípek's furniture to date, it is the total lack of preconceptions behind his choice of materials. He has used steel, copper, brass, wood, MDF and, most famously, rattan for a series of chairs for Driade. His most recent pieces for the company, however, see a narrowing of focus in materials and also, perhaps, in theme. Šípek's choice of medium—cherry wood—is conventional enough, but this only serves to accentuate a Hansel and Gretel quality that has always been implicit in his gnarled backrests and frilly tabletops, though never so baldly stated as in these ornately fretted panels and archaic forms. Swimming against every current of contemporary design, Šípek seems, more than ever, to be gazing into the past—not, perhaps, the past as it actually happened (though there are certainly hints of Biedermeier here), but a past of fairytale and myth.

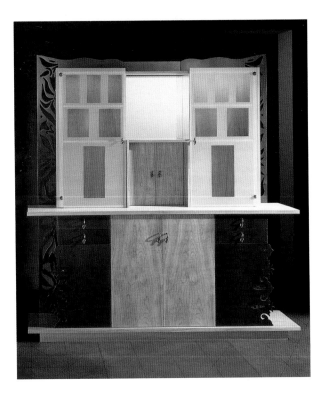

16

15

1 FURNITURE

14 BOŘEK ŠÍPEK

CHAIR, *PRO JP* SERIES

PEARWOOD, LEATHER

H 128cm (50⅜in) W 77cm (30⅜in) D 90cm
(35½in)

MANUFACTURER: WITTMANN DESIGN, UK

15 BOŘEK ŠÍPEK

CHAIR, *LEONORA*

CHERRYWOOD FRAME, EBONIZED OPEN-WORK
SIDES, POLYURETHANE, LEATHER

H 80cm (31½in) W 52cm (20½in) D 49.5cm
(19½in)

MANUFACTURER: ALEPH–DRIADE, ITALY

16 BOŘEK ŠÍPEK

SIDEBOARD, *FELICE*

CHERRYWOOD FRAME, EBONY-COLOURED BACK
AND OPEN-WORK SIDES, CHERRYWOOD AND
LAMINATE TOP, SAND-BLASTED GLASS WITH
TRANSPARENT SQUARES, MIRRORED GLASS,
POLISHED BRASS

H 217cm (85⅜in) W 208cm (81¼in) D 52.2cm
(20⅜in)

MANUFACTURER: ALEPH–DRIADE, ITALY

17 BOŘEK ŠÍPEK

CHAIR, *DORA*

CHERRYWOOD, POLYURETHANE, LEATHER

H 81.5cm (32⅛in) W 44cm (17¼in) D 54cm
(21¼in)

MANUFACTURER: ALEPH–DRIADE, ITALY

17

1 FURNITURE

18 THOMAS ALTHAUS AND VOLKER LAPRELL
CHAIR, *ZSA ZSA*
STAINED OR PAINTED BEECH, ALUMINIUM
H 84cm (33in) W 54cm (21¼in) D 54cm (21¼in)
MANUFACTURER: BROS'S, ITALY

18

19 ENRICO BALERI
STACKING CHAIR, *MIMI*
STEEL, POLYPROPYLENE, POLYAMIDE
The chair has a tilting back.
H 76cm (30in) W 45.5cm (17⅞in) D 48cm
(18⅞in)
MANUFACTURER: BALERI, ITALY

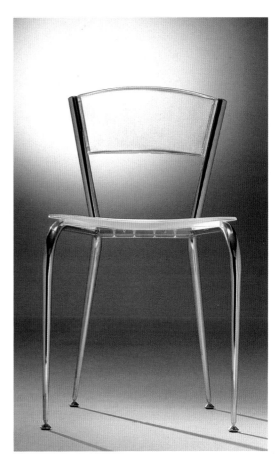

19

20   21   22

With his faultless radar for the mood of the times, **Philippe Starck** first began to voice his misgivings about designer excess three years ago. In *The International Design Yearbook 1989/90* he was worrying about trees and writing poems in praise of plastic. In 1990/91, he declared that 'style' had had its day; despite his earlier doubts, several of his new pieces, like almost everybody else's it seemed, were in wood. Starck has not quite made good his promise to stop designing furniture, but in 1991, as he concentrates on architectural projects and product design, there are signs that the extraordinary flood of designs he unleashed in the 1980s may at last be slowing up. Aleph has launched a number of pieces Starck designed for the Royalton Hotel in New York, including a sofa, armchair and day bed, Idée has introduced the velvet-covered *Miss Paramount* chair, and Kartell has encouraged him to provide progeny for the plastic *Dr Glob* chair and *Miss Balù* table. *Hi-Glob* is a stacking stool and *Super Glob* is a stacking armchair; both marry polypropylene mouldings to tubular steel frames. 'The furnitures must disappear,' says Starck enigmatically. 'As we are not yet able to sit on a current of air, the *Super Glob* discreetly proposes that we should wait comfortably.'

20 PHILIPPE STARCK
ARMCHAIR AND POUFFE, FROM THE
ROYALTON COLLECTION
STEEL FRAME, POLYURETHANE ALUMINIUM
CASTING, REMOVABLE UPHOLSTERY
Armchair: H 113cm (44½in) W 98cm (38⅜in) D
100cm (39½in)
Pouffe: H 45cm (17¾in) W 60cm (23½in)
D 60cm (23½in)
MANUFACTURER: ALEPH–DRIADE, ITALY

21 PHILIPPE STARCK
DAY BED, FROM THE *ROYALTON*
COLLECTION
STEEL FRAME, POLYURETHANE ALUMINIUM
CASTING, REMOVABLE VELVET UPHOLSTERY
H 93cm (36¾in) W 89cm (35in) D 173cm
(68⅛in)
MANUFACTURER: ALEPH–DRIADE, ITALY

22 PHILIPPE STARCK
TWO-SEATER SOFA WITH TWO ARM-
RESTS, FROM THE *ROYALTON*
COLLECTION
POLYURETHANE FOAM, ALUMINIUM CASTING,
PEARWOOD, SEAT AND ARM-RESTS UPHOLSTERED
IN REMOVABLE COTTON FABRIC, VELVET BACK
H 113cm (44½in) W 207cm (81½in) D 100cm
(39½in)
MANUFACTURER: ALEPH–DRIADE, ITALY

23 PHILIPPE STARCK
STACKING CHAIR, *HI-GLOB*
STEEL TUBING, POLYPROPYLENE
H 97cm (38¼in) W 46cm (18¼in) D 46.5cm
(18⅜in)
MANUFACTURER: KARTELL, ITALY

24 PHILIPPE STARCK
STACKING ARMCHAIR, *SUPER GLOB*
STEEL TUBING, POLYPROPYLENE
H 80cm (31½in) W 53.5cm (21⅛in) D 54cm
(21¼in)
MANUFACTURER: KARTELL, ITALY

25 PHILIPPE STARCK
CHAIR, *MISS PARAMOUNT*
WOOD, VELVET
H 103cm (40½in) W 37cm (14½in) D 65cm
(25⅝in)
MANUFACTURER: IDÉE, JAPAN

23

24

25

26

27

1 FURNITURE

26 RICHARD PEDUZZI
STOOL
WILD CHERRYWOOD
H 45cm (17⅝in) W 45cm (17⅝in) D 45cm
(17⅝in)
MANUFACTURER: ÉDITIONS DU NOPAL/MOBILIER
NATIONAL, FRANCE

27 RICHARD PEDUZZI
CHAIR
WILD CHERRYWOOD
H 58cm (22⅞in) W 35.5cm (14in)
MANUFACTURER: ÉDITIONS DU NOPAL/MOBILIER
NATIONAL, FRANCE

28 TOM DEACON
ARMCHAIR, *DEACON*
MAPLE, UPHOLSTERY
H 106cm (41¾in) W 61cm (24in) D 56cm
(22in)
MANUFACTURER: KEILHAUER INDUSTRIES,
CANADA

29 ALDO BARTOLOMEO
CHAIR, *CAMPANINO*
BEECH, LEATHER UPHOLSTERY
H 87cm (34¼in) W 45cm (17⅝in) D 40cm
(15¾in)
MANUFACTURER: STILDOMUS, ITALY

28   29

There are strong traces of **Perry King** and **Santiago Miranda's** *Air Mail Visitor's Chair* for Marcatré in their designs for the American company Atelier International and the Spanish manufacturer Andreu World. It can be seen in the arched front legs and backwards-thrusting 'tricorne' backrest of the *N* chair and even, to a degree, in the upward-curving armrests of their wooden dining chair, *Solea*. King and Miranda's aim is to achieve a certain grace and 'lightness of foot' and, like the *Visitor's Chair*, both designs convey a sense that the structure is tensing, as if the chair is about to pounce.

30 PERRY A. KING AND SANTIAGO MIRANDA
CHAIR, *SOLEA*
WOOD, FOAM, FABRIC
H 75cm (29½in) W 46cm (18¼in) D 52cm (20½in)
MANUFACTURER: ANDREU WORLD, SPAIN

31 PERRY A. KING AND SANTIAGO MIRANDA
CHAIR, *N*
WOOD, STEEL, PLASTIC FOAM, LEATHER OR FABRIC UPHOLSTERY
H 82cm (32¼in) W 59cm (23in) D 56cm (22in)
MANUFACTURER: ATELIER INTERNATIONAL, USA

32 FABIO DI BARTOLOMEI
CHAIR, *SAMURAI*
SOLID BEECH, CURVED MULTI-LAYERED BEECH, PADDED SEAT, LEATHER COVER
H 73cm (28¾in) W 53cm (20⅞in) D 56cm (22in)
MANUFACTURER: SKIPPER, ITALY

1 FURNITURE

33 OSCAR TUSQUETS BLANCA
STACKING CHAIR, *POTRO*
BEECH, WICKER
H 86cm (33⅞in) W 48cm (18⅞in) D 44cm
(17¼in)
MANUFACTURER: CARLOS JANÉ CAMACHO,
SPAIN

34 OSCAR TUSQUETS BLANCA
TABLES, *GACELA*
CHERRYWOOD, CHERRYWOOD VENEER,
PEARWOOD OR EBONY-COLOURED FINISH
Rectangular: H 50.5cm (19⅞in) W 50cm (19⅝in)
D 36.5cm (14⅜in)
Square: H 50.5cm (19⅞in) W 39cm (15⅜in)
D 39cm (15⅜in)
MANUFACTURER: ALEPH–DRIADE, ITALY

35 OSCAR TUSQUETS BLANCA
SOFA, *ALI-BABA*
FIBREGLASS AND SOFT POLYURETHANE FOAM,
STEEL STRUCTURE, WOOL CARPET
H 100cm (39½in) W 200cm (78¾in) D 87cm
(34¼in) 230cm (90½in)
MANUFACTURER: CASAS, SPAIN

33

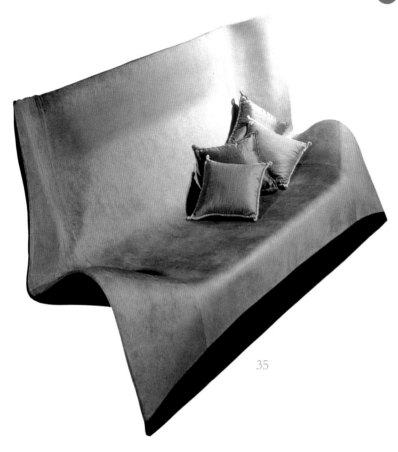

35

It was seeing a carpet draped over furniture in an English country house that gave **Oscar Tusquets Blanca** the idea for his new three-seater sofa for Casas, a playful reinterpretation of a frequently over-formal furniture type. Sometimes, says Tusquets Blanca, people like to sit on the floor to watch television, or to talk with friends. With *Ali-Baba* it is possible to sit either on the floor or on the seat and still enjoy the comfort of the sofa. Three rug designs are available: a Tibetan tiger, a traditional Turkish pattern, and the one shown, which is the most personal to Tusquets Blanca, a labyrinth.

Tusquets Blanca's *Potro* chair is a similarly modest proposal about the aesthetic tyranny of so much 'designer' furniture and the timeless need for simple domestic comfort. 'There are too many tubular chairs with pipes, metal and rubber,' he says. '*Potro* is a little manifesto. It is anti-High Tech.' An attempt to remake the traditional Spanish guitarist's chair, *Potro* ('colt' in Spanish) continues the preoccupation with wood that Tusquets Blanca revealed four years ago with the *Gaulino*. That chair, with its obvious references to Gaudí and Mollino, was enthusiastically received. *Potro*'s determinedly conventional appearance has generated a cooler reception in the Spanish design shops, but its virtues—comfort, lightness and stackability—could transform that in time.

34

35

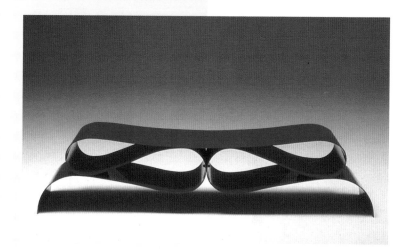

37

36 Jiří Pelcl
Sofa, *Flag*
Metal, velvet
Limited batch production
H 180cm (70⅞in) W 165cm (65in) D 80cm
(31½in)
Manufacturer: Atelier Pelcl,
Czechoslovakia

37 Agenore Fabbri
Bench, *Nastro di Gala*
Enamelled steel
H 37cm (14½in) L 160cm (63in) D 40cm
(15¾in)
Manufacturer: Tecno, Italy

38 Diana Firth
Chaise longue, *Lounge Lizard*
Laminated pine
Limited batch production
H 93cm (36⅜in) W 63cm (24⅞in) L 188cm
(74in)
Manufacturer: Bryan Heighton, New
Zealand

38

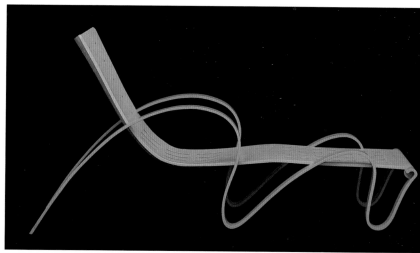

40

39

1 FURNITURE

41

42

43

44

43 FORREST MYERS
BED, *KILIMANJARO 1990*
STEEL, BRASS
One-off
H 48.3cm (19in) W 147.3cm (58in)
D 198.1cm (78in)
MANUFACTURER: ART ET INDUSTRIE, USA

44 RON ARAD
ROCKING CHAIR, *HEART & INDUSTRIE 1990*
STAINLESS STEEL
One-off
H 34cm (13⅜in) W 46cm (18⅛in) D 22cm (8⅜in)
MANUFACTURER: ART ET INDUSTRIE, USA

45 RON ARAD
TABLE, *SPLIT*
BEECH SPLINES, STAINLESS STEEL
Due to the cogging system and the splitting of two legs, the table can extend to twice its size.
H 72cm (28⅜in) W150cm–280cm (59–110¼in) D 88cm (34⅞in)
MANUFACTURER: POLTRONOVA, ITALY

46 RON ARAD
CHAIR, *SPLIT*
DIE-CAST ALUMINIUM, WALNUT
Can be used on its own or as part of a two-seater sofa.
H 75cm (29½in) W 60cm (23½in) 110cm (43⅜in) D 58cm (22⅞in)
MANUFACTURER: POLTRONOVA, ITALY

Ron Arad's exhibition in an old Milanese conservatory building was one of the undisputed triumphs of the 1991 Furniture Fair. Arad enjoyed remarkable success in the 1980s, but it was clear by the end of the decade that the mood had changed and that the metal bashers would need to develop new themes if they were to sustain their reputations. Few can now doubt that Arad has achieved that end. To some observers, his twelve brightly upholstered chairs for Moroso's *Spring* collection (one was not ready for the show) were welcome evidence of a move towards the mainstream. Their surprise value was certainly sufficient to eclipse his other exhibits. The four pieces on pages 36-7, along with the *Split* chair and table for Poltronova, might seem to confirm the impression that the balance of Arad's concerns has shifted. In fact, Arad and his studio, One-Off, continue to experiment with sheet metal in solid volumes and with spring-based pieces which are the uncompromising, less commercial cousins of the Moroso collection. If there is a line separating the 'evolutionary' industrial design of Mario Bellini or Antonio Citterio from the aesthetic radicalism of, say, Gaetano Pesce, then Arad is choosing to remain on the side of the radicals.

45

46

1 FURNITURE

47 INGO MAURER AND TEAM
TABLES, *ONTZ*
MARBLE, STEEL
Support can be adjusted to carry
different table-top dimensions.
H 70cm (27½in) 100cm (39½in) W 140cm
(55⅛in) D 140cm (55⅛in)
MANUFACTURER: INGO MAURER, GERMANY

48 ESTUDI BLANC
TROLLEY, *BARNA*
TUBULAR AND SHEET METAL
H 75cm (29½in) W 56cm (22in),
70cm (27½in) or 85cm (33½in)
MANUFACTURER: GRUPO T, SPAIN

49 LLUIS CLOTET
TROLLEY, *JARDÍN*
ZINC-PLATED AND PAINTED STEEL, GLASS TRAYS,
METHACRYLATE WHEELS, NYLON CORE, SOLID
TYRES
H 71cm (28in) W 143 (56⅜in) D 54cm (21¼in)
MANUFACTURER: BD EDICIONES DE DISEÑO,
SPAIN

47

48

49

In a somewhat straitened Milan Furniture Fair, three designers still seemed to be designing at maximum stretch. Two of them—Ron Arad and Bořek Šípek—are showmen who can be relied upon to deliver a plethora of new pieces in flamboyant style. The third, the Milanese designer **Antonio Citterio,** has an altogether lower profile and a quieter, more functional approach. Yet for Citterio, just as much as for the others, 1991 was a year that revealed his strengths to the full. He showed new pieces with Vitra—the *Area* entrance seating system, designed with Oliver Loew—and a range of attractive easy chairs with Flexform (see pages 44–5), but it was his folding tables and trolleys for Kartell, also designed with Loew and two years in the making, that stood out. Citterio's ambition in revitalising this most undemonstrative but useful of household items were modest. 'I decided to design this series of carts using technological materials and bringing back images that have always belonged to household memories.' Great attention has been paid to the small details of construction that give the *Filippo* and *Battista* trolleys their personality. Some companies might have cut corners by using an existing, mass-produced wheel; Kartell's have been specially made. The trolleys are pleasingly simple designs realised with inordinate care.

50

51

52

50 **ANTONIO CITTERIO AND OLIVER LOEW**
FOLDING EXTENSIBLE TROLLEY, *BATTISTA*
THERMOPLASTIC TECHNOPOLYMER WITH SCRATCH-PROOF FINISHING, PAINTED STEEL, PAINTED ALUMINIUM
Open: H 69cm (27⅛in) W 100cm (39½in) D 54cm (21¼in)
Half-open: H 69cm (27⅛in) W 54cm (21¼in) D 50cm (19⅝in)
Folded: H 69cm (27⅛in) W 54cm (21¼in) D 20cm (7⅞in)
MANUFACTURER: KARTELL, ITALY

51 **ANTONIO CITTERIO AND OLIVER LOEW**
SEATING, *AREA*
ALUMINIUM DIE-CAST FRAME, TESSO OR LEATHER UPHOLSTERY
The bench with two or three seats can be assembled to give a complete and flexible system by using various backs, arms and tables.
H 80cm (31½in) or 94.5cm (37⅛in) W (three-seater) 222cm (87⅜in) D 65cm (25⅝in)
MANUFACTURER: VITRA, GERMANY

52 **ANTONIO CITTERIO AND OLIVER LOEW**
FOLDING TROLLEY, *FILIPPO*
THERMOPLASTIC TECHNOPOLYMER WITH SCRATCH-PROOF FINISHING, PAINTED STEEL, PAINTED ALUMINIUM
Open: H 83cm (32¾in) W 46cm (18⅛in) D 62cm (24⅜in)
Closed: H 83cm (32¾in) W 10cm (4in) D 62cm (24⅜in)
MANUFACTURER: KARTELL, ITALY

1 FURNITURE

54

53 DAKOTA JACKSON
STACKING CHAIR, *VIK-TER*
CHERRYWOOD, WELDED STEEL, EPOXY POWDER
FINISH
H 88.3cm (34¾in) W 48.3cm (19in) D 50.8cm
(20in)
MANUFACTURER: DAKOTA JACKSON, USA

54 ANTONIO CITTERIO
SOFA, *EDUARD*
WOODEN FRAME, POLYURETHANE FILLING, DOWN
SEAT AND CUSHIONS, CASTORS, WOODEN LEGS
H 87cm (34¼in) W 215cm (84⅝in) D 106cm
(41¾in)
MANUFACTURER: FLEXFORM, ITALY

55 ANTONIO CITTERIO
CHAIR, *BODY*
HAND-STITCHED LEATHER, BEECH, WALNUT OR
ROSEWOOD LEGS
H 73cm (28¾in) W 50cm (19⅝in) D 53cm
(20⅞in)
MANUFACTURER: FLEXFORM, ITALY

56 ANTONIO CITTERIO
ARMCHAIR, *AMADEUS*
BEECH AND CHROME-PLATED METAL FRAME,
CANE, POLYURETHANE AND DACRON CUSHIONS,
FRONT CASTORS, WOODEN BACK LEGS
H 67cm (26⅜in) W 68cm (26¾in) D 86cm
(33⅞in)
MANUFACTURER: FLEXFORM, ITALY

53

55

56

46

57

58

59

The presentation pack for **Massimo Iosa Ghini's** 1991 collection for Lisar comes with the designer's now familiar cartoons of science fiction cities, but the iconography, this time, seems more a matter of habit than necessary explanation. The new collection is in dark wood and the traditional material goes some way towards normalizing, if not entirely neutralizing, the aerodynamic energy of Iosa Ghini's furniture. There is a huge credenza, a sideboard and a sofa, as well as smaller pieces such as a lamp stand and coffee table, but it is the bow-shaped *Bonaparte* writing desk and the *Rodi* folding screen that most successfully marry Iosa Ghini's comic-book futurism with this new monumentality of form.

57 MASSIMO IOSA GHINI
WRITING DESK, *BONAPARTE*
WOOD
H 80cm (31½in) W 350cm (137⅜in) D 74cm (29⅛in)
MANUFACTURER: LISAR, ITALY

58 MASSIMO IOSA GHINI
SCREEN, *RODI*
WOOD
H 200cm (78⅜in) W 190cm (74⅞in)
MANUFACTURER: LISAR, ITALY

59 MASSIMO IOSA GHINI
TROLLEY, *INCONTRO*
MOULDED CRYSTAL SHEETS, ANODIZED ALUMINIUM COMPONENTS
H 82cm (32¼in) W 105cm (41⅜in) D 45cm (17¾in)
MANUFACTURER: FIAM, ITALY

60 ENZO MARI
TABLE, *2335 ACANTO*
CAST-IRON ENAMELLED STEEL FRAME WITH SCRATCH-RESISTANT EMBOSSING, 12MM TEMPERED PLATE GLASS
H 72cm (28⅜in) W 200cm (78⅜in) D 100cm (39⅜in)
MANUFACTURER: ZANOTTA, ITALY

60

1 Furniture

61 Jean Nouvel
Armchair, *Elementaire*
Solid samba wood, beech
H 85cm (33⅓in) W 82cm (32⅓in) D 80cm
(31½in)
Manufacturer: Ligne Roset, France

62 Peter Maly
Chaise longue, *Koga*
Solid beech, Oregon and Okoumé plywood
H 88cm (34⅜in) W 174cm (68½in) D 86cm
(33¾in)
Manufacturer: Ligne Roset, France

63 Hans Hollein
Chaise longue, *Berggasse*
Wood, expanded polyurethane, fabric
H 90cm (35½in) L 233cm (91¾in) D 74cm
(29⅛in)
Manufacturer: Poltronova, Italy

64 Toshiyuki Kita
Chair, *Fido*
Bent plywood, steel, cast aluminium,
polyurethane foam, fabric or leather
upholstery
H 91cm (35¾in) W 46cm (18⅛in) D 60cm
(23½in)
Manufacturer: Moroso, Italy

61

62

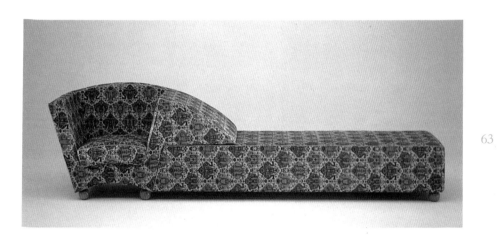

63

64

65

65 SYLVAIN DUBUISSON
BUREAU
HONDURAS MAHOGANY VENEER, LEATHER
Limited batch production
H 72cm (28⅜in) W 190cm (74⅞in) D 100cm
(39½in)
MANUFACTURER: FOURNITURE ÉDITIONS,
FRANCE

66 SYLVAIN DUBUISSON
TABLE, *PORTEFEUILLE*
STEEL, GLASS, CARBON, ALUMINIUM, EPOXY
FINISH
Limited batch production
H 74cm (29⅛in) W 140cm (55⅛in) D 70cm
(27½in)
MANUFACTURER: FOURNITURE ÉDITIONS,
FRANCE

The French designer **Sylvain Dubuisson's**
furniture exemplifies the unpretentious
refinement most valued by *International
Design Yearbook* editor Andrée Putman.
Dubuisson began his career working in the
offices of Ove Arup in London and there is
a powerfully architectural quality to his
simple, clearly drawn forms, whether he is
designing a jug in silver or a table in wood.
Dubuisson's desk is a smaller version of
one that he originally created for the
French Minister of Culture, Jack Lang: a
leather writing area is set into a mahogany
top supported by an irregular section that
looks as though it has been carved from a
huge wooden cone. The curving, carbon-
fibre structure of Dubuisson's folding table
is delineated with the same exacting eye for
the well-placed line.

66

66

68

69

67

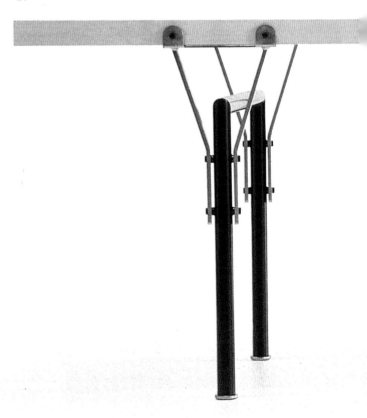

1 FURNITURE

67 LOVE ARBÈN
TABLE, *ARGUS*
SYCAMORE, MATT CHROME STEEL, LACQUERED
STEEL
H 72cm (28⅜in) W 80cm (31½in) L 220cm
(86⅝in)
MANUFACTURER: LAMMHULTS, SWEDEN

68 HARRI KORHONEN
TABLE, *CONIX*
EPOXY-POWDERED STEEL, GLASS
Prototype
H 72cm (28⅜in) Di 90cm (35½in) 110cm (43¾in)
MANUFACTURER: INNO INTERIOR, FINLAND

69 LOVE ARBÈN
TABLE, *BONGO*
MOULDED ALUMINIUM, LACQUERED STEEL
H 72cm (28⅜in) Di 55cm (21¾in)
MANUFACTURER: LAMMHULTS, SWEDEN

70 JONAS BOHLIN
CHAISE LONGUE, *LYRA*
STEEL, LEATHER
H 40cm (15¾in) L 200cm (78¾in) D 75cm
(29½in)
MANUFACTURER: KÄLLEMO, SWEDEN

70

1 FURNITURE

71

71 HARTMUT ESSLINGER
REVOLVING CHAIR, COR PROJECT
PRESSED ALUMINIUM, LEATHER UPHOLSTERY
H 102cm (40⅛in) W 67cm (26⅜in) D 63cm
(24⅞in)
MANUFACTURER: COR WOHN- AND
BÜROMÖBEL HELMUT LÜBKE, GERMANY

72 HARTMUT ESSLINGER
REVOLVING CHAIR, COR PROJECT
PRESSED ALUMINIUM, FABRIC UPHOLSTERY
H 92cm (36⅛in) W 67cm (26⅜in) D 63cm
(24⅞in)
MANUFACTURER: COR WOHN- AND
BÜROMÖBEL HELMUT LÜBKE, GERMANY

73 EMILIO AMBASZ
OFFICE CHAIR, *QUALIS*
ELECTRO-WELDED STEEL, FABRIC, FOAM
Tilts backwards and forwards as
user moves.
H 80–89cm (31½in–35in) W 58cm (22⅞in)
D 60cm (23½in)
MANUFACTURER: TECNO, ITALY

74 ROY FLEETWOOD
SOFA, *WING*
CHROMED BASE, LEATHER UPHOLSTERY, GLASS
TABLE TOPS
H 80cm (31½in) W 225cm (88⅜in) D 49cm
(19¼in)
MANUFACTURER: VITRA, GERMANY

72

73

74

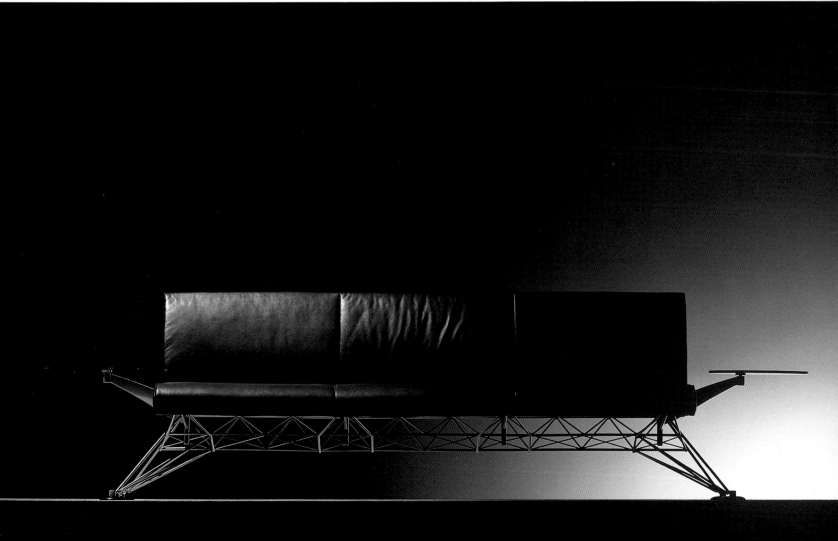

75

76

1 FURNITURE

75 PAUL MATHIEU AND MICHAEL RAY
LOW TABLE, *LÉGER REGEL*
MAHOGANY
H 40cm (15¾in) W 80cm (31½in) L 120cm (47¼in)
MANUFACTURER: ÉCART INTERNATIONAL, FRANCE

76 PAUL MATHIEU AND MICHAEL RAY
SOFA, *SISTER MARGARET*
WOOD, CANVAS, LEATHER
H 87cm (34¼in) W 189cm (74½in)
D 90cm (35½in)
MANUFACTURER: ÉCART INTERNATIONAL, FRANCE

77 PAUL MATHIEU AND MICHAEL RAY
CHAIR, *POLLITT*
MAPLE
H 75.5cm (29¾in) Seat H 45cm (17¾in)
W 49cm (19¼in) D 59cm (23in) Seat D 34cm (13⅜in)
MANUFACTURER: ÉCART INTERNATIONAL, FRANCE

78 PAUL MATHIEU AND MICHAEL RAY
ARMCHAIR, *SISTER MARGARET*
WOOD, CANVAS, LEATHER
H 93cm (36⅝in) Seat H 40cm (15¾in) W 97cm (38¼in) D 90cm (35½in)
MANUFACTURER: ÉCART INTERNATIONAL, FRANCE

Paul Mathieu and **Michael Ray's** new pieces for Écart were originally part of a larger group of twenty prototypes designed for the Marmont Hotel on Sunset Boulevard in Los Angeles. The client eventually said no to their ideas, but Andrée Putman agreed to put seven of the designs into production. For Mathieu and Ray, who have backgrounds in fashion illustration and photography and have collaborated for six years, the collection is a considerable departure from their earlier sculptural one-offs. Their aim, achieved with some elegance, was to create furniture of indeterminate period that looked as if it had been accumulating in the Marmont since the hotel was built in the late 1920s. The names of the pieces derive from the parts played by Hollywood actors who were regular guests. The maple-wood *Pollitt* dining chair, for instance, is a tribute to Elizabeth Taylor, who starred as Maggie Pollitt in *Cat on a Hot Tin Roof*.

77

78

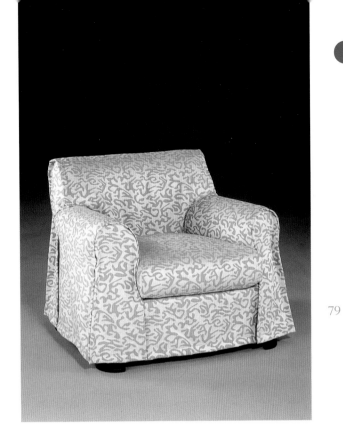

79

It is a sure sign of the way in which the mood in Milan has changed that Cassina's *Segni di Casa* collection represents a conscious attempt by one of Italy's most distinguished manufacturers to reposition itself. It is time, the company declares, to strike a new balance between innovation and significance on the one hand, and saleability and distribution on the other. Cassina believes that it should be possible to address the needs of a wider audience without compromising the standards of quality that have always been its goal.

Segni di Casa has been designed by **Francesco Binfarè**, for many years the co-ordinator of Cassina's contemporary design collection. It consists of fifteen pieces—tables, chairs, armchairs, two- and three-seater sofas—and a range of twenty-five furnishing fabrics. If there is innovation here, as Cassina hopes, it lies perhaps in the comprehensiveness and flexibility of the range as a whole, rather than in the aesthetics of individual pieces which, by the company's previous standards, are conservative. The most ingenious of Binfarè's designs is the *Lom* table. Polyester tablets swivel out from underneath to support either the tabletop extensions or, alternatively, a large square Okoumé-wood frame. This accessory, the *Cornice*, can also be used with the *Angel* shelf unit.

80

1 FURNITURE

79 FRANCESCO BINFARÈ
ARMCHAIR, *LADONA*, FROM THE
SEGNI DI CASA COLLECTION
STEEL STRUCTURE, POLYURETHANE FOAM RUBBER
SEAT, POLYESTER WADDING ON BACK AND ARMS
H 80cm (31½in) W 98cm (38⅜in) D 90cm
(35½in)
MANUFACTURER: CASSINA, ITALY

80 FRANCESCO BINFARÈ
EXTENSIBLE TABLE, *LOM*, FROM THE
SEGNI DI CASA COLLECTION
NATURAL OAK, FORGED METAL
Rectangular: H 75cm (29½in) W 130cm (51⅛in)
extensible to 260cm (102¾in) D 90cm (35½in)
Square: H 75cm (29½in) W 130cm (51⅛in) D
130cm (51⅛in)
MANUFACTURER: CASSINA, ITALY

81 ROBERTO PAMIO
TABLE, *EXECUTIVE*
WOOD, PLYWOOD, NICKELIZED STEEL, LEATHER
H 72cm (28¾in) W 25cm (9¾in) D 130cm
(51⅛in)
MANUFACTURER: MATTEO GRASSI, ITALY

81

60

82 GEMMA BERNAL AND RAMÓN ISERN
CHAIR, *FINA*
STEEL, UPHOLSTERY
H 86cm (33⅞in) W 40cm (15¾in) D 46cm (18⅛in)
MANUFACTURER: GRUPO T, SPAIN

83 GEMMA BERNAL AND RAMÓN ISERN
STOOL, *FINA*
METAL STRUCTURE, POLYURETHANE OR ASH VENEER SEAT
Left: H 94cm (37in) W 34cm (13⅜in) D 32cm (12½in)
Right: H 84cm (33in) W 34cm (13⅜in) D 32cm (12½in)
MANUFACTURER: GRUPO T, SPAIN

84 JORGE PENSI
ARMCHAIR, *ARANDA*
MOULDED RIGID POLYURETHANE, BEECH, FOAM, DACRON
H 78cm (30¾in) W 65cm (25⅜in) D 68cm (26¾in)
MANUFACTURER: KRON, SPAIN

85 JORGE PENSI
STOOL, *MANHATTAN*
STEEL, ALUMINIUM
H 84cm (33in) W 40cm (15¾in) D 40cm (15¾in)
MANUFACTURER: AMAT, SPAIN

82

83

84

85

1 Furniture

86

86 Axel Kufus
Shelf system, *FNP*
MDF, aluminium
H 113cm (44½in) 223cm (87¾in) 260cm (102⅜in) 333cm (131⅛in) W 105–451cm (41½–177⅝in) D 34cm (13⅜in)
Manufacturer: Nils Holger Moormann, Germany

87 Jasper Morrison
Four-Legged Table
Plywood, stainless steel
Limited batch production
H 75cm (29½in) W 180cm (70⅝in) D 65cm (25⅝in)
Manufacturer: SCP, UK

88 Jasper Morrison
Cabinets, from the collection *Universal System*
Beech plywood, aluminium
Left to right:
H 64cm (25⅛in) W 49cm (19¼in) D 56cm (22in)
H 156cm (61⅜in) W 74cm (29⅛in) D 40cm (15¾in)
H 64cm (25⅛in) W 148cm (58¼in) D 40cm (15¾in)
H 116cm (45⅝in) W 74cm (29⅛in) D 40cm (15¾in)
Manufacturer: Cappellini Arte, Italy

89 Jasper Morrison
Stool, *Ottoman*
Beech, aluminium, wool
Limited batch production
H 42cm (16½in) W 105cm (41⅜in) D 50cm (19⅝in)
Manufacturer: SCP, UK

Jasper Morrison is simply not capable of excess. His pieces are so pared down, so monastic in their severity, so uncompromising in their rejection of redundant detail or gratuitous effect that they have the appearance of archetypes. Morrison's table for SCP is not so far away from what a non-designer would draw if asked to sketch a 'table'. It is highly unlikely, however, that such a drawing would display the precision of thought that allows Morrison to play the radiused corners of his table's plywood top against the fractional protrusion of its tiny circular feet.

Morrison's *Universal System* for Cappellini is his most ambitious furniture project to date: twenty-five cupboards, sideboards and chests of drawers in eight basic sizes, made from untreated beech plywood, with aluminium feet or white nylon industrial castors. The system has ironic echoes of Utility furniture and 1950s functionalism, and there is a characteristic note of humour in the way that Morrison has avoided using handles only to replace them with their conceptual image: finger-sized apertures in the shape of keyholes. His reluctance to use anything that cannot be justified as essential extends to the construction: all fixings are achieved by wood joints rather than nails or screws.

87

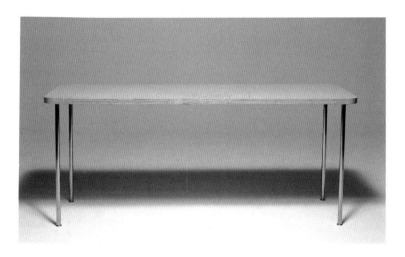

88

89

90

91

1 FURNITURE

90 NIGEL COATES

WARDROBE/SHELVES, *DELFINO*

FIRE-RETARDANT PAINTED METAL STRUCTURE,
SILVER-FINISHED BRASS SUPPORTS AND DRESS
HANGER TUBES, LACQUERED WOODEN SHELVES,
ANTHRACITE WOODEN HATBOX, SAIL-LIKE DOORS
IN ELASTICIZED FABRIC
H 225cm (88⅝in) W 70cm (27½in) D 45cm
(17¾in)
MANUFACTURER: ARREDAESSE, ITALY

91 NIGEL COATES

CHAIR, *CAVALIER*

OAK, EXPANDED POLYURETHANE, LEATHER
H 95cm (37½in) W 48cm (18¼in) D 76cm (30in)
MANUFACTURER: POLTRONOVA, ITALY

92 NIGEL COATES

OUTDOOR CHAIR, *CAVALIER*

OAK
H 95cm (37½in) W 42cm (16½in) D 60cm
(23½in)
MANUFACTURER: POLTRONOVA, ITALY

93

92

93 NIGEL COATES

ARMCHAIR, *TONGUE*

BEECH, COTTON/LINEN OR LEATHER COVER
H 78cm (30¾in) W 95cm (37½in) D 95cm
(37½in)
MANUFACTURER: SCP, UK

The *Delfino* wardrobe/shelving system by **Nigel Coates** for Arredaesse was one of the most imaginative pieces introduced at Milan. It had an extravagance of form and an adventurousness in its approach to the role furniture plays in our everyday lives that was a reminder of earlier, more experimental fairs. This is an example of furniture not simply as fashionable accessory but, to use Coates's words, as a potential 'territory of experience'. The idea for *Delfino* dates back some years to Coates's time as a member of the radical architecture group NATO (Narrative Architecture Today). For NATO's 'Albionize Your Living Room' project, Coates devised a hanging system that concealed clothing inside organic-looking pods of cloth. In *Delfino*, these pods are made of a Lycra-knit fabric, bonded to Neoprene. As always with Coates, the visual associations are plentiful. The pods recall the sails of windsurfers; the structure—stabilized by the wall, but not hanging from it—suggests building-site scaffolding, a long-time obsession. There is also something undeniably erotic about its tactile properties—a quality that is invariably present in Coates's work, whether he is being self-consciously experimental, as in some of his Japanese interiors, or designing a dignified, upholstered armchair for SCP.

1 FURNITURE

94 KONSTANTIN GRCIC
ADJUSTABLE SIDE TABLES, *TAM TAM*
AND *TOM TOM*
BEECH, MDF, STEEL
Limited batch production
Left, Tam Tam: H 50cm (19⅝in) Di 45cm
(17¾in)
Right, Tom Tom: H 70cm (27½in) W 44cm
(17¼in) D 44cm (17¼in)
MANUFACTURER: SCP, UK

95 MATTHEW HILTON
ARMCHAIR, *BALZAC*
BEECH, FEATHERS, WOOL
Limited batch production
H 85cm (33½in) W 80cm (31½in) D 98cm
(38⅝in)
MANUFACTURER: SCP, UK

95

96 MARC NEWSON
CHAISE LONGUE, *ORGONE*
PRINTED GLASS RESIN
H 38cm (15in) W 181cm (71⅜in) D 74cm
(29⅛in)
MANUFACTURER: CAPPELLINI ARTE, ITALY

97 MARC NEWSON
WICKER CHAIR 1990
WICKER
H 84cm (33in) W 76cm (30in) D 113cm
(44½in)
MANUFACTURER: IDÉE, JAPAN

96

94

97

Marc Newson is one of the most recent recruits to the select circuit of design stars whose faces and furniture emblazon the pages of interior design magazines around the world. This is an overheated, unreal and not always very helpful process, as Andrée Putman has cause to remark in her Foreword, but in Newson's case one has to conclude that the fuss has genuine cause. On the evidence of the last four years, the young Australian is an indisputable original; his fluorescent *Embryo* chair and riveted *Lockheed Lounge* chaise longue are signs of a sensibility every bit as individual and clearly defined as that of the early Šípek, Arad or Starck.

Newson mixes a liking for the swollen, organic shapes of 1950s industrial styling with an open-air enthusiasm for the surfing culture of Bondi beach. Nowhere is the latter more apparent than in his *Orgone* chaise longue, designed in 1989 and now put into production by Cappellini, alongside pieces from Tom Dixon and Jasper Morrison. Luridly bright colours, three conical legs and a glass-resin sheen give the piece the look of a mutating surfboard. Given these reference points, Newson's latest pieces for the Tokyo company Idée, the first to spot and underwrite his potential, are not at all what one might expect. It is not form that interests him, Newson says, but the emotions that his pieces generate. Formally, this collection of chairs and chaise longues—inflated, almost cartoonish, with the familiar pinched waists—is no great departure. But the distinctly low-tech cladding, of wicker and felt, makes for a curiously unsettling mixture of the natural and the synthetic.

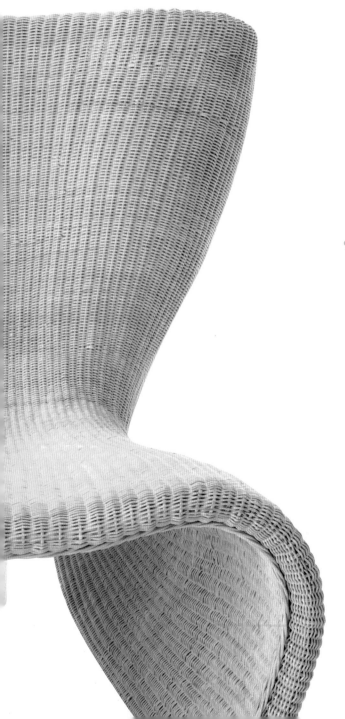

98

1 FURNITURE

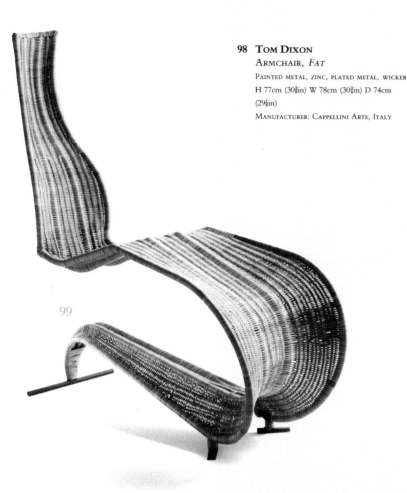

99

98 TOM DIXON
ARMCHAIR, *FAT*
PAINTED METAL, ZINC, PLATED METAL, WICKER
H 77cm (30⅜in) W 78cm (30¾in) D 74cm
(29⅛in)
MANUFACTURER: CAPPELLINI ARTE, ITALY

99 TOM DIXON
CHAISE LONGUE, *BOLIDE I*
PAINTED METAL, ZINC, PLATED METAL, WICKER
H 100cm (39½in) W 42cm (16½in) D 54cm
(21¼in)
MANUFACTURER: CAPPELLINI ARTE, ITALY

100 TOM DIXON
CHAIR, *BOLIDE II*
One-off
TUBULAR STEEL FRAME, FELT UPHOLSTERY
H 100cm (39½in) W 42cm (16½in) D 54cm
(21¼in)
MANUFACTURER: EUROLOUNGE, UK

Tom Dixon has come a long way since his first
'salvage' furniture welded together ladles, pots and
pans in surreal but weirdly logical constructions.
In some ways, however, Dixon's concerns are the
same. The early chairs, stools and light fittings
made a virtue of revealing the ingenuity with
which he had assembled his ad hoc components,
and the processes of his first pieces for Cappellini
are equally explicit. 'I prefer to let processes be
seen,' says Dixon, 'to leave each machining
stage—joints, fillets and weldings—clearly visible
in the finished product.'

With the wicker and iron *Fat* chair and
Bolide I chaise longue, Dixon confirms that he has
been able to achieve the transition from one-off
craftsman to production designer. In the process,
he has exchanged the baroque complexity of his
earlier work for a more organic language of plant
and animal forms. *Fat* has the lightness and
structural transparency of leaves on a tree; *Bolide I*
possesses the coiled energy of a snake. Like Ron
Arad, with whom he is often bracketed, Dixon
likes to reinterpret an established furniture shape
using different materials. *Bolide II*, manufactured
by Eurolounge, substitutes felt for the original
version's wicker, and boldly drawn curves for its
sinuous lines.

101

102

1 FURNITURE

101 KRISTIAN GAVOILLE
ARMCHAIR, *MASSAI*
ALCANTARA, CAST BRONZE
Limited batch production
H 88cm (34⅝in) W 104cm (41in) D 103cm
(40½in)
MANUFACTURER: NÉOTÙ, FRANCE

102 KRISTIAN GAVOILLE
CHEST, *WALTER*
CHERRYWOOD
Limited batch production
H 65cm (25⅝in) W 198cm (77⅞in) D 46cm
(18⅛in)
MANUFACTURER: NÉOTÙ, FRANCE

**103 ELISABETH GAROUSTE AND
MATTIA BONETTI**
SOFA, *CORBEILLE*
VELOUR, BRONZE
Limited batch production
H 115cm (45¼in) W 200cm (78¾in) D 100cm
(39½in)
MANUFACTURER: NÉOTÙ, FRANCE

**104 ELISABETH GAROUSTE AND
MATTIA BONETTI**
MUSIC CABINET
WROUGHT IRON, TERRACOTTA
H 162cm (63¾in) W 84cm (33in) D 40cm
(15¾in)
MANUFACTURER: NÉOTÙ, FRANCE

Néotù, the Parisian gallery established six years ago by Pierre Staudenmeyer and Gérard Delmon, occupies a unique position in French design. To date, Staudenmeyer and Delmon have put more than four hundred pieces into production, in editions ranging from 1 to 500 in size. Always prepared to back their own hunches, they have supported and promoted many of the most creative furniture designers in France, from established figures such as Garouste and Bonetti, to younger designers such as **Kristian Gavoille**.

One of the most remarkable pieces to have emerged from Néotù in the last year—to have emerged from anywhere—is Gavoille's *Massai* armchair. To call the piece elephantine goes some way toward capturing a sense of its overwhelming, almost repellent presence and leathery physical bulk. Gavoille used to work for Philippe Starck (he collaborated on the Royalton and Paramount hotels and the Nani Nani building in Japan) and he reveals himself here to possess an imagination every bit as intuitive and intense. He likes to give his furniture the unsettling air that it has been surprised in a state of temporary repose. In *Massai*, the sense of impending movement comes from the way that Gavoille twists the armrests and angles the pointed bronze feet; in the *Walter* chest of drawers, it comes from three log-like supports, which look free-rolling, although they are in reality fixed.

104

1 FURNITURE

72

**105 LAURA AGNOLETTO AND MARZIO
RUSCONI CLERICI**
SMALL TABLE, *Legs*
GLASS, WOOD, RUBBER
Prototype
H 35cm (13¾in) W 100cm (39⅜in) D 35cm
(13¾in)
MANUFACTURER: AMEDEI TRE, ITALY

106 MARTIN SZEKELY
WARDROBE, *SF*
SYCAMORE
Limited batch production
H 175cm (68⅞in) W 72cm (28⅜in) D 35cm
(13¾in)
MANUFACTURER: NÉOTÙ, FRANCE

107 MARTIN SZEKELY
LOW TABLE, *TB*
SYCAMORE
Limited batch production
H 39cm (15⅜in) W 121cm (47⅝in) D 61.5cm
(24⅛in)
MANUFACTURER: NÉOTÙ, FRANCE

108 MARTIN SZEKELY
SOFA, *EX*
SLATE, SATIN
Limited batch production
H 97cm (38⅛in) W 223cm (87¾in) D 107cm
(42⅛in)
MANUFACTURER: NÉOTÙ, FRANCE

105

106

107

108

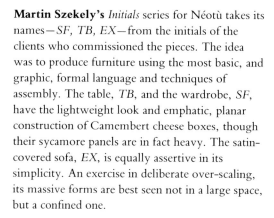

Martin Szekely's *Initials* series for Néotù takes its names—*SF, TB, EX*—from the initials of the clients who commissioned the pieces. The idea was to produce furniture using the most basic, and graphic, formal language and techniques of assembly. The table, *TB*, and the wardrobe, *SF*, have the lightweight look and emphatic, planar construction of Camembert cheese boxes, though their sycamore panels are in fact heavy. The satin-covered sofa, *EX*, is equally assertive in its simplicity. An exercise in deliberate over-scaling, its massive forms are best seen not in a large space, but a confined one.

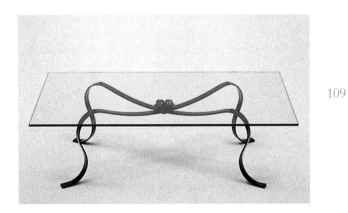

109

110

111

1 FURNITURE

109 ANNA ANSELMI
COFFEE TABLE, *POPPY*
WROUGHT IRON, CRYSTAL
H 38cm (15in) W 140cm (55½in) D 70cm
(27½in)
MANUFACTURER: BIEFFEPLAST, ITALY

110 VICO MAGISTRETTI
TABLE, *SHINE*
CHERRYWOOD, ALUMINIUM
H 73½cm (28½in) W 150cm (59in) D 130cm
(51¼in)
MANUFACTURER: EDIZIONI DE PADOVA, ITALY

111 MARCO ZANUSO
TABLE
METAL, GLASS
H 70cm (27½in) Di 45cm (17¾in)
MANUFACTURER: ARTELANO, FRANCE

112 PASCAL MOURGUE
TABLE, *PIROUETTE*
CAST IRON, CAST ALUMINIUM, GLASS
H 73cm (28¾in) W 60cm (23½in) L 60cm
(23½in)
MANUFACTURER: FERMOB, FRANCE

113 PASCAL MOURGUE
CHAIR, *RIO*
WOOD, IRON
H 72cm (28¾in) W 47cm (18½in) D 48cm
(18⅞in)
MANUFACTURER: ARTELANO, FRANCE

112

113

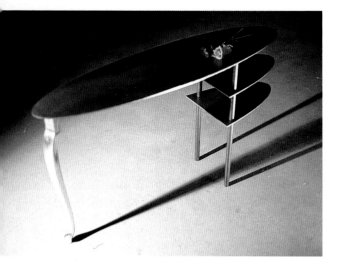

114

114 MICHEL FEITH
TABLE, *FRISCO*
STEEL
Limited batch production
H 70cm (27½in) W 130cm (51¼in) D 20cm
(7⅞in)
MANUFACTURER: MÖBEL PERDU, GERMANY

115 MICHEL FEITH
TABLE, *OPFERSCHALE*
STEEL
Limited batch production
H 70cm (27½in) Di 100cm (39½in)
MANUFACTURER: MÖBEL PERDU, GERMANY

116 GEORG APPELTSHAUSER
SWIVEL TABLE, *INTERMEZZO*, FROM
THE *METAMORPHOSEN* COLLECTION
STEEL, GLASS
H 43cm (16⅞in) Di 100cm (39½in)
MANUFACTURER: DRAENERT, GERMANY

117 GUEN BERTHEAU-SUZUKI
TABLE, *TURN OVER*
CHROMED STEEL, SUS, SAND-BLASTED GLASS
The top can be put on in any
direction.
H 68cm (26¾in) Di 80cm (31½in)
MANUFACTURER: ISHIMARU, JAPAN

115

116

117

118

119

118 PATRICK NAGGAR
CHAIR, *SEPIK RIVER*
BENT PLY CHERRY VENEER, RAWHIDE LACING,
BENT STEEL FRAME
H 96.5cm (38in) W 26.7cm (10½in) D 55.9cm
(22in)
MANUFACTURER: ARC INTERNATIONAL, USA

119 PATRICK NAGGAR
CHAIRS, *CELESTE* IN *DAY* AND
NIGHT VERSIONS
RIGHT, DAY: MAPLE, GOLD LEAF, LEATHER
UPHOLSTERY
LEFT, NIGHT: WENGE, CORIAN INLAY, LEATHER
UPHOLSTERY
H 87.6cm (34½in) W 40.6cm (16in) D 44.6cm
(17⅜in)
MANUFACTURER: ARC INTERNATIONAL, USA

120 KEVIN WALZ
CHAIR, *JERSEY*
MOULDED URETHANE, ENAMELLED STEEL
Limited batch production
H 80cm (31½in) W 52cm (20½in) D 55.3cm
(21¾in)
MANUFACTURER: ARC INTERNATIONAL, USA

120

121   122

123

With the departure of Ettore Sottsass, Memphis was left with a world-famous name, a catalogue of authentic design classics, and no obvious role for the future. It responded by redefining its brief, naming itself **Meta Memphis**, and commissioning pieces not from designers and architects but from leading names in the visual arts. Most pieces in the first collection of 1989 were at least notionally functional, although the line between furniture and sculpture was sometimes shakily drawn. The second collection is more ambiguous. Sol Lewitt's coffee table could be nothing else, but it is hard to imagine many people wanting to sit and read with the formality demanded by Alighiero e Boetti's reading desk, although the cherry-wood structure has undoubted elegance and grace. Meta Memphis remains a highly watchable experiment, but many will feel, on the evidence so far, that the validity of its hypothesis is open to doubt.

1 Furniture

81

121 MICHELE DE LUCCHI
SOFA AND CHAIR, *DUBLINO*, FROM THE *JOYCE* COLLECTION
WOOD, POLYURETHANE, LEATHER UPHOLSTERY
Sofa: H 72cm (28⅜in) W 218cm (85⅞in) D 89cm (35in)
Chair: H 72cm (28⅜in) W 98cm (38⅜in) D 89cm (35in)
MANUFACTURER: MOROSO, ITALY

122 MICHELE DE LUCCHI
WRITING DESK, *CELEO*
PEARWOOD, CRYSTAL
H 117cm (46in) W 137cm (54in) D 60cm (23½in)
MANUFACTURER: GLASS DESIGN, ITALY

123 ALIGHIERO E BOETTI
DESK, *LEGGI*
CHERRYWOOD
Reading desk with drawers and fold-up top.
Prototype
H 130cm (51⅛in) W 45cm (17¾in) D 63cm (24⅞in)
MANUFACTURER: MEMPHIS, ITALY

124 MARCO BAGNOLI
SHELF, *CIOTOLA*
WOOD WITH SILVER LAYER
H 27cm (10½in) W 155cm (61in) D 57cm (22⅜in)
MANUFACTURER: MEMPHIS, ITALY

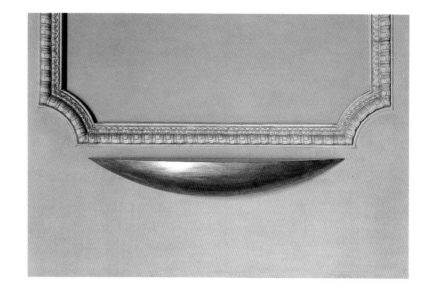

124

125 SOL LEWITT
TABLE
WOOD, CRYSTAL
H 45cm (17¾in) W 165cm (65in) D 45cm (17¾in)
MANUFACTURER: MEMPHIS, ITALY

125

126

126 ACHILLE CASTIGLIONI AND MICHELE DE LUCCHI
DESK WITH CABINET, *SANGIROLAMO*
CHERRYWOOD OR ROSEWOOD
The cabinet comprises a set of items that may be combined in a variety of ways, including a slotted unit designed to take technical equipment.
Desk: H 73cm (28¾in) W 303cm (119⅜in)
Cabinet: H 115cm (45¼in) W 303cm (119⅜in) D 50cm (19⅝in)
MANUFACTURER: HIGH VISIBILITY FOR OLIVETTI SYNTHESIS, ITALY

127 ACHILLE CASTIGLIONI
SHELVES, *712 JOY*
PLYWOOD ELEMENTS WITH STEEL REINFORCING, STOVE-ENAMELLED STEEL SUPPORTS
H 190cm (74⅞in) W 96cm (37⅞in) D 30cm (11¾in)
MANUFACTURER: ZANOTTA, ITALY

128 ACHILLE CASTIGLIONI
BEDSIDE TABLE, *480 ISI*
CAST-IRON BASE, BLACK-LACQUERED MDF FRAME
H 120cm (47¼in) W 30cm (11¾in) D 20cm (7⅞in)
MANUFACTURER: ZANOTTA, ITALY

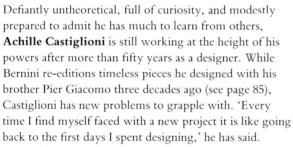

Defiantly untheoretical, full of curiosity, and modestly prepared to admit he has much to learn from others, **Achille Castiglioni** is still working at the height of his powers after more than fifty years as a designer. While Bernini re-editions timeless pieces he designed with his brother Pier Giacomo three decades ago (see page 85), Castiglioni has new problems to grapple with. 'Every time I find myself faced with a new project it is like going back to the first days I spent designing,' he has said.

The *Joy* shelf unit, designed for Zanotta, is a wonderful example of his wit. Castiglioni has always acknowledged the importance of art as an indirect influence on design and this is a piece that is both sculptural—a much-abused word—yet certain about its purpose as furniture. It is also a generous piece. Castiglioni does not prescribe what to do with the shelves (three-, four-, five-, six- and seven-shelf versions are available); he leaves the precise arrangement of the sculpture, which turns around a central pole, for the user.

A similar, though necessarily more structured, flexibility underpins the *Sangirolamo* system which Castiglioni has designed with Michele De Lucchi for Olivetti Synthesis. The aim was to devise a means of organising and containing the technology of the modern office (at home or work) without allowing it to dominate its setting. *Sangirolamo* consists of a desk, a console table with sliding smoked-glass doors for fax, personal computer, printer, television and video recorder, and a set of bookshelves in floor-based and console-mounted versions. All are traditional in appearance and all are in wood, suggesting that the softening of forms already seen in the living room may soon get into the office.

129

129 ACHILLE CASTIGLIONI
TABLE, *SOLONE*
CHROMED EXTRUDED ALUMINIUM LEGS WITH
CAST-IRON BASES, GLASS TOP
Limited batch production
H 75cm (29½in) Di 125cm (49⅛in) 140cm
(55½in) 155cm (61in)
MANUFACTURER: MARCATRÉ, ITALY

**130 ACHILLE AND PIER GIACOMO
CASTIGLIONI**
CHAIR AND FOOTSTOOL, *SAN LUCA*
WOOD, LEATHER
Re-edition from 1961
Chair: H 96cm (37⅞in) W 87cm (34¼in)
D 100cm (39⅜in)
Footstool: H 38cm (15in) W 57cm (22⅜in)
D 57cm (22⅜in)
MANUFACTURER: BERNINI, ITALY

**131 ACHILLE AND PIER GIACOMO
CASTIGLIONI**
WALL BOOKCASE
BEECH PLYWOOD FINISHED IN BEECH OR
NATURAL LAMINATE
The shelves are hung by means of
fine steel cable attached to a brass
disc fixed to the wall.
Re-edition from 1957
H 182cm (71⅝in) W 105cm (41½in) D 30cm
(11⅞in)
MANUFACTURER: BERNINI, ITALY

131

130

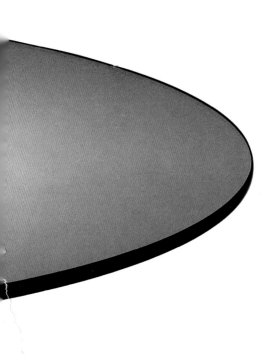

133

132

134

1 FURNITURE

132 CHARLES AND RAY EAMES
EAMES SCREEN
PLYWOOD, ASH VENEER, FLEXIBLE CONNECTION
WITH COTTON STRIP
Re-edition from 1940
H 172cm (67¾in) W (8 units) 204cm (80¾in)
W (6 units) 153cm (60¼in)
MANUFACTURER: VITRA, GERMANY

133 CARLO MOLLINO
BEDSIDE TABLE, *CARLINO*
BLACK-LACQUERED WOOD, BLACK PLATE GLASS
Re-edition from 1933
H 75cm (29½in) W 45cm (17¾in) D 28cm (11in)
MANUFACTURER: ZANOTTA, ITALY

134 CARLO MOLLINO
TABLE, *REALE*
ASH, GLASS, GRANITE
Re-edition from 1946
H 71.1cm (28in) W 200cm (78¾in) D 92.7cm
(36½in)
MANUFACTURER: ICF/UNIKA VAEV, USA

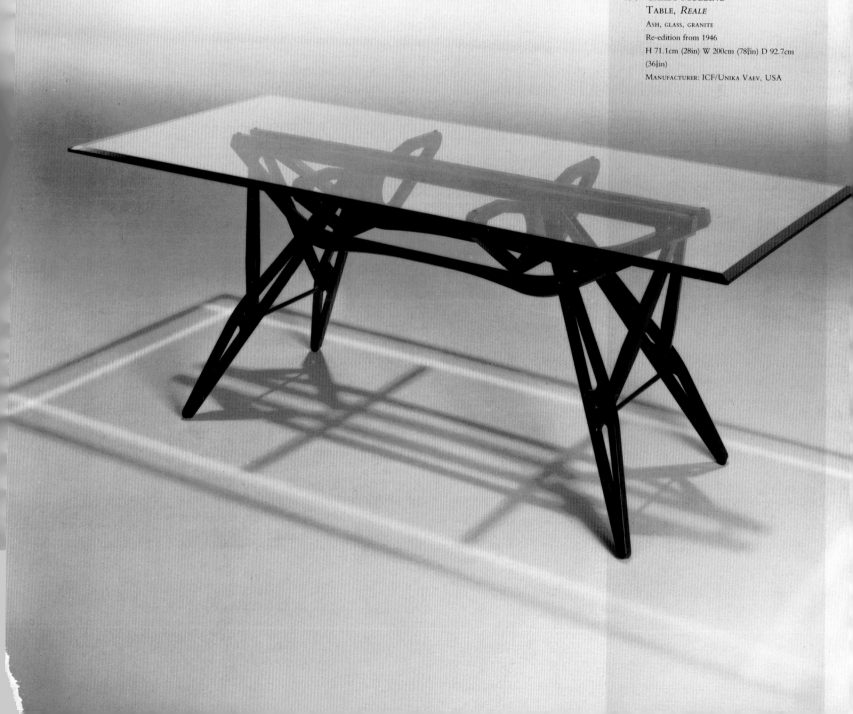

1 FURNITURE

135 RICHARD NEUTRA
SIDE CHAIR
STAINLESS STEEL, FABRIC, LEATHER, ALCANTARA
Re-edition from 1947
H 83cm (32¾in) W 40cm (15¾in) D 47cm
(18½in)
MANUFACTURER: PROSPETTIVE, ITALY

136 RICHARD NEUTRA
CANTILEVER CHAIR
STAINLESS STEEL, FABRIC, LEATHER, ALCANTARA
Re-edition from 1929
H 64cm (25¼in) W 56cm (22in) D 70cm (27½in)
MANUFACTURER: PROSPETTIVE, ITALY

137 RICHARD NEUTRA
TABLE, *CAMEL*
WOOD
The legs can be re-positioned to
adjust the height.
Re-edition from 1940
H 72cm (28¾in) W 205cm (80¾in) D 90cm
(35½in)
MANUFACTURER: PROSPETTIVE, ITALY

138 RICHARD NEUTRA
SEATING, *ALPHA*
WOOD, FABRIC, LEATHER, ALCANTARA
Re-edition from 1929
H 90cm (35½in) W 106cm (41¾in) D 84cm
(33in)
MANUFACTURER: PROSPETTIVE, ITALY

1991 was a year of welcome re-editions of furniture by Mollino, Castiglioni and Eames; nothing is more welcome, however, than the long-lost pieces by the Austrian-born architect **Richard Neutra**. A member of that first generation of modernists which included Le Corbusier and Mies van der Rohe, he created a number of designs for his own architectural projects; when Prospettive acquired the rights from his son Dion in 1989, they became available for the first time. The early version of the *Cantilever Chair*, created for the steel-framed Lovell House four years after Neutra moved to the US in 1923, emerges as a superbly understated masterpiece of 1920s modernism that is arguably the equal of designs by Le Corbusier and Marcel Breuer. It is likely to find an enthusiastic new audience. So, too, is the *Camel* table, inspired by the sight of a camel curling its legs to lie down. The wood or steel legs can be reversed so that the piece can function as a dining table or a coffee table. Nine of Neutra's pieces are now in production and more will follow, including examples of his lamps.

135

136

137

138

2

2

LIGHTIN

The 1991/92 lighting collections were marked less by bold innovation and decisive breaks with the past than by a steady exploration of the possibilities opened up in previous years by new lightweight light sources. There are designers who concentrate on the quality of light, producing fittings which are quietly elegant rather than sculpturally assertive, and there is another camp which treats the light-fitting as an occasion for expression and poetry, whimsy and humour. What both groups share is a liking for bold, clearly defined shapes and a degree of structural simplicity. There is nothing in this collection to compare with the exuberance of Castiglioni's bulb-encrusted *Taraxacum '88* ceiling lamp of four years ago.

Now that a lamp can assume almost any form, aesthetic restraint becomes an even more purposeful statement. The pendant lamps by Andrée Putman, King and Miranda, and Lovegrove and Brown have a timeless classical confidence. Designs such as Afra and Tobia Scarpa's *Pierrot* task lamp and Josep Lluscà's *Avalon* bedside light are closer to this functionalist philosophy than they might appear at first sight. Their idiosyncratic imagery is not predetermined by the designer's whim, it is a by-product of careful analysis of the lighting problem.

For Agnoletto and Clerici the starting point is far more conceptual. Their *Sputnik* lamp, a bare bulb on a flexible stalk, is an idea (about art, industry and space technology) rather than a practical solution. With *Lucellino*, on the other hand, Ingo Maurer seems almost to mock the aerial freedom he was one of the first to exploit with *YaYa Ho*—he simply attaches a handful of feathers to some ordinary light bulbs.

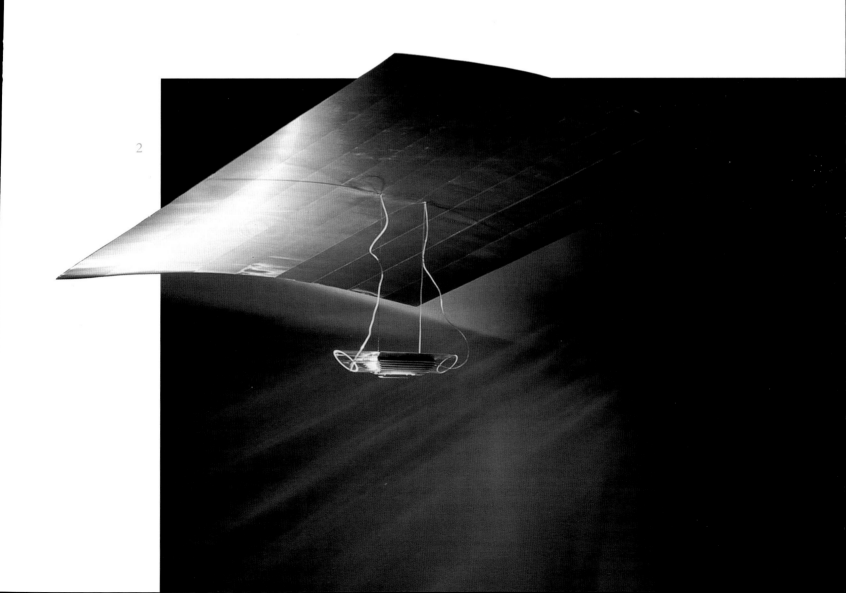

Previous spread

1 INGO MAURER
CEILING LAMP, *LUCELLINO*
LIGHT BULB, FEATHERS, WIRES
A low-voltage halogen bulb is
made to look like an ordinary
incandescent bulb.
Prototype
Takes one 12V halogen bulb.
H 10cm (4in) W 15cm (6in) L 20cm (7⅞in)
MANUFACTURER: INGO MAURER, GERMANY

2 INGO MAURER
CEILING LAMP, *SCOOPER*
METAL, GLASS
The glass tube both carries and
covers the light source. The
reflector (sail) is made of a new
material used in space aeronautics.
Takes one 300/500W 12V halogen bulb.
H 50cm (19⅝in) W 170cm (66⅞in) L 150cm
(59in)
MANUFACTURER: INGO MAURER, GERMANY

3

4

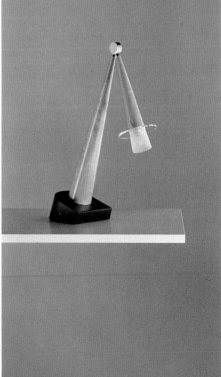

5

Many designers have exploited the anthropomorphic possibilities of the task lamp, but this was not the intention of **Afra** and **Tobia Scarpa** when they began the two years of development that would lead to the creation of *Pierrot*, their latest project for Flos. Early drawings show a tall, conical base, which metamorphosed over time into two flat legs, with arms similarly profiled. This structure is made of the same composite board used for printed circuitry and serves the double function of conducting the current without need of wires. Bird-like and whimsical, the lamp has a personality sufficiently distinctive to make it stand out from the crowd of competitors in this already saturated area of the market.

6

2 LIGHTING

7 PATRICK MAGNIN
DESK LAMP, *ZOOM*

ENAMELLED ALUMINIUM STRUCTURE,
THERMOPLASTIC POLYESTER BASE,
POLYCARBONATE ALUMINIUM REFLECTOR

The base houses the transformer
and rests on conical rollers which
permit a rotatory movement.

Takes one 50W 12V halogen bulb.
Base: W 10.5cm (4⅛in)
Arm: L 123cm (48⅜in)
MANUFACTURER: ARTELUCE, ITALY

8 PERRY A. KING AND SANTIAGO MIRANDA
SUSPENDED SPOTLIGHT, *HALO*

ALUMINIUM, PLASTIC

Takes one 50W 12V halogen bulb.
H 116cm (45⅝in) W 11cm (4⅜in) H of lamp
6.2cm (2⅜in)
MANUFACTURER: ARTELUCE FLOS, ITALY

9 PERRY A. KING AND SANTIAGO MIRANDA
SUSPENDED LIGHT, *ALOA*

ALUMINIUM, FROSTED GLASS

Takes one 20/30/50W 12V halogen bulb.
Shade 3.6cm (1½in) W 23cm (9in)
MANUFACTURER: ARTELUCE FLOS, ITALY

7

9

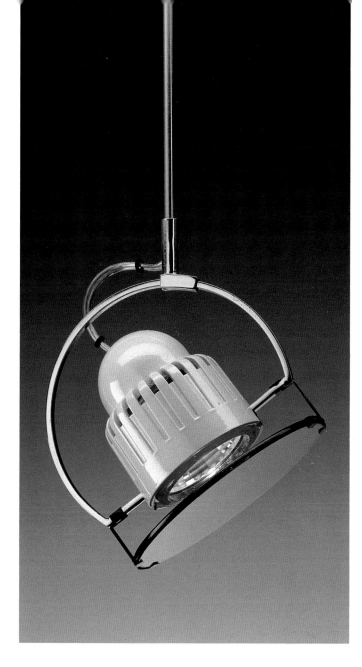

8

The relationship between **Perry King** and **Santiago Miranda** and the Italian company Arteluce Flos is now over fifteen years old. During this time, the Anglo-Spanish duo have created more than twenty lamps; their first, the *Jill* uplighter of 1977, is still the most popular and commercially successful. What distinguishes all of these designs, as the recent monograph *King and Miranda: The Poetry of the Machine* makes clear, is the interplay of technology and poetry, and their attempt to reconcile science and art. After the initial minimalism of *Jill* and the ceiling-mounted *Aurora* of 1982, which was similarly influential, the designers moved in the mid-1980s into more ornate designs, such as the bewinged *Gabriel* table lamp. King and Miranda's two most recent light fittings for Arteluce Flos, *Halo* and *Aloa*, suggest a return to less elaborately engineered and expressive forms. *Halo* is an adjustable spotlight in aluminium and plastic that reapplies the semicircular frame of the pair's earlier *RAI* spotlight (see *The International Design Yearbook 1989/90*). *Aloa*, a pendant light, has been treated with more of a flourish, particularly in the hoop of aluminium that encircles the frosted glass diffuser, but it, too, provides evidence of a new sobriety in their thinking.

11

10

2 LIGHTING

10 PHILIPS CORPORATE INDUSTRIAL DESIGN

POCKET LAMP

ANODIZED ALUMINIUM, SUEDE-COATED PLASTIC

The on/off switch is integrated in the sliding cover.

Takes one 2W 4V halogen bulb.

H 11cm (4⅜in) W 6cm (2⅜in) D 2.5cm (1in)

MANUFACTURER: PHILIPS ELECTRONICS, THE NETHERLANDS

11 KENNETH GRANGE AND JOHAN SANTER

DISPLAY LIGHTING SYSTEM

MOULDED HIGH TEMPERATURE PLASTICS, DIE-CAST ALLOY

A complete range of low voltage track and rose mounted display lights using a 5cm (2in) diameter dichroic reflector lamp unit.

Takes 12V lightstream M range bulbs.

MANUFACTURER: THORN LIGHTING, UK

11

12

13

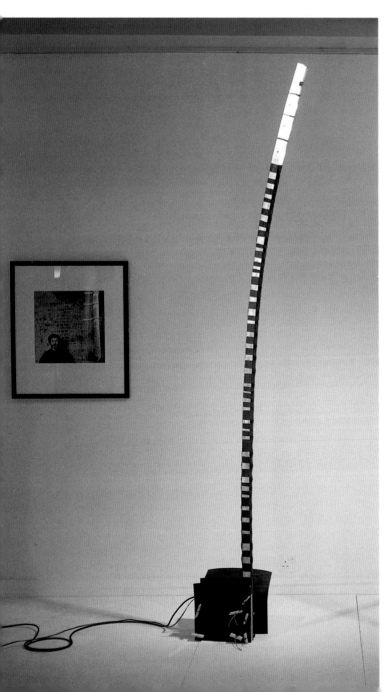

2 LIGHTING

12 PUCCI DE ROSSI
TABLE LAMP
ZINC
Takes one 100W bulb.
H 65cm (25⅜in) Di 25cm (9⅞in)
MANUFACTURER: NÉOTÙ, FRANCE

13 THOMAS EISL
FLOOR LAMP
ALUMINIUM, RUBBER
One-off
Takes four 20W bulbs.
H 245cm (96½in)
MANUFACTURER: THOMAS EISL, UK

14 FRANZ WEST
SWINGING LAMP
IRON
Limited batch production
Takes two halogen bulbs.
L 180cm (70⅞in)
MANUFACTURER: MEMPHIS, ITALY

15 BOŘEK ŠÍPEK
WARDROBE WITH ILLUMINATION
BASE STEEL (ST37), WOOD, BRASS TUBE,
LACQUERED SHEET STEEL
The light is aimed towards the ceiling.
Takes one low voltage halogen bulb with transformer.
H 210cm (82⅜in) W 52cm (20½in) Di 43cm (16⅞in)
MANUFACTURER: VITRA, GERMANY

14

15

The immateriality of light and its many cultural and poetic associations might be expected to make a profound impact on lighting design. But the form of the contemporary lamp, despite the liberating technological miniaturization of the 1980s, is still in most cases pragmatically determined. When designers do treat lighting as an opportunity to explore the fantastic or symbolic, the results can be so whimsical that it is not always apparent one is looking at a lamp. **Bořek Šípek's** *Wardrobe* for Vitra combines its function as a clothes-hanger with a frilly-rimmed uplighter that blossoms from the spiky central column like the flower of an exotic cactus. **Pucci de Rossi's** lamp for Néotù, however, resembles a crudely formed artefact from some forgotten age of zinc.

The master of this kind of lighting design is **Thomas Eisl,** an Austrian artist resident in London whose laterally conceived constructions have made him an *International Design Yearbook* regular. Eisl's lights are improvisations (though always deeply pondered) using ordinary materials available to anyone: bricks, blocks of wood or, in this case, strips of aluminium and rubber. No matter how far he strays from conventional notions of appropriate form, his designs always retain a sense of the delicacy and magic of light.

16

2 LIGHTING

16 DAL MONDO
CANDELABRA
WOVEN WIRE
H 122cm (48in) Di 114cm (44⅞in)
MANUFACTURER: CAPPELLINI ARTE, ITALY

17 MAURO CANFORI
FLOOR LAMP, *MANTIDE 315*
BLACK LACQUERED METAL BASE AND STEM,
WHITE LACQUERED ALUMINIUM REFLECTOR, SILK-
SCREENED POLYCARBONATE DIFFUSER
A dimmer facility gives indirect
and diffused light.
Takes one max 60W incandescent bulb or one
max 300W halogen tubular bulb.
H 190cm (74⅞in) Reflector Di 48cm (18⅝in)
MANUFACTURER: OLUCE, ITALY

18 RICCARDO DALISI
FLOOR LAMP, *SISTER 365*
LACQUERED METAL STRUCTURE, ADJUSTABLE
SILK-SCREENED POLYCARBONATE DIFFUSER
Takes one max 150W incandescent bulb.
H 180cm (70⅞in) 210cm (82⅝in) W 90cm
(35½in)
MANUFACTURER: OLUCE, ITALY

17

18

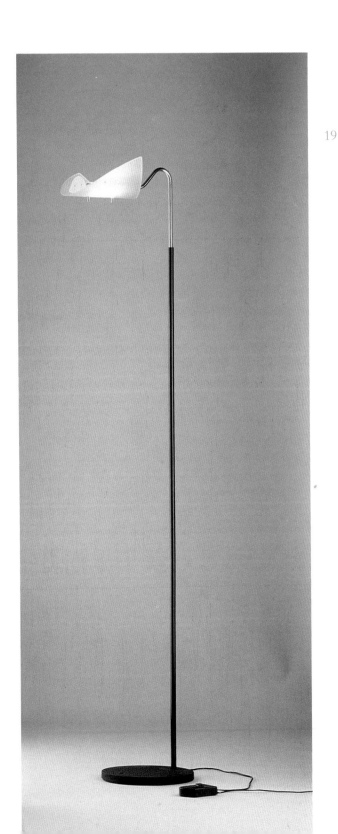

19   20

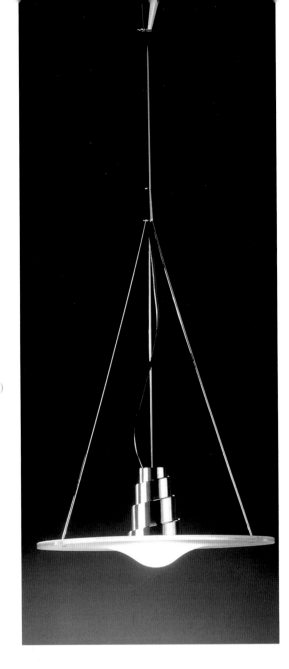

2 LIGHTING

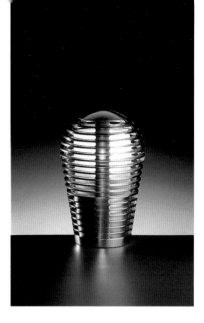

19 JORGE GARCIA GARAY
FLOOR LAMP, *ASTRA*
BLACK OR CHROMED METAL, BENT SAND-
BLASTED CRYSTAL SHADE
Takes one max 500W bulb.
H 190cm (74⅞in) W 40cm (15¾in) D 25cm
(9⅞in)
MANUFACTURER: GARCIA GARAY, SPAIN

**20 ROSS LOVEGROVE AND JULIAN
BROWN**
EXTENSIBLE SUSPENDED LAMP,
BAB-ILIS
METAL, MATT PRESSED-GLASS DIFFUSER,
CHROMIUM-PLATED FINISH
Takes one 100W GLS bulb.
L 35cm (13¾in) Di 13cm (5⅛in)
MANUFACTURER: METALARTE, SPAIN

21 SERGI AND OSCAR DEVESA
TABLE LAMP, *ZEN*
ANODIZED ALUMINIUM, CHROMED AND PAINTED
IRON
Fully articulated to permit
movement in any direction from
the base.
Takes one 100W bulb.
H 61cm (24in) W 13.6cm (5⅜in)
MANUFACTURER: METALARTE, SPAIN

22 HANS ANSEMS
FLOOR AND WALL LAMPS, *ZEUS*
STEEL, DULL SATIN GLASS
Each takes one 300W tungsten halogen bulb.
Floor: H 222.5cm (87⅞in) W 67cm (26¾in)
Wall: W 67cm (26⅜in) D 22cm (8⅜in)
MANUFACTURER: LUXO ITALIANA, ITALY

21

22

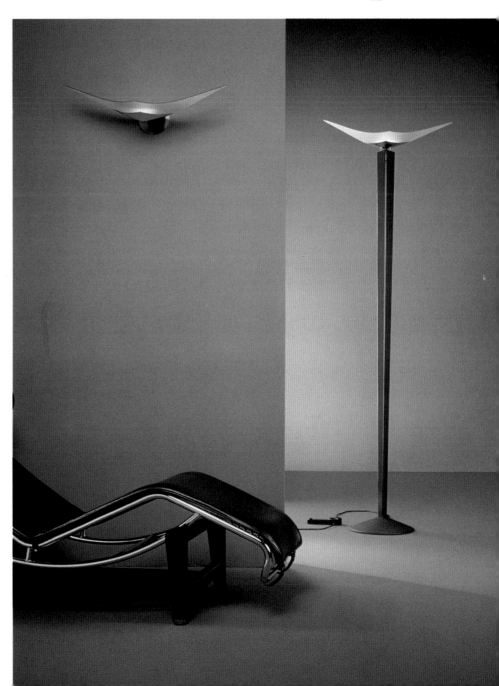

2 LIGHTING

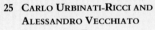

23 ANDRÉE PUTMAN
SUSPENDED LAMP, *LINDA*
SATIN ALUMINIUM, POLISHED CHROME
Smaller model takes two, larger model four
150W halogen bulbs.
L 122cm (48in) or 244cm (96in) D 7.5cm (3in)
MANUFACTURER: BALDINGER ARCHITECTURAL
LIGHTING, USA

23

24 ANDRÉE PUTMAN
SUSPENDED LAMP, *CONSTANTIN*
CHROME, WITH ACRYLIC, ALABASTER OR GLASS
DIFFUSER
Casts translucent light downwards
while radiating indirect light
upwards.
66cm model takes three 60 or 75W
incandescent bulbs or six compact fluorescent
bulbs. Other models take three 75 or 100W
incandescent bulbs or six compact fluorescent
bulbs.
Diffuser D 12.5cm (5in) Di 66cm (26in)
D 15cm (6in) Di 91.5cm (36in)
D 18.5cm (7¼in) Di 107cm (42in)
MANUFACTURER: BALDINGER
ARCHITECTURAL LIGHTING, USA

24

**25 CARLO URBINATI-RICCI AND
ALESSANDRO VECCHIATO**
WALL LIGHT, *FOLIO*
BLOWN GLASS
Takes one 150W halogen bulb.
W 33cm (13in) L 25cm (9⅞in) D 8cm (3⅛in)
MANUFACTURER: FOSCARINI MURANO, ITALY

26 MASATOSHI SAKAEGI
WALL LIGHT/LIGHTING GRAPHIC
TRANSLUCENT BOARD, FLUORESCENT BULB
The reflectors can be angled to
create varying light patterns.
Limited batch production
H 77cm (30⅜in) W 73cm (28¾in) D 14cm (5½in)
MANUFACTURER: SAKAEGI DESIGN STUDIO,
JAPAN

There is more than a hint of heroic
1930s modernism in **Andrée Putman's**
designs for the New York company
Baldinger. Putman established her own
company, Écart International, to
manufacture classic pieces by Eileen
Gray and Robert Mallet-Stevens, and
their simplicity of line and rigorous
taste—at once luxurious and
functionally austere—have become an
essential component of her own
approach. She has created two wall
sconces and three pendant lamps,
including the triangular-profiled *Linda*
and the centrepiece of the collection,
Constantin. Acrylic, alabaster or glass
bowls are suspended from a metal stem
which has the immaculately engineered
appearance of a precision tool. There is
also a chandelier version nearly seven
feet across, with four glass globes
mounted on extended arms.

25

26

25

26

105

27

28

29

30

27 ALIEN ASSOCIATES
TABLE LAMP, *SHUFFO*
NICKEL-PLATED BRASS, ACRYLIC
The lamp operates by picking up
power from the base via the legs.
Limited batch production
Takes one 10W 12V halogen bulb.
H 16cm (6⅜in) Di 18cm (7⅛in)
Base Di 30cm (11¾in)
MANUFACTURER: WOKA LAMPS, AUSTRIA

28 SERGIO ASTI
TABLE LAMP, *PARIGI 1991*
GLASS
Takes one 60W or 100W bulb.
H 308cm (149⅝in) 300cm (118in) Di 400cm
(157½in) 300cm (118in)
MANUFACTURER: CANDLE, ITALY

**29 LAURA AGNOLETTO AND MARZIO
RUSCONI CLERICI**
FLOOR LAMP, *SPUTNIK I*
RUBBER, PERSPEX AND AN INDUSTRIAL WHEEL
Prototype
Takes one 125W bulb.
H 130cm (51⅛in) Di 50cm (19⅝in)
MANUFACTURER: AMEDEI TRE, ITALY

30 TILL LEESER
FLOOR LAMP, *METEOR*
METAL, STONE
Limited batch production
Takes one 50W 12V halogen bulb.
H 200cm (78¾in) W 30cm (11¾in) D 30cm (11⅝in)
MANUFACTURER: TILL LEESER DESIGN,
GERMANY

31

The *Avalon* lamp by **Josep Lluscà** for Blauet has won many admirers for its simple charm and velvet-textured metallic finish. For Lluscà, it was a return to the conical shape of the *Bolonia* lamp he designed for Metalarte (see *International Design Yearbook 1989/90*). Like its predecessor, *Avalon* is intended for bedside reading, and tackles the problem with some ingenuity. The shade, a miniature coolie hat, can be tilted to direct the light and shield the eyes from stray beams, using a handle that projects like a miniature cigarette from below. These anthropomorphic details, and the lamp's strong tactile appeal, combine to give it the quality of an adult toy. Yet its form is in no way gratuitous: it has arisen from Lluscà's careful definition of the reader's lighting needs.

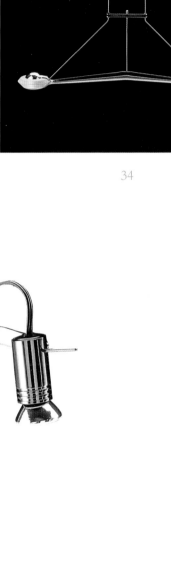

2 LIGHTING

31 JOSEP LLUSCÀ
TABLE LAMP, *AVALON*
SHEET METAL, PRESSED GLASS
A double-position switch allows
two types of light. A swivel joint
in the lampshade allows it to be set
in any direction.
TAKES ONE 50W 12V HALOGEN BULB.
H 25cm (9⅞in) W 9.5cm (3¾in)
MANUFACTURER: BLAUET, SPAIN

32 JOSEP LLUSCÀ
FLOOR LAMP, *SAETA*
STEEL STRUCTURE, CAST-IRON BASE, MATT
METALLIZED GREY LACQUER, CHROME-PLATED
BLACK OR WHITE FINISH
TAKES ONE 50W HALOGEN BULB.
H 120cm (47¼in) W 48cm (18⅞in)
MANUFACTURER: BLAUET, SPAIN

33 JOSEP LLUSCÀ
TABLE LAMP, *SAETA*
STEEL STRUCTURE, BLACK POLYURETHANE BASE,
ALUMINIUM REFLECTOR, MATT GLASS
PROTECTION, SILVER-PLATED OR BLACK CHROME
FINISH
TAKES ONE 20W 12V HALOGEN BULB.
H 48cm (18⅞in) W 48cm (18⅞in)
MANUFACTURER: BLAUET, SPAIN

34

34 JOSEP LLUSCÀ
EXTENSIBLE SUSPENDED LAMP,
GAVINA
INJECTED ALUMINIUM STRUCTURE, NATURAL
FINISH, EXTENSIBLE CHROME-PLATED STEEL RODS,
DOUBLE SHADE WITH GLASS DIFFUSER
TAKES TWO 50W 12V HALOGEN BULBS.
L 104cm–177cm (41in–69¾in) W 71cm (28in)
MANUFACTURER: BLAUET, SPAIN

32

33

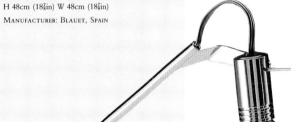

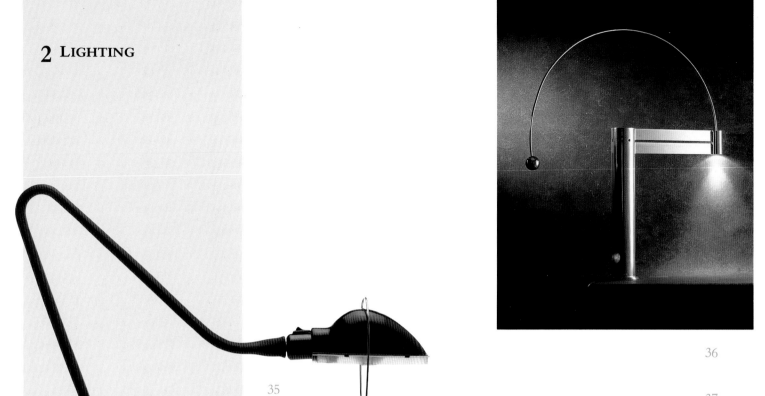

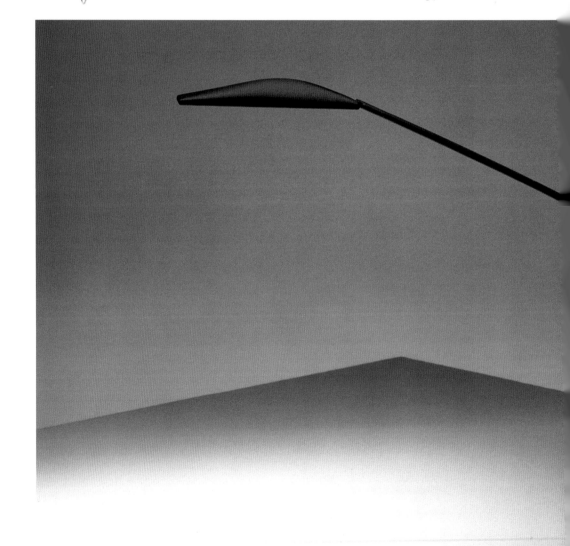

35

36

37

35 ASSOCIATE DESIGNERS
TABLE LAMP, *BRAVO*

STEEL, ALUMINIUM, PLASTIC, ELASTOMER
Prototype
Takes one incandescent, halogen or PL bulb.
Arm: W 2.8cm (1⅛in) L 88cm (34⅝in)
D 1.4cm (½in)
Head: W 10cm (4in) L 20cm (7⅞in)
MANUFACTURER: BRAVO-U, SPAIN

36 PIERRE LALLEMAND
DESK LAMP, *PARADOXE*

CAST ALUMINIUM
Limited batch production
Takes one low-tension 12V dichroic bulb.
H 60cm (23½in)
MANUFACTURER: MOONLIGHT DESIGN, BELGIUM

37 MARIO BARBAGLIA AND MARCO COLOMBO
TABLE LAMP, *DOVE REVERB*
TECHNOPOLYMERS
Light intensity is adjusted by the approach of a hand.
Takes one 50W 24V halogen bulb.
H min 27cm (10½in) max 96cm (37⅞in)
Base: W 11cm (4⅜in)
Lamp: W 84cm (33in)
MANUFACTURER: PAF, ITALY

38 JOSEP MASSANA, JOSEP TREMOLEDA AND JOSEP MORA
TABLE AND CLAMP LAMP, *ROMANA*
IRON, ANODIZED ALUMINIUM
Fully articulated to give light in any direction.
Takes 100W incandescent bulbs.
H 61cm (24in) L 86cm (33⅞in)
MANUFACTURER: MOBLES 114, SPAIN

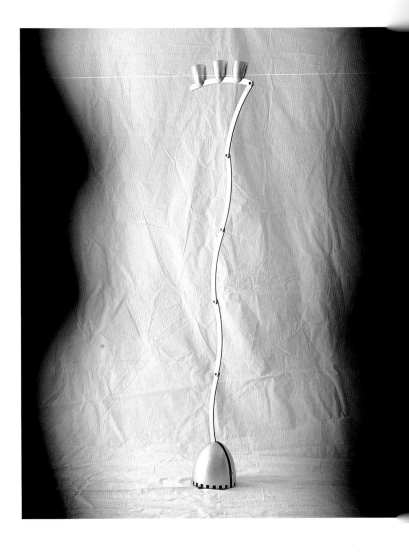

The *Alien* lamp by the German designer **Siggi Fischer** is a kit of parts which sets the highest premium on versatility. Broken down into its cast-aluminium components, *Alien* looks like nothing in particular. Assembled, it can function as a table lamp or, with its six-part articulated arm fully extended, as a floor-standing uplighter. Depending on the configuration, up to three egg cup-sized lamps can be clipped to the frame. As with Josep Lluscà's *Avalon* reading lamp, a friendly appearance and ease of handling act as an encouragement to play.

2 LIGHTING

39 SIGGI FISCHER
TABLE LAMP, *ALIEN*
MATT CHROME METAL, CAST ALUMINIUM
Fully collapsible with six folding parts.
Three clip-on lamps take 200W 12V bulbs.
Max H 180cm (70⅞in) Di 18cm (7⅛in)
MANUFACTURER: THOMAS SCHULTE, GERMANY

40 YAMADA DESIGN STUDIO
READING LAMP, *COMODINO*
MOULDED PLASTIC, STEEL
Can be used with rechargeable battery or AC adaptor, giving different light intensities.
Takes a max of one 4.8V bulb.
H 34cm (13⅜in) Di 10.4cm (4⅛in)
MANUFACTURER: CLASSICON, GERMANY

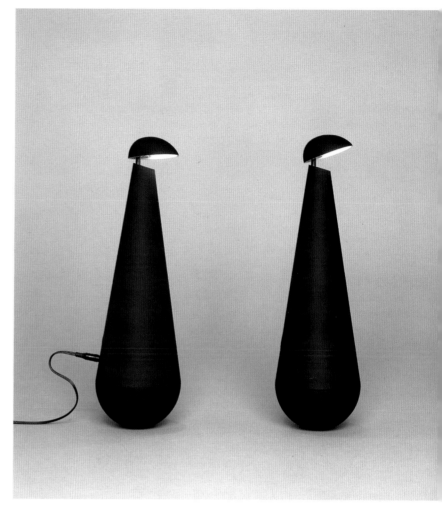

40

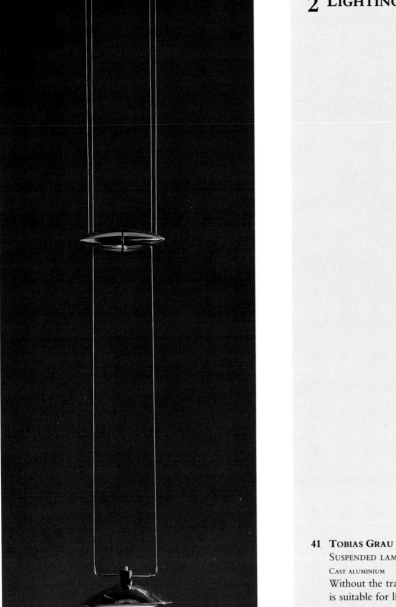

41

42

41 TOBIAS GRAU
SUSPENDED LAMP, *TAI*
CAST ALUMINIUM
Without the transformer the lamp
is suitable for lighting systems.
Takes one 50W halogen bulb.
H variable Di 18cm (7½in)
MANUFACTURER: TOBIAS GRAU, GERMANY

42 TOBIAS GRAU
TABLE LAMP, *KALLISTO*
CAST BRONZE, MURANO GLASS SHADE
Limited batch production
Takes one max 100W incandescent bulb.
H 70cm (27½in) W 50cm (19⅝in)
MANUFACTURER: TOBIAS GRAU, GERMANY

43 HERBERT WEINAND
FLOOR LAMP, *TRIBELLI*
STEEL, OPAQUE GLASS
Produced in three parts.
Takes one 60W opaque bulb.
H 133cm (52⅜in) W 14cm (5½in) D 14cm (5½in)
MANUFACTURER: GALERIE WEINAND, GERMANY

44

2 LIGHTING

44   TERENCE WOODGATE
LIGHTING SYSTEM, *INFINITE*
EXTRUDED AND DIE-CAST ALUMINIUM
Full movability guaranteed by 360–
degree swivel action of spotlights
and the hinged coupler joining
straight and curved tracks.
Horizontal track elements of low-
voltage modular lengths plus track
modules with a 450-degree arc
which could create a 3-metre
circle, both having top and
underside clip facilities for
spotlights.
Takes dichroic or tungsten halogen bulbs.
Four spotlight types:
20W capsule with 2 beam sizes
50W capsule with 20 beam widths
50W capsule with choice of wide and narrow
beam reflectors
75W capsule with choice of wide, medium and
narrow beam reflectors
MANUFACTURER: CONCORD, UK

45   ROY FLEETWOOD
SPOTLIGHT, *EMANON*
CAST ALUMINIUM, SHEET STEEL, PLASTIC
Takes one 750W or one 1,000W tungsten
halogen bulb.
H 60.5cm (23⅜in) W 31.6cm (12⅜in) L 62cm
(24⅜in) Di 15cm (6in)
MANUFACTURER: ERCO LEUCHTEN, GERMANY

45

Roy Fleetwood's first two collaborations with Erco were structural lighting support systems—*Axis* and *Gantry*—of exceptional elegance and technical ingenuity. For his third project he has turned his attention to the light source. The *Emanon* projectors—Fleetwood calls them 'light cannons'—are for use primarily on stage, or for trade fairs and exhibitions, but they could equally well be applied to architectural interiors. The system is modular, made of lightweight aluminium castings, and components can be slotted into the basic assembly with ease.

The same careful resolution of functional requirements and aesthetics is to be found in **Terence Woodgate's** low-voltage lighting system for Concord. *Infinite's* two-sided track can be organised into loops, waves, zig-zags and double-decker configurations; the spotlights can project upwards or downwards, on stalks of variable length.

3

1

3

TABLEW

2

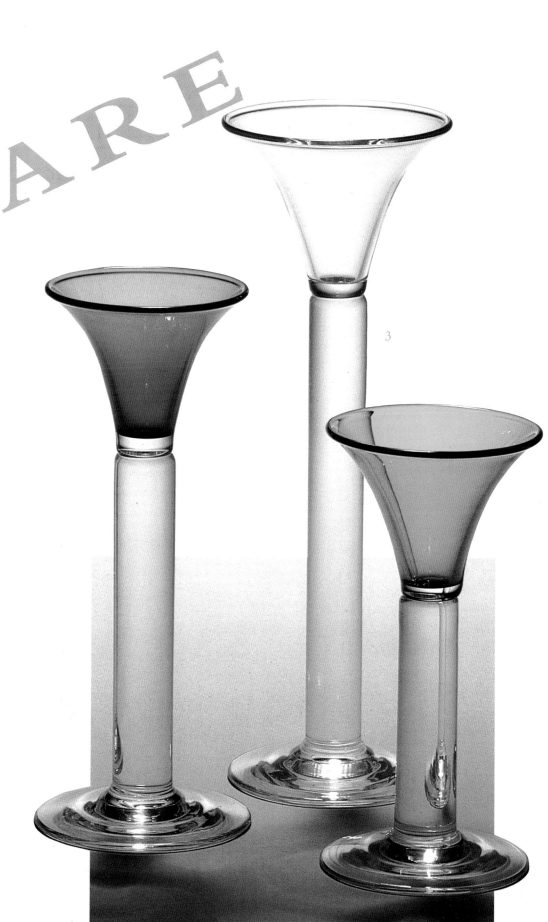

ARE

3

Of all the categories in this edition of the *Yearbook*, tableware is the section that seems most rigorously to define Andrée Putman's personal vision. Other guest editors might have made many of the same choices in furniture, lighting or product design, but there is a unity and coherence to her choice of tableware that reflects, not an unexpected consistency among designers working in this area, so much as the consistency of the selector's own sensibility and taste.

The strictures that Andrée Putman applies to furniture are doubled here. There is little place for the eccentric, the loud or the peculiar in this most intimate area of design. With a few exceptions (Bořek Šípek is the most notable), the pieces she has selected, whether classical or modernist, evince the same rejection of formal complexity, and superfluous ornament and style. Lines are taut, sinuous, precise; outlines meticulously drawn. The vivacity of Sergio Asti's pure white vases and Masatoshi Sakaegi's plates comes from the way that irregular edges play against each other like hillside contours. Pattern, where it is used at all, is bright and graphic, a definer of shape, as in Maryse Boxer's plates and Monica Guggisberg and Philip Baldwin's blown-glass bowls, which are rich in colour, unpretentious in form and—a vital consideration—comfortable to live with.

Yet there are some pieces in Andrée Putman's selection which suggest the more informal and even playful possibilities of tableware. Quirky details—the suggestion of trees and buildings—enliven the otherwise smooth white sides of Olivier Gagnère's terracotta vase, while Yamo's egg cup is not really a 'cup' at all; it is a collection of springy metal arms that fondle the egg as you eat.

3 TABLEWARE

Previous spread

1 MONICA GUGGISBERG AND PHILIP BALDWIN
OVERLAY BOWL
SAND-BLASTED SWEDISH HALF-CRYSTAL (5% LEAD),
KUGLER COLOURS
Limited batch production
H 14cm (5½in) Di 23cm (9in)
MANUFACTURER: VERRERIE DE NONFOUX,
SWITZERLAND

2 MONICA GUGGISBERG AND PHILIP BALDWIN
BASE BOWLS
SWEDISH HALF-CRYSTAL (5% LEAD), KUGLER COLOURS
Left to right:
H 14.5cm (5¾in) Di 22cm (8⅝in)
H 12cm (4¾in) Di 18cm (7⅛in)
H 17.5cm (6⅞in) Di 27cm (10½in)
MANUFACTURER: VERRERIE DE NONFOUX,
SWITZERLAND

3 MONICA GUGGISBERG AND PHILIP BALDWIN
CANDLESTICKS
SWEDISH HALF-CRYSTAL (5% LEAD), KUGLER COLOURS
Left to right:
H 24cm (9⅜in) Di 9cm (3½in)
H 30cm (11⅞in) Di 9cm (3½in)
H 17cm (6⅝in) Di 9cm (3½in)
MANUFACTURER: VERRERIE DE NONFOUX,
SWITZERLAND

4

5

6

7

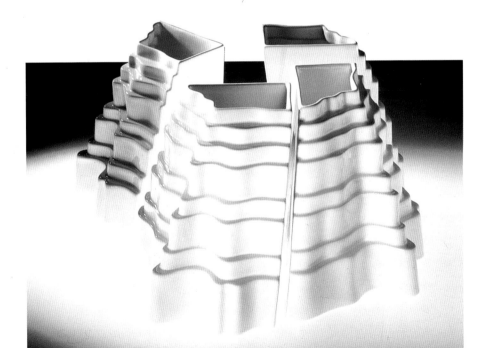

This spread

4 Lino Sabattini
Plate, *R/3*
Porcelain
Prototype
H 4cm (1½in) Di 25.5cm (10in)
Manufacturer: Sabattini Argenteria, Italy

5 Masatoshi Sakaegi
Plates, from the *Clay Wave*
collection
Ceramic
Top to bottom:
W 10.8cm (4¼in) Di 12.3cm (4⅞in)
W 17.8cm (7in) Di 20.2cm (8in)
W 22.7cm (9in) Di 25.8cm (10¼in)
W 29.5cm (11⅝in) Di 34cm (13⅜in)
Manufacturer: Sakaegi Design Studio, Japan

6 Sergio Asti
Dishes
Bone china
W 10cm (4in) L 10cm (4in)
Manufacturer: Oun Corporation, Japan

7 Sergio Asti
Vase, *Collina*
Ceramic, in four pieces
H 24cm (9⅜in) W 20.5cm (8¼in) L 22cm (8⅝in)
Manufacturer: Anthologie Quartett,
Germany

3 TABLEWARE

8 **GUIDO ANTONIO NIEST**
OIL LAMP
SAND-BLASTED SILVER-PLATED BRASS CUP,
ALUMINIUM STAND
Uses paraffin oil and a fibreglass
wick. The flame lasts approximately
three hours.
One-off
H 35cm (13¾in) Di 5cm (2in)
MANUFACTURER: ATELIER CANAIMA, ITALY

9 **MARCO ZANUSO**
VASE, *CEDAR*
CERAMIC
Limited batch production
H 30cm (11⅞in) W 22cm (8⅝in)
MANUFACTURER: ITALO BOSA, ITALY

10 **ANDREAS WEBER**
CANDLESTICK, *ISADORA*
STAINLESS STEEL, GLASS
H 32cm (12½in) Di 12cm (4¾in)
MANUFACTURER: ARTIPRESENT, GERMANY

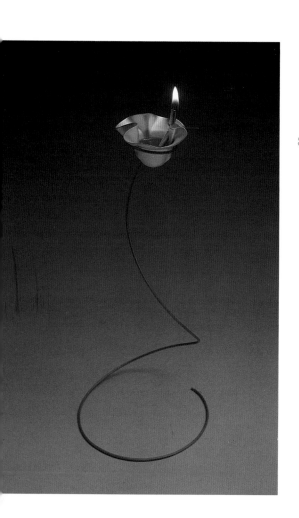

8

9   10

11

3 Tableware

11 Oscar Tusquets Blanca
Candlestick, *Salvador*
Matt or silver-coloured bronze
H 29cm (11$\frac{3}{8}$in) D 9cm (3$\frac{1}{2}$in)
Manufacturer: Driade, Italy

12 Oscar Tusquets Blanca
Cutlery, *Victoria*
Stainless steel
Left to right:
Butter knife: L 13.8cm (5$\frac{3}{8}$in)
Tablespoon: L 19.9cm (7$\frac{7}{8}$in)
Table fork: L 20.2cm (8in)
Table knife: L 22.8cm (9in)
Fish fork: L 19.9cm (7$\frac{7}{8}$in)
Fish knife: L 20.9cm (8$\frac{1}{4}$in)
Coffee spoon: L 10.5cm (4$\frac{1}{8}$in)
Teaspoon: L 13cm (5$\frac{1}{8}$in)
Fruit knife: L 19.6cm (7$\frac{3}{4}$in)
Fruit fork: L 19.3cm (7$\frac{5}{8}$in)
Dessertspoon: L 19.9cm (7$\frac{7}{8}$in)
Sauce spoon: L 19.7cm (7$\frac{3}{4}$in)
Manufacturer: Driade, Italy

13 Oscar Tusquets Blanca
Tea service, *Victoria*
White porcelain with a red base
Left to right:
Tray: H 1.8cm ($\frac{3}{4}$in) Di 32cm (12$\frac{1}{2}$in)
Teacup: H 6cm (2$\frac{3}{8}$in) W 12.2cm (4$\frac{7}{8}$in) Di 10cm (4in)
Saucer: H 1.8cm ($\frac{3}{4}$in) Di 15.6cm (6$\frac{1}{8}$in)
Large teapot: H 16.6cm (6$\frac{1}{2}$in) W 22.3cm (8$\frac{3}{4}$in) Di 15.2cm (6in)
Small teapot: H 10.8cm (4$\frac{1}{4}$in) W 17.6cm (6$\frac{7}{8}$in) Di 12cm (4$\frac{3}{4}$in)
Manufacturer: Driade, Italy

A gentle Catalan humour pervades the work of **Oscar Tusquets Blanca**. He will happily concede that his *Salvador* candlestick, a tribute to his friend Salvador Dalí, is more reminiscent of a Giacometti sculpture than of the notorious Surrealist, and the same generosity of spirit underlies *Victoria*, his first set of cutlery, for Driade's series *Follies*. The company asked Tusquets Blanca for functional designs in marked contrast to the flamboyance of Bořek Šípek's tableware. This request, combined with the complaints of his wife Victoria Roqué, a chef of seventeen years' standing, that designers never examine the way in which their pieces are used, led him to create cutlery with the utmost respect for tradition and table. Tusquets Blanca's designs are long and elegant, with a subtle, decorative twist in the handles. The coffee spoon is illustrated with a coffee bean, the fruit knife with an apple, and the fish knife and fork with fish heads; other motifs are abstract rather than figurative. The *Victoria* china, another first for Tusquets Blanca, is equally dignified in its restraint, but given warmth by the red bases of the raised tea cups and other pieces, which reflect a warm, almost subliminal glow on to saucers and table tops.

13

12

14

15

14 BOŘEK ŠÍPEK
CUTLERY
GOLD-PLATED STAINLESS STEEL
Left to right:
Knife: L 22.1cm (8¾in)
Fork: L 24.7cm (9¾in)
Tablespoon: L 24.7cm (9¾in)
Coffee spoon: L 16.5cm (6½in)
MANUFACTURER: ALTEREGO, THE NETHERLANDS

15 BOŘEK ŠÍPEK
BOWLS AND PLATES
PORCELAIN
Saucers: H 3.5cm (1⅜in) Di 9.5cm (3¾in)
Large bowl: H 7cm (2¾in) Di 15cm (6in)
Small bowls: H 7cm (2¾in) Di 8cm (3⅛in)
Plates: Di 21cm (8¼in)
MANUFACTURER: ALTEREGO, THE NETHERLANDS

16 BOŘEK ŠÍPEK
VASE, *AMELIA*
BOHEMIAN CRYSTAL
Consists of an inner and outer vase.
H 44cm (17¼in) W 18cm (7⅛in)
D 18cm (7⅛in)
MANUFACTURER: DRIADE, ITALY

17 BOŘEK ŠÍPEK
BOWL, *DIVIZNA*
CRYSTAL
Limited edition
H 41cm (16⅛in) Di 32cm (12½in)
MANUFACTURER: STELTMAN EDITIONS, THE
NETHERLANDS

18 BOŘEK ŠÍPEK
SOUP TUREEN
PORCELAIN
H 32cm (12½in) W 33cm (13in) D 26cm (10¼in)
MANUFACTURER: DRIADE, ITALY

19 BOŘEK ŠÍPEK
GLASSES
CRYSTAL
H 27cm (10½in) Di 12cm (4¾in)
MANUFACTURER: ALTEREGO, THE NETHERLANDS

At a time when many companies are advancing with caution and favouring the saleable and safe, **Bořek Šípek** continues to design china and glassware that overturn expectation and defy all precedent except for his own. His latest clutch of commissions for Driade and Alterego continue the line of poetic experiment seen in previous pieces for the same companies. This year, too, there is the *Divizna* bowl in green, blue, yellow and red crystal for Steltman Editions in Amsterdam. As a designer, Šípek inhabits some dark fairytale landscape of his own imagining. His pieces are ceremonial trappings imposed on the ordinary routines of everyday life. 'I'm not doing this for everyday,' he says. 'I'm working for Sunday.' He insists that his intrusive, idiosyncratic pieces, encrusted with ornament, produce a reaction in the viewer, whether pleasure or dislike. If there is a private mythology behind them, it is not one that he is prepared to divulge.

18

17

16

19

20 NIGEL COATES
VASE, *CHOKER*
GLASS, CAST IRON
Prototype
H 35cm (13¾in) W 18cm (7⅛in)
MANUFACTURER: SCP, UK

21 SYLVAIN DUBUISSON
CARAFE, *L'AIGUIÈRE RETROUVÉE*
SOLID SILVER 925
Limited batch production
H 27cm (10⅝in) Capacity 75cl
MANUFACTURER: ALGORYTHME, FRANCE

22 MICHAEL ROWE
CONICAL VESSEL
TINNED BRASS
One-off
H 28.5cm (11¼in) W 26cm (10¼in)
L 40cm (15¾in)
MANUFACTURER: MICHAEL ROWE, UK

The first range of glass vases for SCP by
Nigel Coates is, like his furniture, a
development of ideas and techniques first
explored in his architectural commissions.
Coates has specified glass details for
projects such as the chandelier in the Jigsaw
shop in London's Brompton Road, and the
new vases have a similar organic
exuberance. This design, 'a kind of late
twentieth-century metamorphosis of an
amphora', encapsulates a collision of
cultures and times—a constant theme of the
Japanese architecture and interior design
projects which have brought Coates to
fame. In the production version, the stand
will be made in vitreous enamel to impart
an even more ancient air. The vase will be
available in several sizes: as the jug
decreases across the range, so the lip
becomes larger and more flared in a
characteristically fluid progression of form.

23

24

3 TABLEWARE

23 MARIE-CLAUDE LALIQUE
VASE, *CLÉMATITES*
CRYSTAL
H 21.3cm (8⅜in) D 16.3cm (6⅜in)
MANUFACTURER: LALIQUE, FRANCE

24 MARIE-CLAUDE LALIQUE
VASE, *NYMPHALE*
CRYSTAL
H 21.3cm (8⅜in) D 16.3cm (6⅜in)
MANUFACTURER: LALIQUE, FRANCE

25 OLIVIER GAGNÈRE
VASE, *BAS RELIEF*
PAINTED TERRACOTTA
Limited batch production
H 29cm (11⅜in) Di 20cm (7⅞in)
MANUFACTURER: OLIVIER GAGNÈRE, FRANCE

26 OLIVIER GAGNÈRE
PLATE, *VERRE À ANNEAUX*
HAND-BLOWN MURANO GLASS
Di 40cm (15¾in)
MANUFACTURER: OLIVIER GAGNÈRE, FRANCE

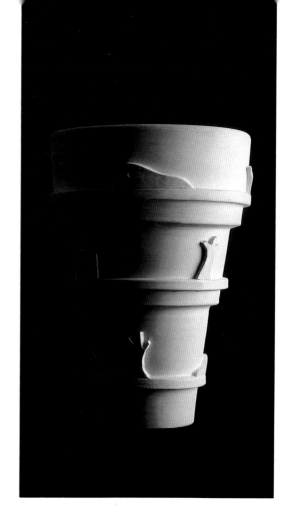

25

26

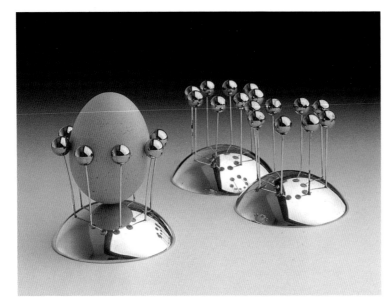

27

28

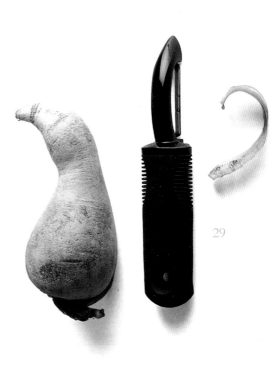

29

3 Tableware

27 Yamo
Egg cups, *Acte 1*
Aluminium
H 6cm (2⅜in) Di 6.5cm (2½in)
Manufacturer: Techniland, France

28 Davide Mercatali
Saucepan, *Queen*
Aluminium, steel, plastic
H 15cm (6in) Di 24cm (9⅜in)
Manufacturer: Indy, Italy

29 Davin Stowell and Tucker Viemeister for Smart Design
Potato peeler, *Good Grips* range of kitchen equipment
Stainless steel, Santoprene handle
H 2.8cm (1⅛in) W 3.5cm (1⅜in)
L 11cm (4⅜in)
Manufacturer: Oxo International, USA

30 Rena Dumas
Teapot, *Complice*
Silver, metal, wicker
Comprises teapot, tea caddy and box containing two tumblers.
H 9.5cm (3¾in) W 18cm (7⅛in) D 11cm (4⅜in)
Manufacturer: Ercuis, France

31 Erik Magnussen
Butter dish
Stainless steel
H 5.6cm (2⅛in) W 10.5cm (4⅛in)
D 8cm (3⅛in)
Manufacturer: A/S Stelton, Denmark

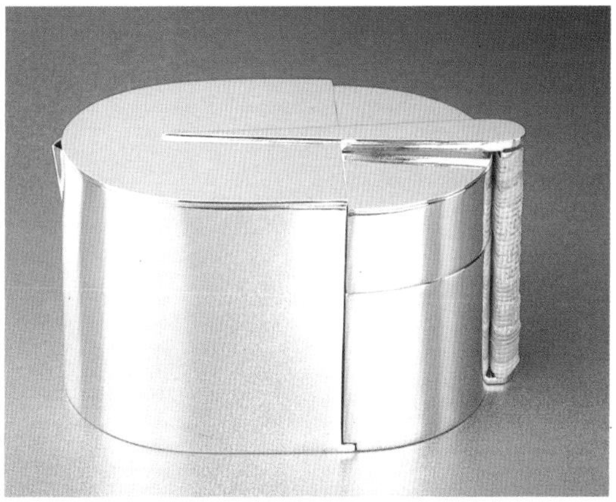

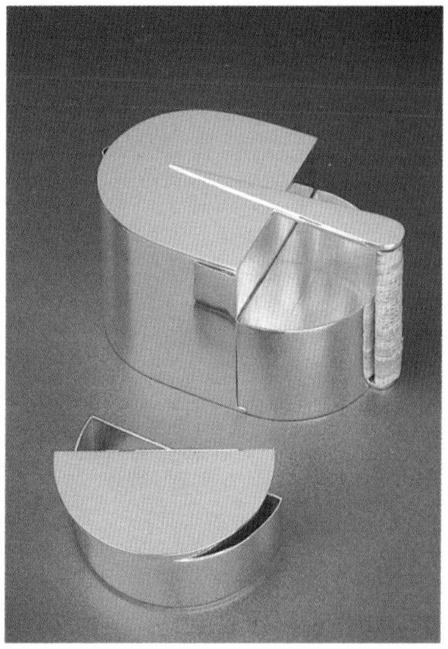

30

31

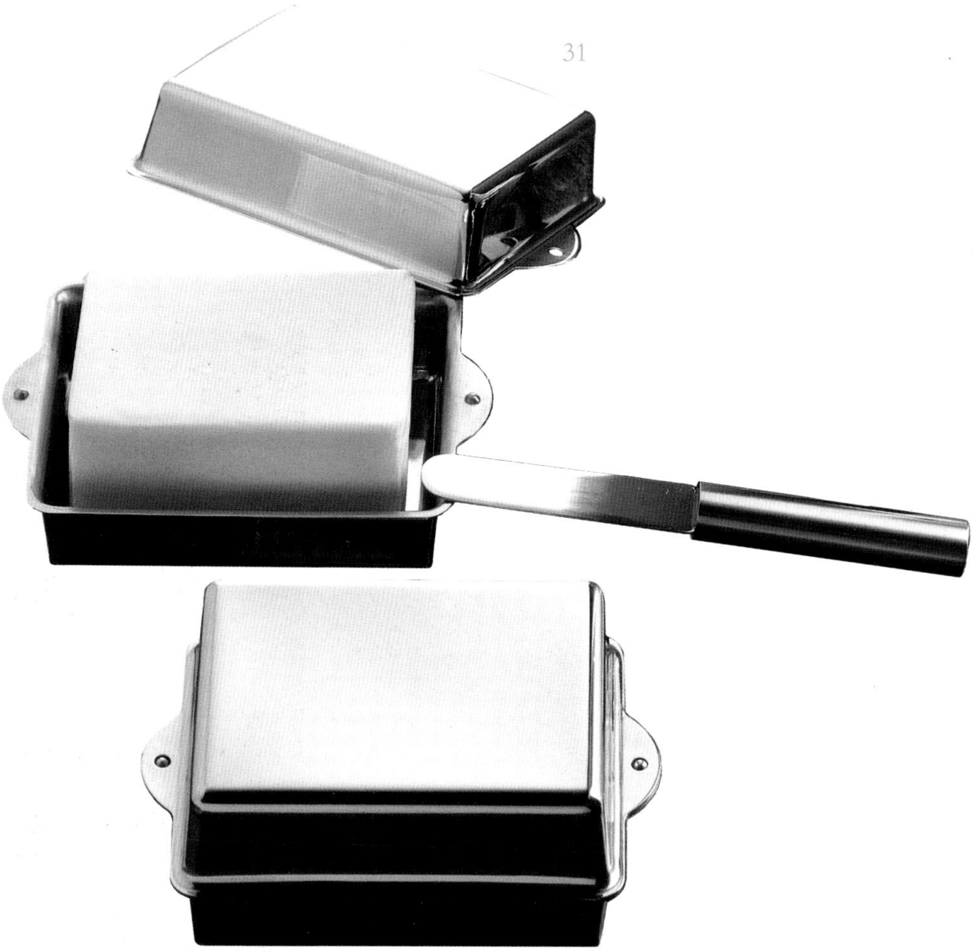

32 ECKHARD SCHUSSLER FOR STUDIO PROTOS
GLASSES, *AMARNA*
Prototype
Left to right:
Sherry: H 28cm (11in) Di 8cm (3⅛in)
Champagne: H 32cm (12½in) Di 7cm (2¾in)
Wine: H 30cm (11¾in) Di 7.5cm (3in)
MANUFACTURER: ANTHOLOGIE QUARTETT,
GERMANY

33 ALAIN CARRÉ
GLASSES, *CRYSTAL PALACE*
CRYSTAL, HAND-PRESSED STEM, BLOWN BOWL
Left to right:
White wine: H 18.3cm (7¼in) Di 7cm (2¾in)
Red wine: H 20cm (7⅞in) Di 7.8cm (3⅛in)
Champagne: H 22cm (8⅝in) Di 6cm (2⅜in)
Goblet: H 21cm (8¼in) Di 8cm (3⅛in)
MANUFACTURER: SASAKI GLASS, JAPAN

34 ALESSANDRO ZULIANI
CONDIMENT SET
BLOWN GLASS
Limited batch production
Oil/vinegar: H 14cm (5½in) Di 4cm (1½in)
Salt/pepper: H 6cm (2⅜in) Di 2.5cm (1in)
MANUFACTURER: TEMPI DI CARTA, ITALY

35 ALESSANDRO ZULIANI
VASES, *VETRI*
BLOWN GLASS
The flowers are suspended in a vacuum.
Limited batch production
H 150cm (59in) Base Di 22cm (8⅝in)
MANUFACTURER: TEMPI DI CARTA, ITALY

32

33

34

35

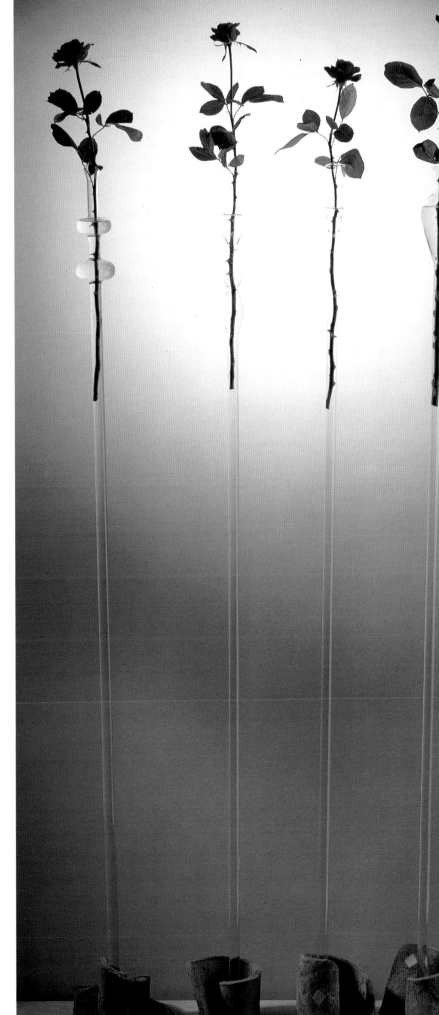

36

37

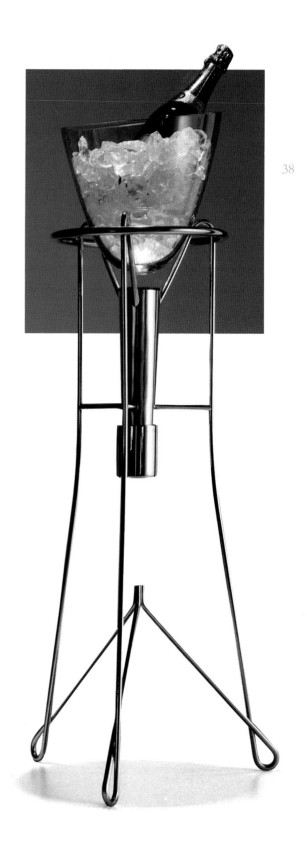

38

39

In the last three years, **Ross Lovegrove** and his partner Julian Brown have established themselves as industrial designers with a refined eye for detail and an acute feeling for textural effect. Lovegrove, now working alone, created this champagne valet for a private client who was building a house in the Arizona desert. The one-off piece was designed with an eye on eventual mass production. It conceals a powerful, cordless torch within its central stem, which doubles as a vase. Light shines up into the blown glass bowl, illuminating the ice; with flowers in the vase, it gives the valet a desert bloom. The three feet formed by bent steel rods are unforced details which arise elegantly from the production process.

36 ANNETTE MEECH
DECANTER AND GLASSES, *BOBBIN*
24% LEAD CRYSTAL, GLASS
Limited batch production
Decanter: H 38cm (15in) Di 9cm (3½in)
Glasses: H 20cm (7⅞in) Di 8cm (3⅛in)
MANUFACTURER: ANNETTE MEECH, UK

37 DAL MONDO
VASE
TERRACOTTA
H 21cm (8¼in) Di 19.5cm (7⅝in)
MANUFACTURER: CAPPELLINI ARTE, ITALY

38 ROSS LOVEGROVE
CHAMPAGNE VALET
GLASS BOWL, NICKEL-PLATED STEEL FRAME, TORCH, GOLD-PLATED VASE
Prototype
H 80cm (31½in) D 35cm (13¾in)
MANUFACTURER: FORUM, UK

39 CARLO MORETTI
GLASSES, *SOFFIO ROSA*
MURANO CRYSTAL
Left to right:
Small glass: H 9cm (3½in) Di 11cm (4⅜in)
Wine glass: H 10.5cm (4¼in) Di 7.5cm (3in)
Water glass: H 12.5cm (5in) Di 8cm (3⅛in)
MANUFACTURER: CARLO MORETTI, ITALY

40

41

40 **MICHAEL GRAVES**
SALAD SERVERS
SILVER-PLATED DIE-CUT BRASS, ACID-ETCHED
ENGRAVING
L 27.9cm (11in) D 1.9cm (¾in)
MANUFACTURER: SWID POWELL, USA

41 **MARIA GRAZIA FIOCCO**
SERVING CONTAINERS, FROM THE *OASI*
COLLECTION
STEEL, SILVER, GILDED STEEL HANDLES
Rectangular hors-d'oeuvre dish: H 1.7cm (¾in) W
32cm (12½in) D 25.6cm (10⅛in)
Round tray: H 1.3cm (½in) Di 33cm (13in)
Rectangular tray: H 1.7cm (¾in) W 40cm (15¾in)
D 29cm (11⅜in)
MANUFACTURER: GNUTTI, ITALY

42 **MARIA GRAZIA FIOCCO**
SERVING CONTAINERS, FROM THE
RAINBOW COLLECTION
PLASTIC
Salad bowl: H 13.4cm (5¼in) Di 28.4cm (11¼in)
Salad servers: W of handle 2cm (¾in) W of end
7.5cm (3in) L 32cm (12½in)
Ice bucket: H 17.4cm (6⅞in) Di 17.5cm (6⅞in)
Wine cooler: H 22.5cm (8⅞in) Di 14cm (5½in)
Ice tongs: W 5cm (2in) L 19cm (7½in)
MANUFACTURER: BIESSE, ITALY

42

43

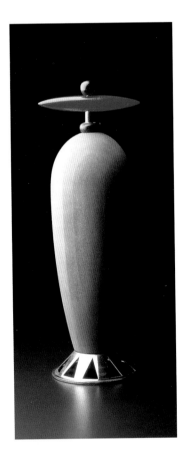

44

Pieces by **Carsten Jørgensen** have the clarity of outline and the sense of rightness and balance that come from paring away superfluous detail and striving at all costs for formal simplicity. Even Jørgensen's touches of whimsy, such as the elliptical red handle and flared steel base that give his pepper grinder a slightly Memphis look, are applied with restraint. The *Teapot 2000*, designed for the Tea Council, is an attempt at innovation in an area in which there might seem to be little remaining room for improvement. A plunger similar in principle to that of a coffee pot allows the user to adjust the strength of the brew.

45

46

43 CARSTEN JØRGENSEN
SALT AND PEPPER GRINDERS, *TRIANON*
BEECH, CHROME-PLATED BRASS, STEEL, DELRIN
Cone: H 11cm (4⅜in) Di 9.4cm (3⅜in)
Sphere: H 11.4cm (4½in) Di 9cm (3½in)
MANUFACTURER: BODUM, SWITZERLAND

44 CARSTEN JØRGENSEN
PEPPER GRINDER
PEARWOOD, STAINLESS STEEL, NYLON
Limited batch production
H 20cm (7⅞in) Di 6.5cm (2½in)
MANUFACTURER: BODUM, SWITZERLAND

45 CARSTEN JØRGENSEN
KETTLE, *OSIRIS*
STAINLESS STEEL, MACROLON
H 10.7cm (4¼in) Di 17cm (6⅜in)
MANUFACTURER: BODUM, SWITZERLAND

46 CARSTEN JØRGENSEN
TEAPOT 2000
BOROSILICATE, GLASS, STAINLESS STEEL,
POLYPROPYLENE
Contains strainer and plunger
infusion system.
H 12.5cm (5in) Di 14.5cm (5⅜in)
MANUFACTURER: BODUM, SWITZERLAND

47

48

3 TABLEWARE

47 MARYSE BOXER
PLATES, *KALEIDOSCOPE*
PORCELAIN
Di 20cm (7⅞in) 25cm (9⅞in) 32cm (12½in) 40cm
(15¾in)
MANUFACTURER: MARYSE BOXER DESIGNS, UK

48 MARYSE BOXER
PLATES, *CONCENTRICS*
MATT-GLAZED EARTHENWARE, GOLD
HAND-PAINTING
Di 23cm (9in) 27cm (10½in)
MANUFACTURER: MARYSE BOXER
DESIGNS, UK

49 ANDRÉE PUTMAN
PLATE, *SKY MAP*
PORCELAIN
Di 27.5cm (10⅞in)
MANUFACTURER: SASAKI CRYSTAL, USA

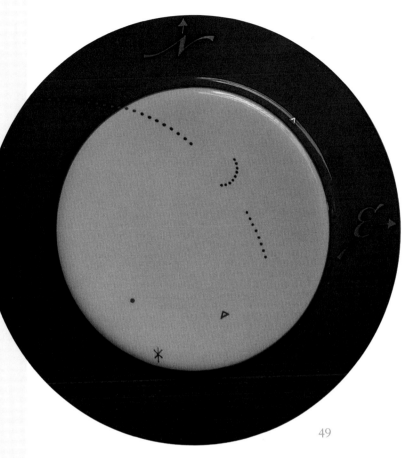

49

4

TEXTILE

If previous *Yearbooks* have been dominated by the jacquards of Junichi Arai, this year it is Hiroshi Awatsuji who makes the strongest impression with a collection of graphically textured cottons. Awatsuji's imagery ranges from natural bark to fields of mathematically regular computer texture, a tension between the organic and the synthetic that also underpins the work of Yoshiki Hishinuma, Kiyoshi Yamamoto and other Japanese textile designers. In both technology and art, the Japanese continue to set a standard of invention that few other countries can match. Arai's *Random Pocket* is a wool and polyester jacquard scattered, as its name suggests, with flattened pockets that look like the empty husks of discarded seed pods.

Europe and America have a long way to go before they can produce cottons and wools as exquisite as this. The liveliest western designs, with the unsurprising exception of Mariscal's cartoon print, are examples of hand-tufted rug-making. Designers such as Helen Yardley in Britain and Carouschka in Sweden have a gift for bold, cut-out shapes and vibrant colours that make their rugs sought-after accents for the unembellished architecture of contemporary interiors. Andreas Brandolini's *Ogar* rug derives its impact not from pattern but from the *trompe-l'oeil* 'shadow' that makes it look as though one rug is floating above another. Brigitte Starck, wife of Philippe, makes an unexpected début with a rug originally conceived for the Royalton Hotel, which is animated by cavorting squiggles.

S

2

3

4 TEXTILES

Previous spread

1 HILTON McCONNICO
RUG, *MANÈGE BLEU*
HAND-TUFTED WOOL
W 180cm (70⅞in) L 270cm (106⅜in)
MANUFACTURER: TOULEMONDE BOCHART,
FRANCE

2 BRIGITTE STARCK
RUG, *ZOO*
WOOL
Limited batch production
Di 250cm (98⅜in)
MANUFACTURER: YVES GASTOU, FRANCE

3 ANDREAS BRANDOLINI
RUG, *OGAR*
HAND-TUFTED WOOL
Limited batch production
W 170cm (66⅜in) L 190cm (74⅞in)
MANUFACTURER: EDITION B-S, GERMANY

4

5

4 TEXTILES

6

This spread

4 MARIO TALLI NENCIONI
FABRIC, *J2175*
LINEN JACQUARD STRETCH (82% LINEN, 2%
LYCRA, 16% COTTON)
W 90cm (35½in) Repeat 20cm (7⅞in)
MANUFACTURER: TELENE, ITALY

5 FINN SKÖDT
UPHOLSTERY FABRIC, *ZINAR*
WOOL
W 144cm (56¾in)
MANUFACTURER: KVADRAT, DENMARK

6 HELLE ABILD
FABRIC
CRÊPE DE CHINE BOTTOM LAYER, SILK ORGANZA
TOP LAYER, SILK-PRINTED
One-off
W 90cm (35½in) Repeat 25cm (9⅞in)
MANUFACTURER: HELLE ABILD, DENMARK

Most of the rug designs by **Helen Yardley** have been one-offs, created to order for architects and domestic clients as the last stage in the process of fitting out an interior. The architectural 'givens' of the project therefore determine the size, colour, compositional stresses and voids of the designs. Yardley intends her rugs to merge seamlessly into their settings; to help this, the abstract elements function as directional indicators or 'road signs', subtly marking out the occupant's movement through the space. Now, responding to the continuous demand for her work, she has produced a number of limited edition pieces. The new rugs reprise the Matisse-derived vocabulary of her commissioned projects, while being designed to suit as wide a range of situations as possible. As with the customized rugs, the designs are rigorously edited in content and formally precise in design.

7

8

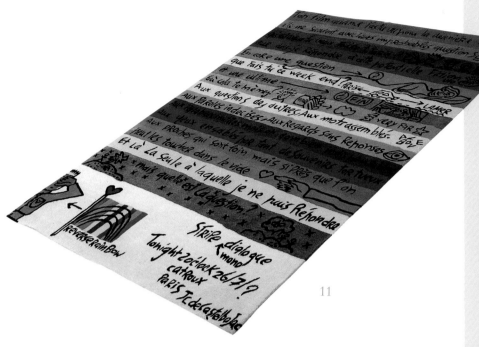

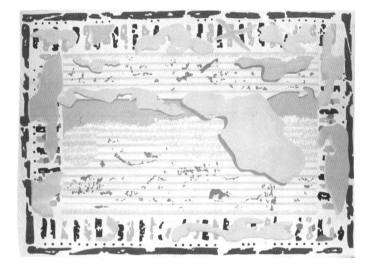

11

10

9

7 HELEN YARDLEY
RUG
HAND-TUFTED WOOL
Limited edition
W 243cm (95⅝in) L 152cm (60⅛in)
MANUFACTURER: A/Z STUDIOS, UK

8 HELEN YARDLEY
RUG
HAND-TUFTED WOOL
Limited edition
W 240cm (94½in) L 190cm (74⅞in)
MANUFACTURER: A/Z STUDIOS, UK

9 ANNABELLE D'HUART
RUG, *TACHKANDE* FROM THE
ATLANTIDE SERIES
GOUACHE ON CANVAS
Limited batch production
L 419.1cm (165in) W 289.6cm (114in)
MANUFACTURER: SOCIÉTÉ DES AMIS DU MUSÉE
NATIONAL D'ART MODERNE, CENTRE GEORGES
POMPIDOU, FRANCE

10 ANNABELLE D'HUART
RUG, *TAGAR* FROM THE *ATLANTIDE*
SERIES
GOUACHE ON CANVAS
Limited batch production
L 419.1cm (165in) W 289.6 cm (114in)
MANUFACTURER: SOCIÉTÉ DES AMIS DU MUSÉE
NATIONAL D'ART MODERNE, CENTRE GEORGES
POMPIDOU, FRANCE

11 JEAN-CHARLES DE CASTELBAJAC
RUG, *STRIPE DIALOGUE*
80% WOOL, 20% NYLON
Also available in acrylic
W 170cm (66⅞in) L 240cm (94½in)
MANUFACTURER: LIGNE ROSET, FRANCE

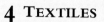

12

13

14

12 REIKO SUDO
FABRIC, *BIG CABLE*
COTTON JACQUARD
Reversible double-weave structure.
The crinkled surface is created by
using two yarns tightly twisted in
opposite directions.
W 89cm (35in) Repeat 39cm (15⅜in)
MANUFACTURER: NUNO, JAPAN

13 REIKO SUDO
FABRIC, *PIN-TACK*
COTTON AND RAYON JACQUARD
Double-weave cloth with warps at
different tensions, alternating
between areas using one or many
yarns to create the pleats.
W 117cm (46in) Repeat 5cm (2in)
MANUFACTURER: NUNO, JAPAN

14 REIKO SUDO
FABRIC, *PATCHWORK EMBROIDERY*
RAYON WITH MACHINED RAYON EMBROIDERY
W 97cm (38¼in) Repeat 10cm (4in)
MANUFACTURER: NUNO, JAPAN

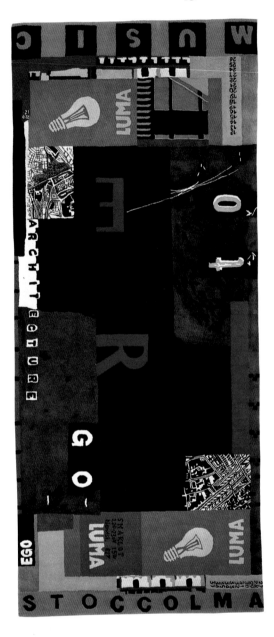

4 TEXTILES

15 CAROUSCHKA
RUG, *LUMA*
HAND-TUFTED WOOL
One-off
W 170cm (67⅛in) L 400cm (157½in)
MANUFACTURER: THAILAND CARPET
MANUFACTURING, THAILAND

16 CAROUSCHKA
RUG, *STOCKHOLMS POSTEN*
HAND-TUFTED WOOL
One-off
W 205cm (80¾in) L 334cm (131½in)
MANUFACTURER: THAILAND CARPET
MANUFACTURING, THAILAND

17 CAROUSCHKA
RUG, *SOVJETIQUES*
HAND-TUFTED WOOL
One-off
W 180cm (70⅞in) L 385cm (151½in)
MANUFACTURER: THAILAND CARPET
MANUFACTURING, THAILAND

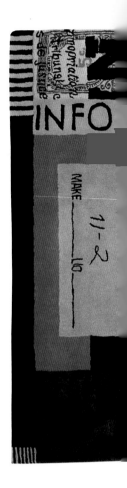

16

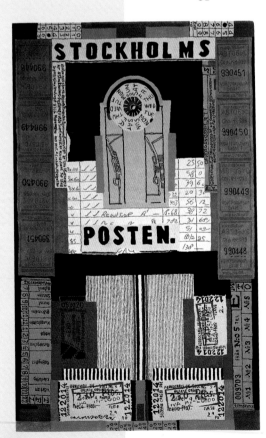

17

Frustration with existing designs for rugs led the Swedish interior designer **Carouschka** to start producing her own in the mid-1980s. She continues to work as a designer of theatre sets and exhibitions, and to paint, but hand-tufted rugs have become an increasingly important part of her output. Carouschka draws on a repertoire of collage techniques and motifs familiar from twentieth-century art, from Cubism onwards, to create intricate typographic designs capable of working as compositions from four or more viewpoints. The tickets, diagrams, parking permits and newspaper headlines she scatters across her rugs form a visual diary of her personal memories and travels.

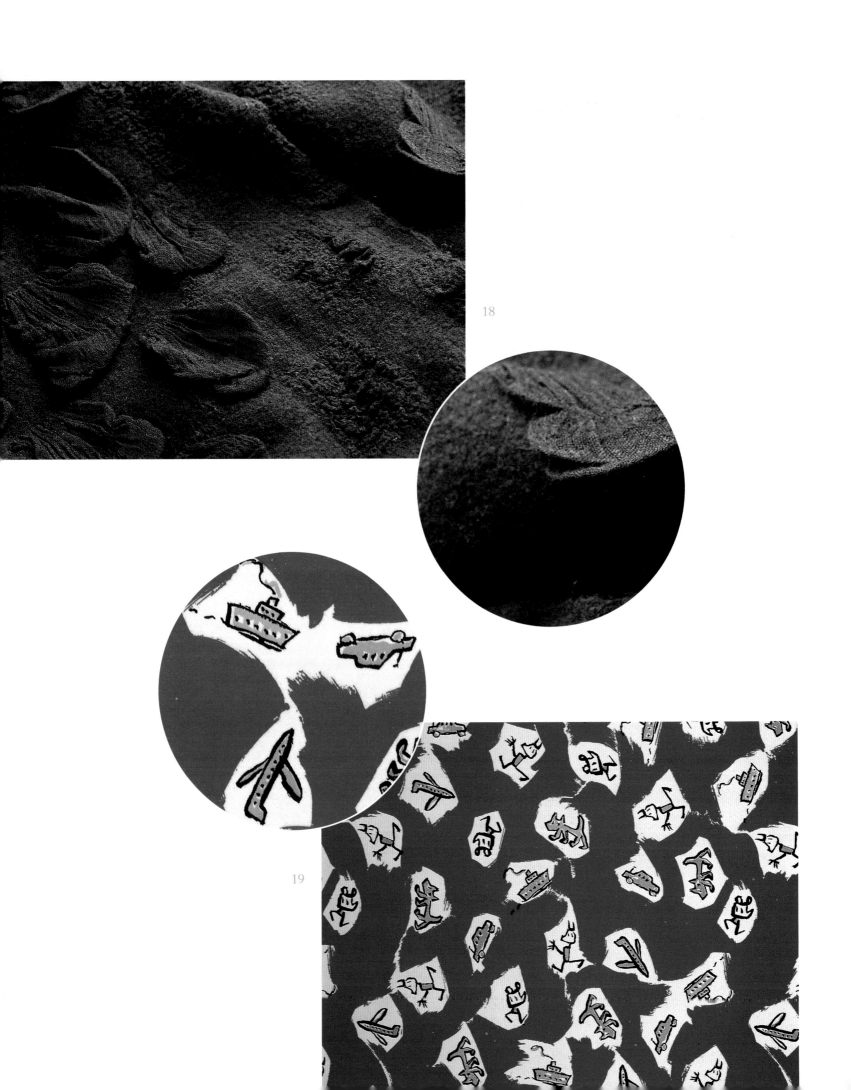

18

19

4 TEXTILES

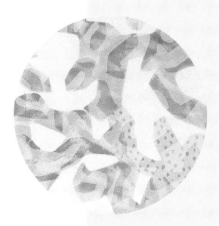

18 JUNICHI ARAI
FABRIC, *RANDOM POCKET*
WOOL, POLYESTER JACQUARD
During the finishing process water
is thrown randomly at the fabric
causing it to shrink and pucker in
an irregular pattern.
W 80cm (31½in) Repeat 25cm (9⅞in)
MANUFACTURER: NUNO, JAPAN

19 JAVIER MARISCAL
FABRIC, *MUÑECOS*
COTTON PRINTED WITH SIX INKS
W 75cm (29½in)
MANUFACTURER: TRÁFICO DE MODAS, SPAIN

**20 LYNNE WILSON AND FRANCESCO
BINFARÈ**
FABRICS, FROM THE *SEGNI
SULL'ACQUA* COLLECTION
COTTON, POLYESTER AND COTTON JACQUARD
Series of simple woven fabrics
which can be used alone or
overprinted to create a coordinated
but differentiated collection.
W 140cm (55⅛in) Repeat 40cm (15¾in)
MANUFACTURER: ASSIA FOR CASSINA, ITALY

20

22

21

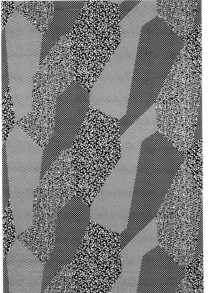

23

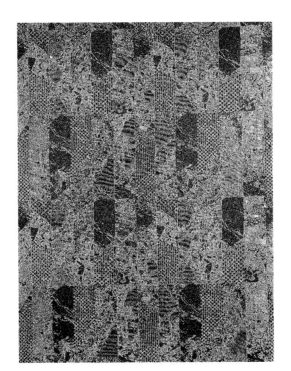

24

4 TEXTILES

21 HIROSHI AWATSUJI
FABRIC FOR INTERIOR DESIGN,
KIRIKO
COTTON
W 130cm (51⅛in) Repeat 64cm (25¼in)
MANUFACTURER: FUJIE TEXTILE, JAPAN

22 HIROSHI AWATSUJI
FABRIC FOR INTERIOR DESIGN,
TAMRONG
COTTON, RAYON
W 140cm (55⅛in) Repeat 64cm (25¼in)
MANUFACTURER: FUJIE TEXTILE, JAPAN

23 HIROSHI AWATSUJI
FABRIC FOR INTERIOR DESIGN,
BABYLON
POLYESTER, RAYON
W 137cm (54in) Repeat 48cm (18⅞in)
MANUFACTURER: FUJIE TEXTILE, JAPAN

24 HIROSHI AWATSUJI
FABRIC FOR INTERIOR DESIGN,
FUMON
COTTON
W 130cm (51⅛in) Repeat 81cm (31⅞in)
MANUFACTURER: FUJIE TEXTILE, JAPAN

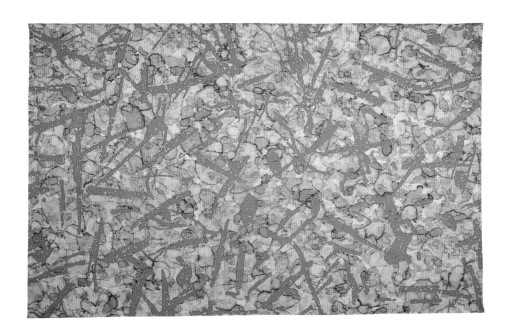

25

25 KIYOSHI YAMAMOTO
WALL HANGINGS, *FOREST*
COTTON, MULTIPLE COLOUR JET PRINTING
Limited batch production
H 300cm (118in) W 450cm (177½in)
MANUFACTURER: FUJI EIGHT, JAPAN

26 YOSHIKI HISHINUMA
FABRIC, *CHECK PRINT*
POLYESTER
W 100cm (39½in) Repeat 80cm (31½in)
MANUFACTURER: HISHINUMA ASSOCIATES,
JAPAN

27 YOSHIKI HISHINUMA
FABRIC
COTTON, STAINLESS STEEL FIBRES
W 100cm (39½in) Repeat 70cm (27½in)
MANUFACTURER: HISHINUMA ASSOCIATES,
JAPAN

Japanese textile designs have an energy, boldness and command of the most advanced manufacturing techniques that put them in a class of their own. Many patterns take the form of all-over 'fields' with no obvious beginning or end, like abstract expressionist drip paintings rather than conventional modules with obvious repeats. A distinctly Japanese conception of the natural world underpins many of these images. The series *Forest* by **Kiyoshi Yamamoto,** cotton wall hangings created with multiple colour-jet printing, are composed of calligraphic strokes that suggest the dense matting of branches and undergrowth without representing them in a literal way.

Yoshiki Hishinuma, on the other hand, addresses the alternative conceptions of beauty that arise from a consideration of the countryside and cityscape. It is not enough, he says, to import fragile images of natural wonder into the urban environment—they will be overwhelmed. Hishinuma wants to discover a way of representing the city's own 'artificial' beauty in his designs for clothing and textiles. His cotton fabric woven with shiny steel threads conveys a sense of surging, elemental forces using sophisticated industrial materials and techniques.

26

27

28

4 TEXTILES

28 KOLOMAN MOSER
CARPET, FROM THE *CLASSIC*
COLLECTION
POLYAMIDE
W 400cm (157½in)
Width repeat 100cm (39½in) Length repeat
93cm (36⅝in)
MANUFACTURER: VORWERK, GERMANY

29 JOSEF HOFFMANN
CARPET, FROM THE *CLASSIC*
COLLECTION
POLYAMIDE
W 400cm (157½in)
Width repeat 50cm (19⅝in) Length repeat
92.5cm (36⅜in)
MANUFACTURER: VORWERK, GERMANY

The German carpet manufacturer **Vorwerk** attracted considerable international attention with its last two collections of designs. The first, *Dialog*, brought together painters and architects of the calibre of David Hockney, Roy Lichtenstein and Arata Isozaki to suggest that the carpet had become an unjustly overlooked medium for adventurous design; *Dialog 2* added graphic designer Milton Glaser and architects Richard Meier and Zaha Hadid, among others, to the fold. This year, Vorwerk has looked to the past rather than the future for its new collection, a decision that seems to reflect the mood of conservative reflection and recessionary caution currently permeating the world of design. Vorwerk's *Classic* series introduces Art Nouveau designs by Josef Hoffmann, Joseph Maria Olbrich, Peter Behrens, Henry van de Velde, Koloman Moser and Richard Riemerschmid, as well as turn-of-the-century patterns by the company's own studio. These designs, selected from among the thousands that filled the pattern books of the period, were always intended for industrial production. Vorwerk has been careful, however, to respect the artists' wishes by using only those patterns which were designed originally for use as floor coverings. Hard-wearing timbrelle fibres make the carpets suitable for contract work as well as residential settings.

29

5

1

2

.. -5

PRODUC

T S

3

4

Ever since Lisa Krohn and Tucker Viemeister endowed their electronic phonebook with a folding hinge suggestive of a paper phonebook (*International Design Yearbook 1988/89*), theorists have been debating the merits of product semantics. The semantic approach allows immaterial and supposedly alienating electronic functions to be symbolized—and thereby humanized and made accessible—in concrete terms. It is an attractive idea, but on the evidence of this selection it has yet to be widely applied with anything like the literalness of Krohn and Viemeister's prototype.

What is apparent, however, in a remarkable number of the products collected here is the continuing softening, rounding and—in its most developed manifestation—*streamlining* of plastic form. Massimo Iosa Ghini's spectacles, Mark Newson's *Mystery* clock and Hedda Beese's slender wedge of a telephone attempt to reduce the object to the least possible number of lines and planes. In cameras, speakers and suitcases, orthogonal lines and boxy constructions are giving way to semicircular profiles and cylindrical form. Even computer disk drives, a quintessentially intimidating 'black box' product (though in reality most are grey), are being domesticated with waves and curves.

While familiar functions are being interpreted in a new way (see Philips's three-inch television and cordless personal CD), and the Japanese are retro-styling everything from cameras to cars in an apparently successful attempt to stimulate image-conscious consumers, a few designers are engaging with the more demanding industrial design task of devising new forms for new functions. Sony's *Data Discman* and Sottsass Associati's *Angel Note Access Terminal* are technically innovative, but not so different in appearance, despite their miniature size, from a thousand other computer terminals. Kenneth Grange's *VPi386*, however, offers an entirely new screen-based but keyboard-free approach to data collection *and* it is beautiful to look at and handle. Of all the sections in the *Yearbook*, product design was the one most warmly commended by Andrée Putman for the standard of its entries.

5 PRODUCTS

Previous spread

1 MASSIMO IOSA GHINI
SPECTACLES, *9500*
INJECTION-MOULDED SPX
W 15.5cm (6⅛in) D 4.5cm (1¾in)
MANUFACTURER: SILHOUETTE INTERNATIONAL,
AUSTRIA

2 MASSIMO IOSA GHINI
SPECTACLES CASE
INJECTION-MOULDED PLASTIC, LEATHER, LYCRA
W 20cm (7⅞in) D 8cm (3⅛in)
MANUFACTURER: SILHOUETTE INTERNATIONAL,
AUSTRIA

3 MASSIMO IOSA GHINI
SPECTACLES, *9502*
INJECTION-MOULDED SPX
W 15cm (6in) D 4.2cm (1⅝in)
MANUFACTURER: SILHOUETTE INTERNATIONAL,
AUSTRIA

4 MASSIMO IOSA GHINI
BOX, *IGM 2*
PEARWOOD
Prototype
H 10.5cm (4⅛in) W 31cm (12¼in) D 31cm
(12¼in)
MANUFACTURER: DESIGN WERKSTÄTTE, AUSTRIA

5

6

7

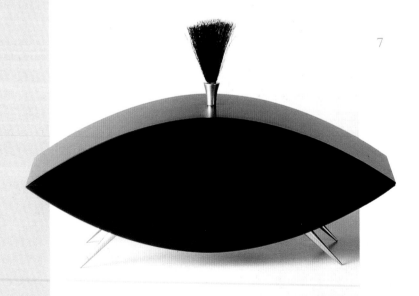

This spread

5 MARTIN SZEKELY
BOX, *WODAN*
PEARWOOD
H 23cm (9in) W 12cm (4¾in) D 12cm (4¾in)
MANUFACTURER: FRANZ SCHATZL, DESIGN
WERKSTÄTTE, AUSTRIA

6 MARTIN SZEKELY
BOX, *KOSMAS*
PEARWOOD
H 16cm (6⅜in) W 8cm (3⅛in) D 8cm (3⅛in)
MANUFACTURER: FRANZ SCHATZL, DESIGN
WERKSTÄTTE, AUSTRIA

7 SIGI MAYER
BOX, *WILDER KAISER 17*
BLACK VARNISHED MDF, ALUMINIUM, CHAMOIS
HAIR
H 22cm (8⅜in) W 35cm (13¾in) D 12cm (4¾in)
MANUFACTURER: FRANZ SCHATZL, DESIGN
WERKSTÄTTE, AUSTRIA

8 MASAFUMI SEKINE
TIERED BOXES
PEWTER, HAMMERED DECORATION
One-off
H 20cm (7⅞in) Di 20cm (7⅞in)
MANUFACTURER: MASAFUMI SEKINE, JAPAN

9 MASAFUMI SEKINE
BOX
PEWTER
One-off
H 30cm (11⅞in) W 53cm (20⅞in) D 35cm
(13¾in)
MANUFACTURER: MASAFUMI SEKINE, JAPAN

8

9

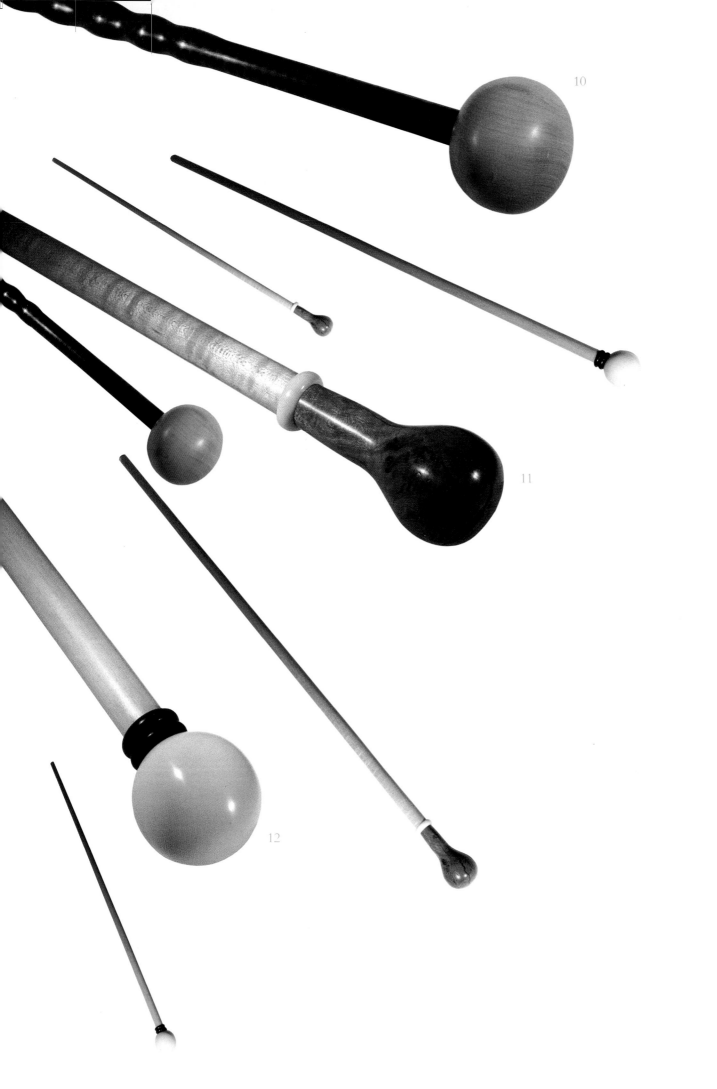

10

11

12

Like the hat, the walking stick is one of those items of personal apparel which are irretrievably bound to a forgotten dress code and a more formal way of living. Carrying a stick simply because it looked good and imparted a certain style would seem impossibly affected now. For those who do need extra support when walking, **Jan-Kees de Jager's** ball-handled sticks in boxwood, juniper-bush root and bronze are an elegant reminder of the pleasures of the promenade and the stroll.

10 JAN-KEES DE JAGER
WALKING STICK, *LONG WAY TO GO*
LETTERWOOD, BOXWOOD, BRONZE
Limited batch production
H 115cm (45¼in) Di of handle 5.5cm (2⅛in) Di of stick 1.5cm (⅝in)
MANUFACTURER: JAN-KEES DE JAGER, THE NETHERLANDS

11 JAN-KEES DE JAGER
WALKING STICK, *WALK-ON*
BIRD'S-EYE MAPLE, TAGUA NUT, JUNIPER-BUSH ROOT
H 89cm (35in) Di 4.5cm (1¾in)
MANUFACTURER: JAN-KEES DE JAGER, THE NETHERLANDS

12 JAN-KEES DE JAGER
WALKING STICK, *WAVE YOUR WAND*
PEQUINO AMARELLO, RUBBER, POLYESTER
H 85cm (33½in) Di of handle 5cm (2in) Di of stick 1.8cm (⅝in)
MANUFACTURER: JAN-KEES DE JAGER, THE NETHERLANDS

13 JAN-KEES DE JAGER
BOX, *TURNER*
BIRD'S-EYE MAPLE
H 4cm (1½in) Di 18cm (7¼in)
MANUFACTURER: JAN-KEES DE JAGER, THE NETHERLANDS

13

14

15

14 TAKENOBU IGARASHI
TRAVEL KIT, *HYVÄLYSTI*
TRAVEL CASE: LEATHER
H 11.5cm (4½in) W 16.5cm (6½in) D 4.5cm
(1¾in)
NAIL CLIPPERS: STAINLESS STEEL
H 1.1cm (⅜in) W 1.1cm (⅜in) L 6.5cm (2½in)
NAIL FILE: ABS PLASTIC
H 0.4cm (¼in) W 1cm (⅜in) L 12cm (4¾in)
MIRROR: ABS PLASTIC
H 0.7cm (¼in) W 6cm (2⅜in) D 5.5cm (2⅛in)
COMB: PC ALLOY
H 0.6cm (¼in) W 2.6cm (1in) L 12cm (4¾in)
BOTTLE OPENER: STEEL, BRASS
H 1.4cm (½in) W 1.2cm (⅜in) L 9.5cm (3¾in)
SCISSORS: ABS PLASTIC, HIGH CARBON STAINLESS
STEEL
H 0.6cm (¼in) W 5.9cm (2⅜in) L 9.6cm (3¾in)
TRAVEL CASE: LEATHER
H 6.3cm (2½in) W 6.3cm (2½in) L 16cm (6½in)
RAZOR:
H 2cm (¾in) W 4cm (1½in) L 1.5cm (⅝in)
PEN LIGHT: ALUMINIUM, ABS PLASTIC
H 1.3cm (½in) W 1.3cm (½in) L 9.5cm (3¾in)
TOOTHPICK HOLDER: EPM, BRASS
H 1.3cm (½in) W 1.3cm (½in) L 8cm (3⅛in)
BALL-POINT PEN: EPM, BRASS
H 1.3cm (½in) W 1.3cm (½in) L 12.5cm (5in)
MANUFACTURER: KAI INTERNATIONAL, JAPAN

15 KAZUO KAWASAKI
FOLDING KNIFE
STAINLESS STEEL, TITANIUM
W 1.8cm (¾in) L 17.7cm (7in) D 0.9cm (⅜in)
MANUFACTURER: TAKEFU KNIFE VILLAGE, JAPAN

16 TAKENOBU IGARASHI
PAPER KNIFE, FROM THE *YMD*
COLLECTION
STAINLESS STEEL
H 2cm (¾in) W 3cm (1⅛in) L 22cm (8⅝in)
MANUFACTURER: CLASSICON, GERMANY

As a designer, **Takenobu Igarashi** unites a rare command of both three-dimensional and graphic form. His early posters transformed the raw material of numbers and the Western alphabet into powerful graphic shapes, while his sculptures showed that the designs could be turned into constructions of almost architectural complexity. This background makes Igarashi a product designer of real sensitivity: the shadow cast by the stainless steel handle of his paper knife for ClassiCon is a wonderfully precise description of both volume and line. Igarashi is especially good at designing small objects for personal use. *The International Design Yearbook 1990/91* showed his gardening kit *Hyvälysti*; his follow-up for the same company is a collection of traveller's essentials — clippers, scissors, corkscrew, razor and so on — that demand to be picked up and weighed in the hand.

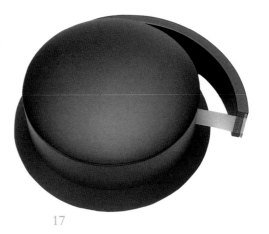

17

18

5 PRODUCTS

17 KENNETH GRANGE

DESK-TOP ADHESIVE TAPE DISPENSER

RUBBER AND PLASTIC MOULDING, DIE-CAST ALLOY

Prototype

H 5cm (2in) Di 14.5cm (5¾in)

MANUFACTURER: KENNETH GRANGE, UK

18 MILES KELLER AND HELEN KERR

DESK SET, *VITESSE*

STAINED AND LACQUERED RUBBERWOOD

Consists of a pencil cup, flat pen holder, dish, letter holder and covered box and business card holder. Most pieces have identical dimensions and can fit together in a line.

H 4cm (1½in) W 10cm (4in) D 17.5cm (6⅞in)

MANUFACTURER: UMBRA, CANADA

19 HIJUNG KASUYA

ORGANIZERS

CARDBOARD, EMBOSSED PAPER

Limited batch production

Left, top to bottom:

Paper box (small): H 26cm (10¼in) W 20cm (7⅞in) D 6.5cm (2½in)

Card file: H 18.3cm (7¼in) W 19.5cm (7¾in) D 4.8cm (1⅞in)

Centre, top to bottom:

Pocket file: H 26cm (10¼in) W 13cm (5⅛in) D 3cm (1⅛in)

Tube: H 8cm (3⅛in) W 44cm (17½in) D 4.8cm (1⅞in)

Memo pad: H 10.3cm (4⅛in) W 10.3cm (4⅛in) D 4.6cm (1⅞in)

Right, top to bottom:

File box: H 31.7cm (12½in) W 25cm (9⅞in) D 7.5cm (3in)

Notebook (A5 size): H 21.5cm (8½in) W 15.8cm (6¼in) D 1.5cm (⅝in)

Notebook (A4 size): H 30.3cm (11⅞in) W 21.4cm (8⅜in) D 1.5cm (⅝in)

Paper box (large): H 32.3cm (12¾in) W 23.5cm (9¼in) D 6.5cm (2½in)

MANUFACTURER: COMS, JAPAN

19

5 PRODUCTS

20 DOUGLAS RICCARDI AND TIBOR KALMAN FOR M & CO.
POCKET WATCH, *SOLO*
BLACK CHROMIUM-PLATED CASE, MINERAL CRYSTAL GLASS, SWISS MOVEMENT
D 0.4cm (⅛in) Di 4cm (1⅝in)
MANUFACTURER: M & CO. LABS, USA

21 TIBOR KALMAN AND EMILY OBERMAN FOR M & CO.
WALL CLOCK, *5 O'CLOCK*
ANODIZED ALUMINIUM, TEMPERED GLASS, GERMAN MOVEMENT
D 4cm (1½in) Di 30.5cm (12in)
MANUFACTURER: M & CO. LABS, USA

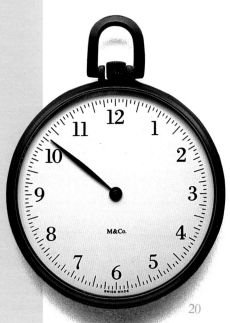

20

22 ALEXANDER BREBNER AND TIBOR KALMAN FOR M & CO.
WRIST-WATCH, *PIE*
18 CARAT GOLD-PLATED BRASS CASE, MINERAL CRYSTAL GLASS, SWISS MOVEMENT
D 0.6cm (¼in) Di 0.6cm (¼in)
MANUFACTURER: M & CO. LABS, USA

23 TIBOR KALMAN AND DOUGLAS RICCARDI FOR M & CO.
PENCIL SET, *MYSTERY*
WOOD, CLOTH
Cloth-bound book with wooden tray containing pencils, 7-inch ruler, paper, paperclips, pencil sharpener, eraser, rubber bands and Italian breath mints.
H 25.5cm (10in) W 19.5cm (7⅝in) D 2.3cm (⅞in)
MANUFACTURER: M & CO. LABS, USA

21

5

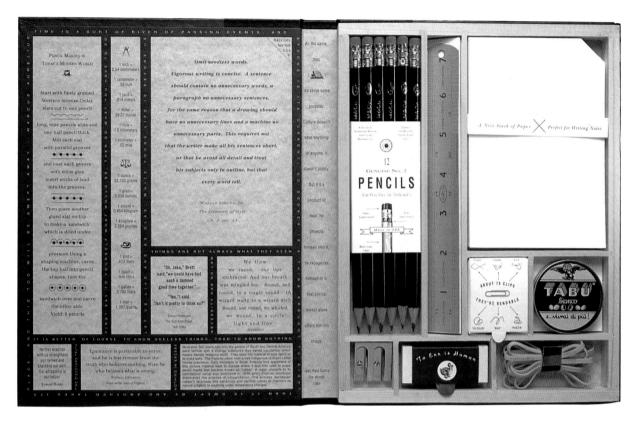

23

22

Tibor Kalman's New York company **M & Co.** can lay claim to being one of the wittiest graphic design teams in America. As an increasingly elaborate sideline, Kalman also runs M & Co. Labs which, since the mid-1980s, has designed and manufactured a range of watches and objects. The watches, in particular, have become a cult due to the subversive ingenuity with which they complicate the seemingly straightforward process of telling the time. (*Askew*, for instance, scrambles the position of every number on the dial except for the twelve.) The company's latest batch of timepieces includes the *Solo* pocket watch with only one hand, the *Pie* wrist-watch, which gives the time in inordinate detail, but only between the hours of nine and twelve, and the single-digit *5 o'Clock* wall clock—'perfect for the office,' say M & Co.

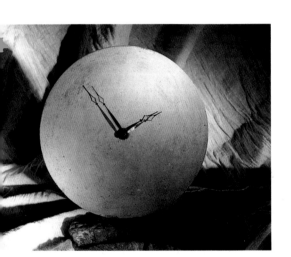

24

25

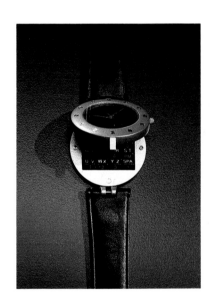

24 NICK CROWE
CLOCK, *RISING MOON*
COPPER, CIMENT FONDU, CHEMICALS
Limited batch production
H 21cm (8¼in) W 18cm (7⅛in) D 6cm (2⅜in)
MANUFACTURER: NICK CROWE, UK

25 EMILIO AMBASZ
COMPUTER WRIST-WATCH
STAINLESS STEEL, GOLD, SILVER, LEATHER
The wrist-watch opens to reveal a
computer display and keypad.
Prototype
H 1–1.2cm (⅜–½in) W 3.4cm (1⅜in)
L 24cm (9⅜in)
MANUFACTURER: ALESSI, ITALY

26 MARC NEWSON
CLOCK, *MYSTERY*
CARBON FIBRE
Limited batch production
Di 80cm (31½in) D 18cm (7⅛in)
MANUFACTURER: IDÉE, JAPAN

27 JOHN LONCZAK
CONTAINER, *PAPERBACK*
POLYETHELENE OR PAPER BOARD
The container is sold flat, then
hooked together with tabs to
create a bin that separates paper,
ready for recycling.
H 7.5cm (3in) W 23cm (9in) D 37cm (14½in)
MANUFACTURER: FORM FARM, USA

28 HEDDA BEESE
TELEPHONE, *BOSSE T410/T415*
INJECTION-MOULDED ABS
Compact telephone with on-hook
dialing and additional loudspeaker
unit.
H 1.4cm (½in) W 7cm (2¾in) L 24cm (9⅜in)
MANUFACTURER: BOSSE TELEKOMSYSTEME,
GERMANY

**29 DAVID DANIELSON FOR HENRY
DREYFUSS ASSOCIATES**
TWO-LINE REMOTE ANSWERING
MACHINE, *1332*
ABS PLASTIC
H 5.5cm (2⅛in) W 17cm (6⅜in) D 73cm (28¾in)
MANUFACTURER: AT&T, USA

28

27

**30 CHRISTOPHER LOEW AND TIM
PARSEY**
CONCEPT BRIEFCASE
INJECTION-MOULDED PLASTIC PARTS WHICH SNAP
TOGETHER
Designed for use with computer
products. One half expands to
increase internal capacity. Used
separately, the halves will fit inside
an attaché case.
Prototype
H 5cm (2in) W 35.5cm (14in) D 35.5cm (14in)
MANUFACTURER: CHRISTOPHER LOEW AND TIM
PARSEY, USA

29

30

5 PRODUCTS

31 PHILIPPE STARCK
KETTLE, *HOT BERTAA*
POLYAMIDE, ALUMINIUM CASTING
H 25cm (9⅞in) Capacity 200cl
MANUFACTURER: ALESSI, ITALY

32 PHILIPPE STARCK
TOOTHBRUSHES
POLYPROPYLENE
H 20cm (7⅞in) W 1.5cm (⅝in)
MANUFACTURER: FLUOCARIL–GOUPIL, FRANCE

33 PHILIPPE STARCK
COLANDER, *MAX LE CHINOIS*
STAINLESS STEEL, BRASS CASTING
H 29cm (11⅜in) Di 30cm (11⅞in)
MANUFACTURER: ALESSI, ITALY

Only **Philippe Starck**, perhaps, could have pulled off the iimprobable feat of turning a toothbrush into a talking point; and only Starck, it is safe to say, could have stamped his personality so unambiguously on an object this humdrum. Starck's attenuated toothbrush stems are the flexible, polypropylene equivalents of the curving horns that have sprouted everywhere from his table lamp for Flos and the corridors of the Royalton Hotel, to the recent *Hot Bertaa* kettle manufactured by Alessi. As always with Starck, the line between the outrageously distinctive and the wilfully obscure is difficult to draw. Many design fans were seduced by one of his other pieces for Alessi, the *Juicy Salif* lemon squeezer—a tall, three-legged structure of undeniable charm. But is the element of over-statement in the lemon squeezer or the toothbrush any different, in the final analysis, from the notorious streamlined pencil sharpener designed by Raymond Loewy? What one is buying, of course, is not so much an object determined by functional necessity as a little piece of Philippe Starck.

33

34

32

34 PHILIPPE STARCK
SPORT BOTTLE
BLOW-MOULDED POLYESTER
H 18.5cm (7¼in) Di 7.5cm (3in)
MANUFACTURER: GLACIER WATER, USA

36

35

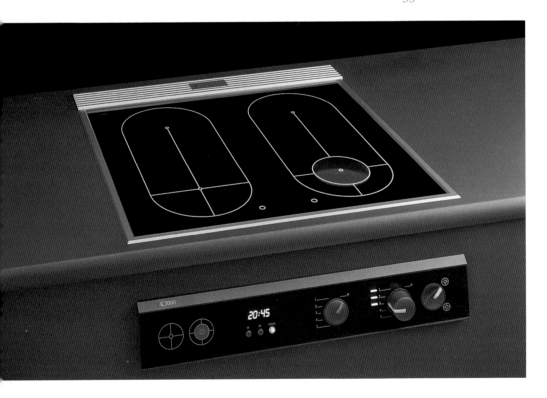

5 PRODUCTS

35 JOSEP LLUSCÀ
GAS HOB
EXTRUDED AND INJECTED ALUMINIUM, OPTICAL
GLASS, INJECTED PLASTIC
Prototype
H 30cm (11⅞in) W 30cm (11⅞in)
MANUFACTURER: CATALANA DE GAS, SPAIN

36 TIMOTHY BROWN
FLOOR-STANDING STOVE
GLASS, STEEL, PLASTIC
Gas range and grill with electric
and microwave oven.
H 85cm (33½in) W 60cm (23½in)
D 50cm (19⅝in)
MANUFACTURER: TOKYO GAS, JAPAN

37 COOP HIMMELBLAU
KITCHEN, *LOFT*
LAMINATE, LACQUERED MDF, ELOXAL
PROCESSED ALUMINIUM, GLASS, PERFORATED
STEEL SHEET
Limited batch production
The dimensions are variable
MANUFACTURER: EWE-KÜCHEN, AUSTRIA

37

Coop Himmelblau were one of seven architectural practices selected by Philip Johnson for the 'Deconstructivist Architecture' show at the Museum of Modern Art, New York, in 1988. Their approach, as that controversial term implies, is angular and disruptive, a collage of shattered planes and colliding beams, as though the geometry of a building has been exploded, then hastily reassembled in not quite the right order. One project, a rooftop remodelling for a firm of Viennese lawyers, was described as looking like a pair of molten chopsticks.

Now Wolf Prix and Helmut Swiczinsky, the firm's principals, have turned their attention to the kitchen, with two new designs for the Austrian company Ewe. *Loft* (page 181) is so conventional in appearance that there is nothing to link it to their previous work, but *Mal-zeit* is open, angular and *deconstructed*. According to Coop Himmelblau, '*Mal-zeit* is the three-dimensional movable version of a drawing describing the artistic and pleasurable preparation of the meal.' This is the kitchen reconceived as technological workstation. The vertical pole forms an axis around which the two arms of the structure pivot; one worktop is motorized and the other perches on the now obligatory I-beam. Surfaces of black iron, Corian and sand-blasted plexiglass lend to the feeling that the act of cooking has been turned into a form of industrial assembly.

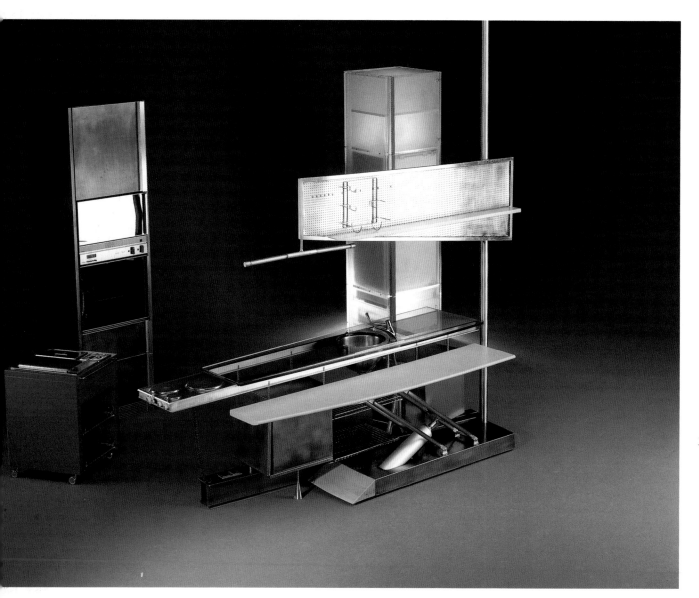

38

5 PRODUCTS

38 COOP HIMMELBLAU
MOVABLE KITCHEN, *MAL-ZEIT*

BLACK IRON, GREEN GLASS, HIGH-GRADE STEEL,
SAND-BLASTED PLEXIGLASS, CORIAN

The bar-plate can be moved up
and down with an electric motor
and rotates on an axis. The kitchen
comes with refrigerator, oven, hot
plate and dishwasher.

Prototype

H 85–205cm (33½–80¾in) W 95cm–270cm (37½–
106⅜in) L 270cm (106⅜in)

MANUFACTURER: EWE-KÜCHEN, AUSTRIA

39 MASAHITO TAKASUNA
KITCHEN, *IZUMI (SPRING)*

STAINLESS STEEL, WOOD, CONCRETE, PLASTICS

The water gushes from the table to
the sink like a spring, with a
subsonic oscillator producing a
mist.

Prototype

H 29cm (11⅜in) W 38.4cm (15¼in) D 11.8cm
(4⅝in)

MANUFACTURER: TOSHIBA CORPORATION, JAPAN

39

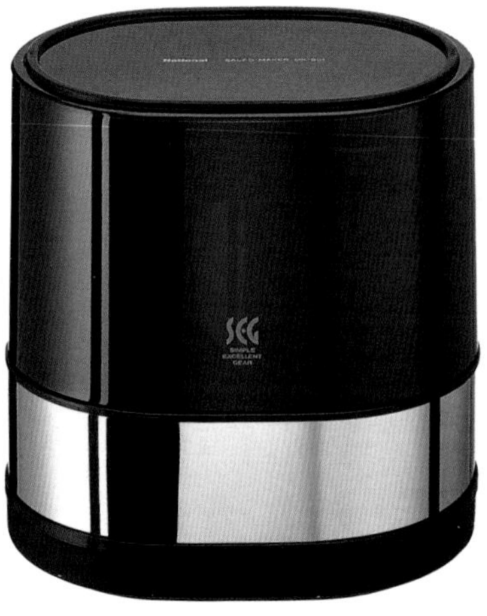

40

41

5 Products

40 Junko Konrai
Salad maker
Stainless steel, plastic
Slices and grates vegetables.
H 20cm (7⅞in) W 19.5cm (7¾in) D 15.5cm (6⅛in)
Manufacturer: Matsushita, Kitchen Appliance Division, Japan

41 Kuno Prey
Drainer/strainer
SAN
The strainer fits all pots with diameters from 18cm (7⅛in) to 24cm (9⅜in).
H 12cm (4¾in) W 28cm (11in) D 1cm (⅜in)
Manufacturer: Rosti Housewares, Denmark

42 Kenneth Grange
Two- and four-slice toasters
Moulded plastic
H 17cm (6⅝in) W 24cm (9⅜in) 37cm (14½in)
D 11.5cm (4½in) 17.5cm (6⅞in)
Manufacturer: Kenwood, UK

43 Bruno Gecchelin
Scales, *Libra*
Nickel-plated device, methacrylate weights, polished brass pans
H 16.5cm (6½in) W 36cm (14⅛in) D 22cm (8⅝in)
Manufacturer: Rede Guzzini, Italy

42

43

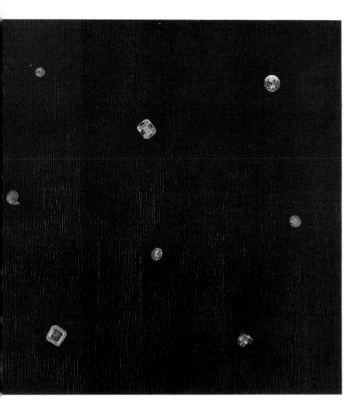

44

45

46

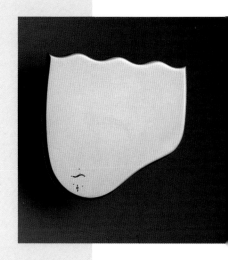

47

44 TRISTRAM FETHERSTONHAUGH
JEWELLED FLOOR
STAINED OAK PANELS WITH PHOTOMECHANICAL
REPRODUCTIONS OF JEWELS, FOSSILS, SILICON
CHIPS OR SPACE JETSAM
One-off
A one-metre square tile, part of a
larger study in surface textures.
MANUFACTURER: TRISTRAM FETHERSTONHAUGH,
UK

45 PATRICK NAGGAR
MIRROR, *PALLAS*
POLISHED CAST ALUMINIUM, EBONIZED WALNUT
Can be either hand-held or
stationary on a base.
H 21cm (8¼in) D 28.5cm (11¼in) Di 22.2cm
(8¾in)
MANUFACTURER: ARC INTERNATIONAL, USA

46 ETTORE SOTTSASS
MIRROR, *ETRUSCO*
BURLWOOD, MAPLE, GOLD LEAF
H 240cm (94½in) W 120cm (47¼in) D 40cm
(15¾in)
MANUFACTURER: GLASS DESIGN, ITALY

47 SYLVAIN DUBUISSON
HAND MIRROR
POLISHED SILVER
Prototype
H 7cm (2¾in) W 7cm (2¾in)
MANUFACTURER: NEW TONE, FRANCE

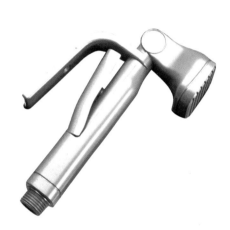

48

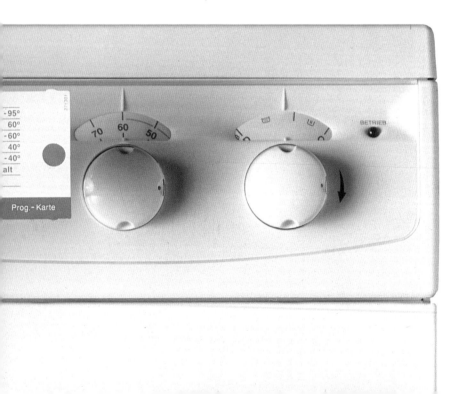

-95°
60°
-60°
-40°
-40°
alt

Prog.- Karte

70 60 50

BETRIEB

49

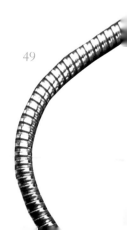

5 PRODUCTS

48 **ROBERTO PEZZETTA**
WASHING MACHINE, *MATURA 9140*
ZINC-COATED STEEL, STAINLESS STEEL,
CARBORAN, ABS, GLASS
H 85cm (33½in) W 60cm (23½in) D 60cm
(23½in)
MANUFACTURER: ZANUSSI, ITALY

49 **JEFFREY KAPEC AND KAZUNA
TANAKA**
HAND-HELD SHOWER
INJECTION-MOULDED ABS, CHROME-PLATED
SHOWER HOSE, DELRIN, BRASS, STAINLESS STEEL
VALVE ASSEMBLY
The shower requires no grip
strength and can be used by the
severely disabled. The spray can be
operated by slipping the device on
or off the wrist, arm or foot.
W 5cm (2in) L 16.5cm (6½in) D 8.9cm (3½in)
MANUFACTURER: LUMEX, USA

50 **RICHARD HEATLY**
TOWEL RAIL, *SALSA*
CHROME-PLATED STEEL, PLASTIC CASTORS
Limited batch production
H 90cm (35½in) D 70cm (27½in)
MANUFACTURER: RICHARD HEATLY, UK

51 **RICHARD HEATLY**
TOWEL RAIL, *ARC*
CHROME-PLATED STEEL
Limited batch production
H 12cm (4¾in) W 67cm (26⅜in) D 9cm (3½in)
MANUFACTURER: RICHARD HEATLY, UK

50

51

52

53

54

5 PRODUCTS

52 TOM FRONING
PORTABLE HEATING SYSTEM, *ENCORE*
INJECTION-MOULDED POLYETHERMIDE
Clockwise from top left:
Floor model: H 10.5cm (4⅛in) W 11.3cm (4½in)
D 5cm (2in)
Floor model: H 3cm (1⅛in) W 9.5cm (3¾in)
D 9.5cm (3¾in)
Table-top model: H 10.5cm (4⅛in) W 11.3cm
(4½in) D 5cm (2in)
Wall model: H 9.5cm (3¾in) W 10cm (4in)
D 3.5cm (1⅜in)
MANUFACTURER: CADET MANUFACTURING,
USA

53 KENNETH GRANGE
GAS-FIRED FAN HEATER
MOULDED PLASTIC, ENAMELLED SHEET STEEL
H 43cm (16⅞in) W 50.5cm (19⅞in) D 18cm
(7⅛in)
MANUFACTURER: HARMAN GAS CORPORATION,
JAPAN

**54 DOUG PATTON, RICHARD JUNG
AND DENNIS GRUDT FOR PATTON
DESIGN**
HEATER/FAN
STYRENE
H 26cm (10¼in) W 25cm (9⅝in) D 10cm (4in)
MANUFACTURER: TATUNG, USA

55 JOSEPH KOSUTH
WITTGENSTEIN'S RADIATOR
CAST IRON TREATED WITH TRANSPARENT PAINT,
CHROMIUM-PLATED METAL LABEL
Crafted and re-issued by Joseph
Kosuth after the original design by
Ludwig Wittgenstein for his
sister's house in Vienna, 1927–8.
H 125cm (49¼in) W 30cm (11⅝in) D 30cm
(11⅞in)
MANUFACTURER: MEMPHIS, ITALY

55

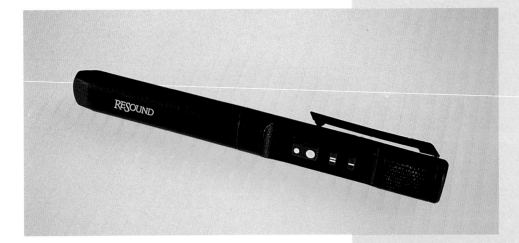

57

56

56 NINABER/PETERS/KROUWEL INDUSTRIAL DESIGN
ELECTRONIC WATER-LEVEL
EXTRUDED ALUMINIUM, PLASTIC, ELECTRONIC COMPONENTS
Measurements are taken by way of light and sound signals.
H 5cm (2in) L 80cm (31½in) D 2cm (¾in)
MANUFACTURER: INCOM, THE NETHERLANDS

57 BRUCE AND SUSAN BURDICK
HEARING CONTROL DEVICE
TUBE EXTRUSIONS, INJECTED-MOULDED PLASTIC PARTS, SHAPED ALUMINIUM PARTS
Shaped like a pen, this discreet device controls the quality and volume of a hearing aid.
L 14.6cm (5¾in)
MANUFACTURER: RESOUND CORPORATION, USA

58 MIKIO KAMEGI
WEATHER CUBE
ABS RESIN
Uses semi-conductor sensors to make accurate weather forecasts. Displays the current time, temperature, atmospheric pressure and humidity, and projects weather conditions eight hours in advance.
H 9cm (3½in) W 9cm (3½in) D 9cm (3½in)
MANUFACTURER: TOSHIBA CORPORATION, JAPAN

59

60

59 CAMERA DESIGN CENTER
CAMERA, *EPOCA*
ABS POLYCARBONATE
H 7.4cm (2⅞in) W 10cm (4in) D 15.5cm (6⅛in)
MANUFACTURER: CANON, JAPAN

60 SHARP AUDIO SYSTEM DESIGN CENTER
CD RADIO-CASSETTE RECORDER, *QT 77CD*
METAL, PLASTIC
H 19.5cm (7⅞in) W 58cm (22⅞in) D 23.8cm (9⅜in)
MANUFACTURER: SHARP CORPORATION, JAPAN

61 KATSUHIKO OGINO
TRAVEL BAGS
INJECTION-MOULDED PLASTIC
Right: H 70cm (27½in) W 50cm (19⅝in) D 22cm (8⅝in)
Left: H 42cm (16½in) W 54cm (21¼in) D 19cm (7½in)
MANUFACTURER: IRIS OHYAMA, JAPAN

61

62

63

5 PRODUCTS

62 TOM DIXON
PARTY FURNITURE
ZINC-PLATED METAL
H 158cm (62⅛in) W 78cm (30¾in) D 93cm
(36⅝in)
MANUFACTURER: CAPPELLINI ARTE, ITALY

63 MARCO ZANUSO
ASHTRAY STAND
METAL, ANTHRACITE, GLASS
H 76cm (30in) Di 30cm (11⅞in)
MANUFACTURER: ARTELANO, FRANCE

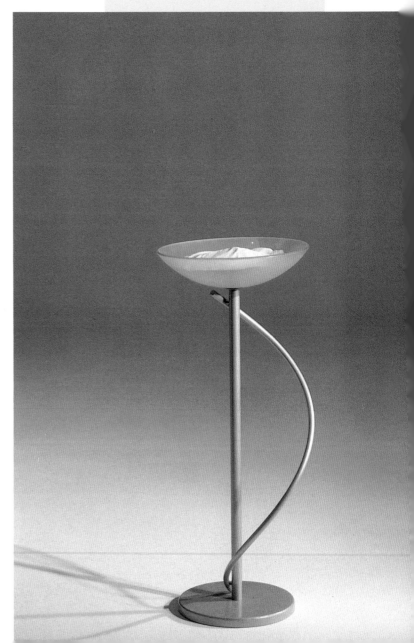

64

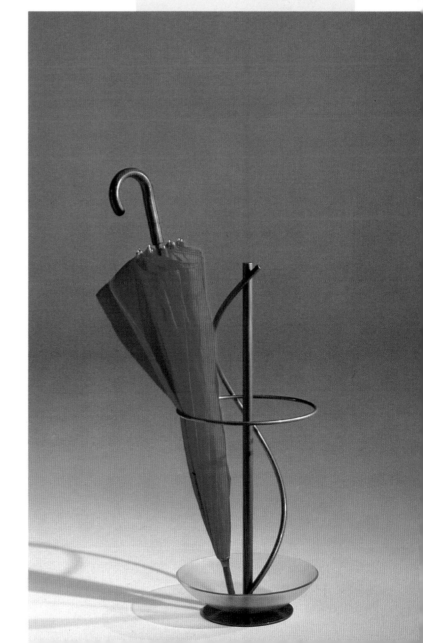

65

64   ANNA ANSELMI   **197**
PLANT STAND, *ECOLOGY*
PAINTED STEEL
Preset for four plants.
H 174cm (68½in) W 48cm (18⅞in)
MANUFACTURER: BIEFFEPLAST, ITALY

65   MARCO ZANUSO
UMBRELLA STAND
METAL, ANTHRACITE, GLASS
H 76cm (30in) Di 30cm (11¾in)
MANUFACTURER: ARTELANO, FRANCE

5 PRODUCTS

66 MAURO CANFORI
PERSONAL COMPUTER UNIT AND
PRINTER TROLLEY,
UBI-PRINT/UBI-BYTE
STEEL, ANTHRACITE ANTI-SCRATCH GREY MDF
Limited batch production
Left to right:
Ubi-Print: H 50cm (19⅝in) W 52cm (20½in)
D 44cm (17¼in)
Ubi-Byte: H 75cm (29½in) W 80cm (31½in)
D 50–75cm (19⅝–29½in)
MANUFACTURER: CIDUE, ITALY

67 MAURO CANFORI
TV OR VIDEO TROLLEY, *UBILUMA*
STEEL, ANTHRACITE ANTI-SCRATCH GREY MDF
Limited batch production
H 106–166cm (41¾–65⅜in) W 70cm (27½in)
D 60cm (23½in)
MANUFACTURER: CIDUE, ITALY

68 MAURO CANFORI
PROJECTOR UNIT, *UBIASA*
TRIANGULAR SECTIONED STEEL, CHROME RODS,
ANTHRACITE ANTI-SCRATCH GREY MDF
Limited batch production
H 108–168cm (42½–66¼in) W 47cm (18½in)
D 44cm (17¼in)
MANUFACTURER: CIDUE, ITALY

68

Despite the fact that we are
surrounded by our electronic
extensions—televisions, video
recorders, personal computers—
they remain an area of storage
which is given very little serious
attention by manufacturers. The
effect is to leave the burgeoning
technology stranded, never quite
integrated into the room. An
unusually elegant and well thought
out exception is the range of trolleys
and stands for Cidue by **Mauro
Canfori**. The *Ubi* series is spare and
angular with tough metal finishes,
and leaves nothing to chance. There
are units to accommodate stereos,
videos, televisions, computers,
printers and slide projectors, as well
as a range of compatible tables and
shelf units.

69

5 PRODUCTS

69 PHILIPS CORPORATE INDUSTRIAL DESIGN

PERSONAL FAX MACHINE, *PFC 20*

INJECTION-MOULDED ABS

H 10.7cm (4¼in) W 26.5cm (10⅜in) D 37cm (14½in)

MANUFACTURER: PHILIPS ELECTRONICS, THE NETHERLANDS

70 MATSUSHITA COMMUNICATION INDUSTRIAL CO. LTD

CORDLESS TELEPHONE WITH ANSWERING MACHINE

PLASTIC

Unit: H 7.8cm (3⅛in) W 18.1cm (7⅛in) D 21.2cm (8⅜in)

Base station and cordless extensions: H 21.4cm (8⅜in) W 5.5cm (2¼in) D 9.4cm (3¾in)

MANUFACTURER: MATSUSHITA, INDUSTRIAL DESIGN CENTRE, JAPAN

71 SHARP INFORMATION SYSTEMS DESIGN CENTER

HOME-COPY FAX MACHINE, *UX-1*

METAL, PLASTIC

H 5.5cm (2¼in) W 32cm (12½in) D 28.4cm (11⅛in)

MANUFACTURER: SHARP CORPORATION, JAPAN

71

70

72

72 SONY CORPORATION
DATA DISCMAN DD-1
PLASTIC
This pocket-sized model accesses information from sources such as catalogues and dictionaries on to a 8cm CD-ROM disc and shows it on a liquid crystal display screen.
H 4.2cm (1⅝in) W 10.7cm (4¼in) D 15.9cm (6¼in)
MANUFACTURER: SONY CORPORATION, JAPAN

73 IMAGE SYSTEMS DESIGN CENTER
PRINTER, *BJ 10E*
PLASTIC
H 4.8cm (1⅞in) W 31cm (12¼in) D 21.5cm (8⅜in)
MANUFACTURER: CANON, JAPAN

74 ETTORE SOTTSASS AND MARCO SUSANI FOR SOTTSASS ASSOCIATI
ELECTRONIC PHONEBOOK, *ANGEL NOTE ACCESS TERMINAL*
ABS, RUBBER
Linked to the central data-base of the Japanese telephone company, Angel Note gives subscribers access to the central directory and, when connected to a phone, enables them to dial numbers directly.
H (closed) 6cm (2⅜in) (open) 17cm (6⅜in) W 20cm (7⅞in) D 23cm (9in)
MANUFACTURER: NTT (NIPPON TELEPHONE/TELEGRAPH), JAPAN

After the *Walkman*, introduced as long ago as 1979, and the *Discman*, its upmarket compact disc cousin, there is a certain inevitability about **Sony's** most recent addition to the series, the *Data Discman*. A data retrieval system for people who find even portable computers too bulky and limiting, the *Data Discman* is one of the first examples of the sort of paperless electronic book that futurologists have fantasized about for decades. Information stored on discs the size of CDs can be called up and displayed on its liquid crystal screen. When the hinged screen is shut, the unit is not much bigger than a postcard.

The most obvious types of literature for storage in this way are dictionaries, catalogues and directories. The *Angel Note Access Terminal*, designed by **Sottsass Associati** for NTT, is a similarly compact device that gives telephone subscribers access to the company's central directory. Like the *Data Discman*, it is a lightweight, attractive object which appears, on the face of it, to answer an obvious need. Considered together, however, the devices raise an interesting question. The logic of this kind of technology—indeed the rationale behind the personal computer— is to concentrate a range of functions in a single processor. No one is going to want to walk around with a briefcase full of miniature terminals, each one dedicated to a different task, and it can only be a matter of time before we see these functions united in a single convenient device.

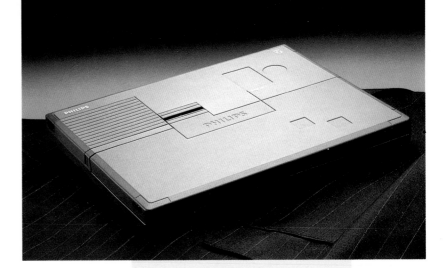

The sight of business people sitting on trains tapping away at lightweight lap-top computers is now almost commonplace, but even this degree of portability presupposes that the user is comfortable using a keyboard in the first place. What about executives who take notes and draft documents by hand? Their communication and data storage needs are no less acute. The electronic notebook designed by **Kenneth Grange** of Pentagram, using technology devised by the Eden Group, is an innovative answer to this problem. It suggests one of the ways in which we can expect to see data-gathering devices develop in the near future. It has no keyboard and looks nothing like a personal computer. Instead, the user writes or draws directly on the screen using the system's electronic pencil/eraser, and commands are activated by touching pictograms in the same way. Data is stored in its memory, and faxes and electronic mail can be exchanged with other users.

Grange believes that there is a fundamental difference between the way in which we perceive computers and other objects. The computer is a tool, something we use, but diaries and cameras are possessions, things that we *own*. To help personalize the notebook and give it tactile appeal, he has used rubberized paint and a book-like leather cover.

75 **KENNETH GRANGE**
PORTABLE FAX MACHINE, *VP1386*
MOULDED PLASTICS
Activated by means of pictograms that are touch-sensitive to the wired pencil/eraser.
H 3.4cm (1⅜in) W 34cm (13⅜in) D 27cm (10½in)
MANUFACTURER: EDEN GROUP, UK

76 **PHILIPS CORPORATE INDUSTRIAL DESIGN**
NOTEBOOK PC, *PCL 101*
INJECTION-MOULDED ABS, POLYCARBONATE
Incorporates compact XT-compatible personal computer with 3½-inch 1.44cm NB floppy disc and liquid crystal display.
H 2.8cm (1⅛in) W 28cm (11in) D 22cm (8⅜in)
MANUFACTURER: PHILIPS ELECTRONICS, THE NETHERLANDS

77 **RICHARD JUNG AND DENNIS GRUDT FOR PATTON DESIGN**
CD STORAGE DEVICE, *OCEAN VISTA*
ABS, ACRYLIC
Stores and transfers information on to a disk.
H 3.5cm (1⅜in) W 12cm (4⅜in) D 9cm (3½in)
MANUFACTURER: OCEAN MICRO SYSTEMS, USA

78 **TOM FRONING**
ADD-ON HARD DISK DRIVE, *TSUNAMI*
INJECTION-MOULDED ABS
For use with Apple Macintosh computers to increase their memory capacity and speed. The drives may be positioned upright or stacked on top of each other.
H 6.1cm (2⅜in) W 2.3cm (⅞in) D 8.3cm (3¼in)
MANUFACTURER: PLUS DEVELOPMENT/LACIE, USA

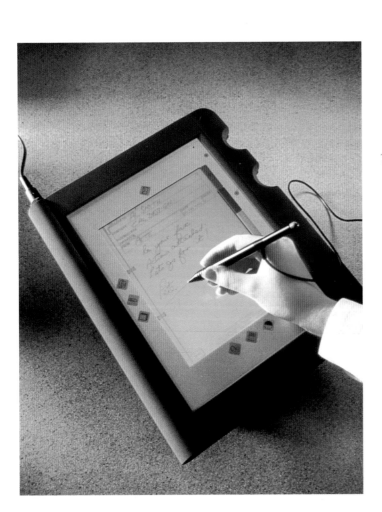

77

78

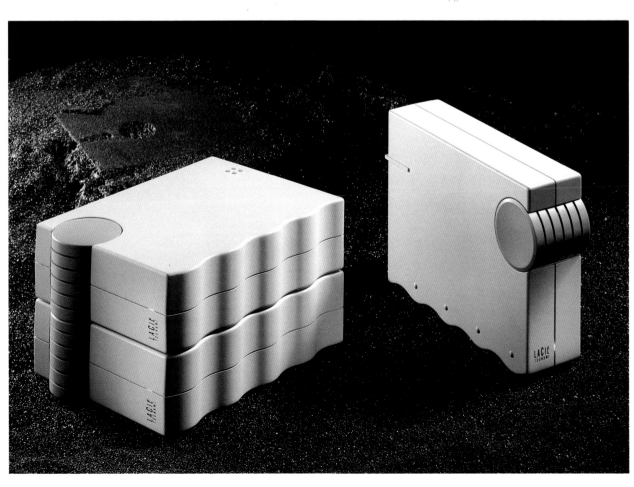

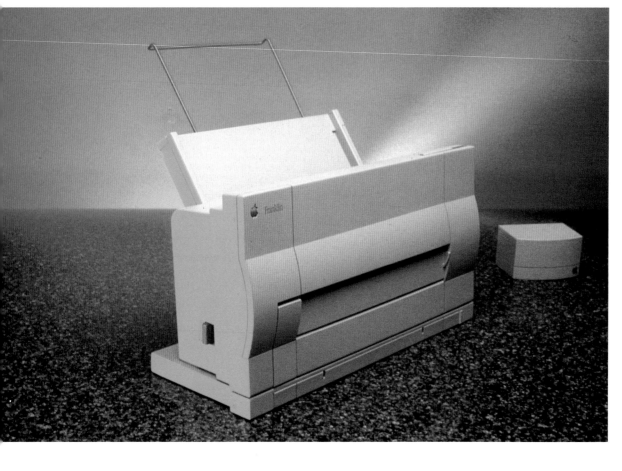

79

The microcomputer craze of the early 1980s left the homes of Europe and America awash with examples of the fledgling technology, but early dreams of computerizing the home accounts have for most people proved disappointing. The technology, at that stage, was simply not powerful or attractive enough. The personal computers that followed were vastly more efficient but, with a few notable exceptions, such as Amstrad's word processor, they were machines designed for the office rather than the home. Apple was the first company to market its products as lifestyle accessories. Unlike its workhorse business competitors, the Apple Macintosh had the softened contours, comfortable presence and modest 'footprint' of a consumer product; it was likeable. Concept models of central processing units designed by **Patton Design** show that Apple is now looking towards a much closer integration of the computer into the home. Shapes are 'soft tech', rounded and unthreatening like kitchen equipment or bathroom scales. Patton's design for the Apple *Style Writer* ink-jet printer, for domestic use and already in production, is not much more elaborate in appearance than a toaster. A vertical construction ensures that the printer takes up as little space on the desktop as possible.

5 PRODUCTS

80

**79 DOUG PATTON, RICHARD JUNG
AND DENNIS GRUDT FOR PATTON
DESIGN**
APPLE COMPUTER INK JET PRINTER,
STYLE WRITER
INJECTION-MOULDED ABS HOUSING
Contains a multi-sheet feeder.
H 16cm (6½in) W 33cm (13in) D 12.5cm (5in)
MANUFACTURER: APPLE COMPUTER, USA

**80 DOUG PATTON FOR PATTON
DESIGN**
APPLE COMPUTER, *GOLDILOCKS II*
ABS, ACRYLIC
One-off
H 14cm (5½in) W 30.5cm (12in) D 19cm (7½in)
MANUFACTURER: APPLE COMPUTER, USA

**81 JOAN CIRANNY FOR PATTON
DESIGN**
APPLE COMPUTER, *GOLDILOCKS II*
ABS, ACRYLIC
One-off
H 10cm (4in) W 30.5cm (12in) D 23cm (9in)
MANUFACTURER: APPLE COMPUTER, USA

81

82 PHILIPS CORPORATE INDUSTRIAL DESIGN
PROJECTION TV, *FL-1*
PLASTICS
H 138cm (54⅜in) W 99cm (39in) D 56cm (22in)
MANUFACTURER: PHILIPS ELECTRONICS, THE NETHERLANDS

83 PHILIPS CORPORATE INDUSTRIAL DESIGN
3-INCH LIQUID CRYSTAL DISPLAY COLOUR TV/MONITOR, *3LC 3000*
ABS PLASTIC, METAL, GLASS
Pocket-sized portable TV which can be used as a view finder/ monitor. It has a sunhood and fluorescent back-lighting.
H 5.5cm (2⅛in) W 10.2cm (4⅛in) D 18.8cm (7⅜in)
MANUFACTURER: PHILIPS, JAPAN

82

83

84 **MATSUSHITA-KOTOBUKI
ELECTRONICS INDUSTRIES**
COMBINATION VCR/21-INCH
COLOUR TV
PLASTIC, STEEL
H 49.8cm (19⅜in) W 55cm (21¾in) D 39.2cm
(15⅜in)
MANUFACTURER: MATSUSHITA, OFFICE
EQUIPMENT DIVISION, JAPAN

85 **MATSUSHITA ELECTRIC
INDUSTRIAL CO.**
LIQUID CRYSTAL DISPLAY VIDEO
PROJECTOR
PLASTIC
H 12.7cm (5in) W 20cm (7⅞in) D 19.4cm
(7⅜in)
MANUFACTURER: MATSUSHITA, TELEVISION
SECTOR, JAPAN

There is more than a dash of Buck Rogers in the
mouldings for the *3LC 3000* television from **Philips**
Japan. The three-inch screen's housing has the emphatic
extrusion of an imaginary space rocket instrument panel
in the days before space flight. This is the same kind of
mannered styling for fun rather than function also seen in
Naoki Sakai's designs for the *Ecru* camera and the limited
edition *Pao* car, which are not so much 'retro' in
approach, according to Sakai, as an attempt to evoke
'future memory'.

   A more straightforward exercise in product
semantics is offered by **Matsushita's** *Liquid Crystal
Display Video Projector*. Though video technology is
electronic rather than photographic, and far more
compact than film, there are obvious symbolic references
to an earlier generation of reel-to-reel projectors in the
shape of the plastic tripod and casing. The image itself can
be projected in either horizontal or vertical formats.

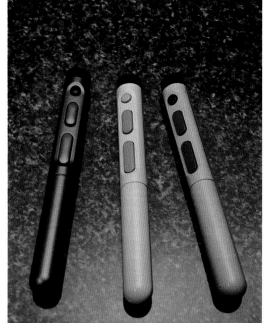

86

87

86 DOUG PATTON AND RICHARD JUNG FOR PATTON DESIGN
PROGRAMMABLE REMOTE CONTROL WITH KEYBOARD
ABS, ACRYLIC
Remote: H 2cm (¾in) W 6.5cm (2½in) L 21.3cm (8⅜in)
Keyboard: H 2cm (¾in) W 15cm (6in) D 9.5cm (3¾in)
MANUFACTURER: MITSUBISHI, USA

87 DOUG PATTON AND RICHARD JUNG FOR PATTON DESIGN
REMOTE CONTROL
ABS, PLASTIC
W 1.5cm (⅝in) L 15cm (6in) Di 1.5cm (⅝in)
MANUFACTURER: MITSUBISHI, USA

88 MICHAEL MCCOY, DALE FAHNSTROM AND DAVID VAN DEN BRANDEN
HOME ENTERTAINMENT SYSTEM, *ELECTRONIC PLANE*
GLASS, ALUMINIUM
The circuit is embedded in the glass, eliminating cables.
H 152.5cm (60in) W 183cm (72in) D 1.4cm (½in)
MANUFACTURER: MICHAEL MCCOY, DALE FAHNSTROM AND DAVID VAN DEN BRANDEN, USA

88

5 PRODUCTS

89 **AJIN TOGASHI**
SPEAKER SYSTEM, *CLEARBALL*
GLASS, METAL, PLASTICS
D 27cm (10½in) Di 24.5cm (9⅝in)
MANUFACTURER: SASAKI GLASS, JAPAN

90 **REIKO TAKADA**
OPTICAL HEADPHONE STEREO
ACRYL, ALUMINIUM
Music generates changes of
movement and colour in the
display panel.
Prototype
H 3cm (1⅛in) W 12.6cm (5in) D 7.3cm (2⅞in)
MANUFACTURER: TOSHIBA CORPORATION, JAPAN

91 **TADAO SHIMIZU**
SPEAKER SYSTEM AND CONTROLS,
NAMI-II
PLASTIC
The system's vertical CD player,
amplifier and speakers are put on
shelves to act as book-ends.
Prototype
Speaker: H 20cm (7⅞in) W 5cm (2in) D 20cm
(7⅞in)
CD player: H 20cm (7⅞in) W 5cm (2in)
D 20cm (7⅞in)
Remote control: H 1.5cm (⅝in) W 6cm (2⅜in)
D 14.8cm (5⅞in)
MANUFACTURER: DESIGN STUDIO TAD, JAPAN

92 **DAVID LEWIS**
AUDIO SYSTEM, *BEOSYSTEM 2500*
GLASS, PLASTICS, ZINC, ALUMINIUM
Contains FM tuner, CD player,
cassette deck and speakers. The
glass doors open automatically at
the approach of a hand.
H 36cm (14⅛in) W 83cm (32⅝in) D 16cm (6⅛in)
MANUFACTURER: BANG & OLUFSEN, DENMARK

89

90

One of the most rigidly observed and least accountable conventions of hi-fi design is that speakers must be rectangular boxes which intrude on their setting as little as possible. This is a restriction that a few of the more adventurous manufacturers are at last beginning to challenge, with speaker designs that give sculptural expression to the transmission of sound, while being far more efficient in acoustic terms than the traditional box.

   Ajin Togashi's *Clearball* speaker system for Sasaki Glass refines a technology first shown in *The International Design Yearbook 1989/90*. It is intriguing in appearance, resembling nothing so much as a pair of transparent eyeballs, while producing a sound image of considerable clarity, depth and width. **Tadao Shimizu's** speakers, on the other hand, combine a decorative, even ornamental, wavy-front finish with the most modest of supplementary functions: they can be used as bookends. The same desire for environmental integration would seem to lie behind **David Lewis's** *Beosystem 2500* for Bang & Olufsen. Lewis simply up-ends the deck (incorporating FM tuner, CD player and cassette) so that its profile conforms to the dynamic tilt of two wafer-thin, blue-fronted speakers.

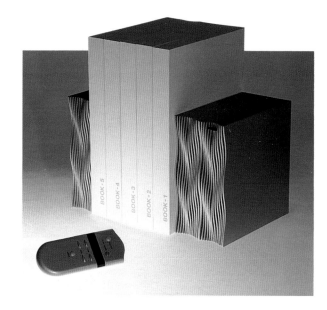

91

92

93

5 PRODUCTS

93 PHILIPS CORPORATE INDUSTRIAL DESIGN
CD SOUND SYSTEM, *FW 2017*
PLASTICS
CD player, cassette recorder and tuner/amplifier including speaker system.
H 21cm (8¼in) W 39cm (15⅜in) D 26cm (10¼in)
MANUFACTURER: PHILIPS ELECTRONICS, THE NETHERLANDS

94

94 PHILIPS CORPORATE INDUSTRIAL DESIGN
HEADPHONE RANGE 90
PLASTICS, METAL
A range of 11 headphones from in-ear to lightweight. Designed around ear and head shapes.
H 14.5cm (5¾in) L 14cm (5½in)
Headband W 0.3–1.3cm (⅛–½in)
MANUFACTURER: PHILIPS ELECTRONICS, THE NETHERLANDS

95 PHILIPS CORPORATE INDUSTRIAL DESIGN

CD PLAYER, *AZ 6819*

METAL BASE, POLYCARBONATE PLASTIC HOUSING

CD player: H 2.6cm (1⅛in) W 16cm (6⅜in)
D (with integrated stand) 25cm (9¾in)
Headphones: H 19cm (7½in) W 17cm (6⅝in)
Stand: H (with headphones) 21cm (8¼in)
MANUFACTURER: PHILIPS ELECTRONICS, THE NETHERLANDS

96 PHILIPS CORPORATE INDUSTRIAL DESIGN

CD SOUND SYSTEM, *AZ 9712*

PLASTICS

Contains CD player, cassette recorder and radio including portable speaker system.

H 66cm (26in) W 19cm (7½in) D 33cm (13in)
MANUFACTURER: PHILIPS ELECTRONICS, THE NETHERLANDS

95

96

98

97

97 HANNES BAUER
COMPACT DISC CONTAINER, *GAP*
LACQUERED MDF, METAL
H 185cm (72⅞in) W 31cm (12⅛in) D 23.5cm
(9¼in)
Without socle W 21cm (8¼in) D 21cm (8¼in)
MANUFACTURER: ANTHOLOGIE QUARTETT,
GERMANY

98 MATSUSHITA ELECTRIC
INDUSTRIAL CO.
PORTABLE CD TUNER SYSTEM
STEEL, PLASTIC
H 5.4cm (2⅛in) W 32.8cm (12⅞in) D 15.2cm
(6in)
MANUFACTURER: MATSUSHITA, AUDIO
DIVISION, JAPAN

99 DOUG PATTON FOR PATTON
DESIGN
CD JUKE-BOX/COMPUTER MEMORY
ABF PLASTIC, ACRYLIC
H 91.5cm (36in) W 14cm (5½in) D 15cm (6in)
MANUFACTURER: APPLE COMPUTER, USA

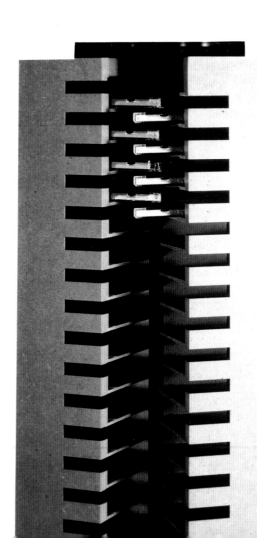

99

Every effort has been made to obtain details about the designers whose work is represented in this book, but in some cases information was not available. The figures following each entry refer to the illustrations of that designer's work (the number before the full point indicates the chapter number).

HELLE ABILD was born in Bergamo in 1964. Since graduating in textile design in 1989, she has worked with fabrics for fashion shows, experimenting with new techniques and materials. She is at present working with the design company Eleven Danes. 4.6

LAURA AGNOLETTO AND MARZIO RUSCONI CLERICI, born 1963 and 1960 respectively, formed their design partnership in 1985. They have lived and worked in Los Angeles and London, and exhibited in international group and solo shows. They create their objects mostly from industrial salvage. 1.105, 2.29

ALIEN ASSOCIATES was founded by Hans Weyers and is based in Belgium. Initially concerned with graphic design, it has expanded its scope to include limited batch production of furniture, lighting and product design. 2.27

ALIGHIERO E BOETTI is one of the 11 European artists commissioned by Meta Memphis to create a range of furniture designed from the standpoint of art rather than design. 1.123

THOMAS ALTHAUS was born in Düsseldorf in 1957, studied at the Secondary Technical School and then attended the F. H. University in Düsseldorf, studying interior and furniture design. He graduated with distinction in 1987 and, until he started running an architectural practice with VOLKER LAPRELL in 1989, worked as a freelance designer and interior architect, collaborating with many major German manufacturers. 1.18

EMILIO AMBASZ was born in Argentina in 1943 and gained a Master's degree in architecture from Princeton University where he was subsequently made a professor. While still in his twenties he helped to found New York's Institute of Architecture and Urban Studies, and served as Curator of Design at the Museum of Modern Art. He has won international recognition and several awards for his work as architect and interior and industrial designer, most recently the 1990 Quaternario Award for high technological achievement. He has exhibited widely, including the 1989 travelling show 'Emilio Ambasz: Architecture, Exhibition, Industrial and Graphic Design' which toured many venues in the USA and Canada. Among his buildings the Museum of American Folk Art and Houston Center Plaza are especially well known. 1.73, 5.25

ANNA ANSELMI, currently art director of Bieffe and Bieffeplast, has received considerable recognition as a designer and has exhibited her work at numerous international furniture fairs. From desks to domestic interiors, she experiments with the concepts of functionalism and rationality within the relevant space—office or home. Anselmi's work is in permanent collections in Munich, San Diego and Philadelphia. 1.109, 5.64

HANS ANSEMS was born in 1951 and studied at the Academy of Art and Sculpture, Arnhem and the École Nationale Supérieure des Arts Décoratifs, Paris. He has worked as a freelance designer and in 1981 founded Ansems Industrial Design. He collaborated with Luxo Italiana in 1982. 2.22

GEORG APPELTSHAUSER was born in Coburg, Germany, in 1942 and served an apprenticeship in watchmaking. He studied precision engineering at the Ulm Technical College from 1970–73. From 1973–78 he studied product design under Professor Lehmann at the Kunstakademie in Stuttgart, and since then has been a self-employed designer and engineer. 1.116

RON ARAD, a furniture, product and interior designer, was born in 1951 in Tel Aviv, Israel. He studied at the Jerusalem Academy of Art and at the Architectural Association, London, graduating in 1979. After working for a firm of London architects, he founded the design company One-Off Ltd in 1981. Ron Arad Associates was formed in 1989. In this year Arad also designed the interior of the public spaces of the new Tel Aviv Opera House with C. Norton and S. McAdam. He has exhibited widely and last year took part in a workshop at the Vitra Design Museum. 1.39–42, 44–46

JUNICHI ARAI was born in 1932 in Gunma Prefecture, Japan. He is a textile manufacturer specializing in sculptural, heavily textured fabrics. In the 1950s he developed the new technique of making and weaving with metallic yarn. He has supplied Issey Miyake and Comme des Garçons, among other leading Japanese designers, and in 1987 he was made an Honorary Member of the Faculty of Royal Designers for Industry. He has exhibited in Japan and the USA and his work can be found in the permanent collections of the Victoria and Albert Museum, London, the Cooper-Hewitt Museum, New York and the Museum of Applied Arts, Finland. 4.18

LOVE ARBÈN is a Swedish architect and furniture designer of international acclaim. He is currently working for Lammhults. 1.67, 69

ASSOCIATE DESIGNERS is a Spanish company founded in 1985. Its activities include all aspects of industrial, architectural, image and graphic design and exhibition production. It operates both nationally and internationally, with offices in Barcelona, Madrid and New York. 2.35

SERGIO ASTI completed his studies at the Milan Polytechnic in 1953, and since then has achieved international recognition as an architect and an interior and industrial designer. He is a charter member of the ADI (the Industrial Design Association). His designs have won numerous awards and have been displayed in several Venice Biennale exhibitions as well as permanent museum collections. Asti has been appointed to many jury panels for architectural and industrial design competitions and has lectured widely in Italy and abroad. 2.28, 3.6, 7

HIROSHI AWATSUJI, a textile designer, was born in Kyoto in 1929 and graduated from the Kyoto Municipal College of Fine Arts, establishing his own design studio in 1958. Since 1964 he has collaborated with the Fujie Textile Company. His principal commissions in Japan include textiles for the government pavilion at Expo 70, and tapestries for the Keio Plaza and Ginza Tokyu hotels. He exhibited at the Victoria and Albert Museum's 'Japan Style' exhibition in 1980, and at the 'Design since 1945' exhibition in Philadelphia. 4.21–24

MARCO BAGNOLI is one of the 11 European artists commissioned by Meta Memphis to create a range of furniture designed from the standpoint of art rather than design. 1.124

ENRICO BALERI studied in Milan and has been involved with a number of companies, including Pluri and Alias, where he held the position of art director until 1983. He then set up Baleri Italia, a firm which has commissioned work from, among others, PHILIPPE STARCK and Alessandro Mendini. Since 1989 Baleri has been the President of Malaparte House Association, which was founded with the purpose of restoring the Villa Malaparte on the island of Capri and using it for cultural events. 1.19

MARIO BARBAGLIA AND MARCO COLOMBO have worked together as interior designers in Milan since 1975. In 1984 they broke into the world of industrial design when they started a collaboration with PAF, creating the PAF Studio Collection, and have won international acclaim. 2.37

CARLO BARTOLI was born in 1931 in Milan, where he studied and began his professional career. He worked initially as an architect and subsequently on industrial and interior design, producing furniture and consumer goods for companies such as Antonangeli, Arflex and Kartell. Since 1988 he has taught advanced industrial design in Rome. Recently his interests have broadened to include architectural and environmental rehabilitation. 1.10

ALDO BARTOLOMEO, born in 1933 in Formia, Italy, is a furniture designer working particularly with metal and wood. His first major design, in 1956, was a chair made of tube and pierced sheet metal. In 1968 he designed the room-divider *Unigramma* with Giorgio de Ferrari, following this with a series of office cabinents, *Unigramma Ufficio*, in 1970. In 1986 he began *Alluminati*, a series of furniture pieces in metal or metal and wood combined. 1.29

HANNES BAUER was born in 1956 and lives in Baden-Baden, Germany. He worked in scenic design until, in 1985, he formed his own company, Möbel & Raum, specializing in interior and furniture design. In 1987 he founded Grono with Jorg Metzmeier and Uwe Schurr. His work has been shown on several occasions at the Zeus exhibition in Milan. He works for Anthologie Quartett among other furniture designers. 5.97

HEDDA BEESE was born in Guhrau, Germany, in 1944 and has degrees in educational sciences and industrial design. She became a designer in 1976 and was elected to the Board of Directors of Design Developments Ltd, London, in 1979. An acclaimed industrial designer, she has lectured in England, Ireland and Germany. From 1981–87 she was Managing Director of Moggridge Associates, London, and became a member of the Chartered Society of Designers, a Fellow of the Royal Society of Arts and a member of the VDID (Verband Deutscher Industrie-Designer e.V.). She has received several awards and her work can be seen in the permanent collection of the Museum of Modern Art, New York. 5.28

GEMMA BERNAL AND RAMÓN ISERN were born in 1949 and 1942 respectively in Barcelona. They studied industrial design at the Eina School, began working together in 1969 and, after various periods apart, formed their current partnership in 1984. They have worked for companies such as Disform, Grupo T, Blauet and Andreu Est., and have been members of the ADP (Association of Professional Designers) since its foundation. They have both lectured at the Eina and the Elisava School in Barcelona and have exhibited widely in Europe. 1.82, 83

GUEN BERTHEAU-SUZUKI is an industrial, furniture and interior designer and architect, born in Paris in 1956. He has a diploma from the Institute of Architecture in Tournai, Belgium and a Master's degree from Tokyo University. After working for Biro et Fernier Architectural Office, Paris and Arata Isozaki and Associates, Japan, he established Guen Bertheau-Suzuki Co. Ltd in 1990. He has exhibited in both Japan and Europe. 1.117

FRANCESCO BINFARÈ was born in Milan in 1939 and founded Cassina in 1969, Braccio di Ferro in 1962 with Gaetano Pesce and Alessandro Mendini, and the Centre of Design and Communication in 1980. He participated at the Venice and Helsinki Biennales and at the Triennale in Milan. He lectures at the Domus Academy in Milan, and has also given many lectures in Europe including seminars at the ICA, London, and the School of Architecture in Strasbourg. 1.79, 80, 4.20

JONAS BOHLIN, born in 1953, is currently working for Källemo. He graduated as an architect in 1981 and works mainly in the fields of interior architecture, stage and exhibition design and furniture. He has exhibited in Sweden and New York. 1.70

FLORIAN BORKENHAGEN was born in Frankfurt in 1959 and studied at the Academy of Fine and Applied Arts. He specializes in interior, set, exhibition, furniture and object design, and in 1990 set up his own studio in Como. 1.9

MARIO BOTTA was born in 1943 in Mendrisio, Switzerland. He attended the Academy of Fine Arts in Milan, then graduated in architecture from the University of Venice. He gained practical experience in Le Corbusier's studio, establishing his own architectural practice in Lugano in 1969. Since 1982 he has been designing furniture for Alias. Two of his chairs are in the study collection of the Museum of Modern Art, New York. 1.3

MARYSE BOXER was born in Tunis and studied art in Tunis and Paris. After being employed as a stylist and colourist for textile and cosmetics companies, she moved to London and created her own establishment, Maryse Boxer Design, concerned with producing a contemporary design concept for the table. Her work has been widely published and she has exhibited at the Centre Georges Pompidou, Paris and the Victoria and Albert Museum, London. 3.47, 48

ANDREAS BRANDOLINI was born in 1951 in Germany. He studied architecture in Berlin and has been a lecturer in industrial design at the Hochschule der Künste, Berlin, and visiting lecturer at the Architectural Association in London, as well as at the Hochschule für Gestaltung, Offenbach and the Hochschule der Künste in Saarbrücken. In 1932 he co-founded Bellefast with Joachim Stanitzek. He has exhibited in Brazil, France, Germany, Italy and Japan. 4.3

ALEXANDER BREBNER now manages The Brebner Company in New York, after spending four years working for M & Co. 5.22

TIMOTHY BROWN received a Master of Design from the Royal College of Art and a Bachelor of Arts in Design for Industry from Newcastle upon Tyne Polytechnic. He has worked for ID Two, San Francisco, Moggridge Associates, London and Seymour Powell, London, and has exhibited in the UK and Japan. His work can be found in the permanent collection of the London Design Museum. 5.36

BRUCE AND SUSAN BURDICK are industrial designers and co-partners of the Burdick Group in San Francisco. Bruce is a graduate of the Art Center College of Design, Los Angeles, and Susan of the Carnegie-Mellon University, Pittsburgh. Their furniture, designed for Herman Miller, is part of the San Francisco Museum of Art's permanent collection. They are the designers of Esprit's merchandizing system and the Echo Scarf showroom, New York. Currently they are working on exhibits for Philips Corporate Museum in The Netherlands and for the Rock and Roll Hall of Fame Museum. Their work has received *Time* magazine's 10 Best Award, Gold and Silver Awards for the Industrial Design Society of America, and the European Ergo Design Award. 5.57

GASPARE CAIROLI is an Italian designer born in Meda in 1952. After graduating, he worked for Cassina and B & B Italia. In 1983 he started his own studio with Elisabetta Donzelli, specializing in furniture design and advertising. His chair, *Terna*, was included in the Cooper-Hewitt Museum collection in 1986. He has been selected for the Compasso d'Oro twice, in 1987 and 1989. 2.5

MAURO CANFORI studied at the European Institute of Design in Milan, as well as Milan University where he specialized in architecture. In 1986 he was made art director for Cidue for whom he designed the *Matta Chair* which was selected at the Milan Forum of Design in 1988. He has exhibited in Paris and Japan. 2.17, 5.66–68

CAROUSCHKA is a Swedish textile designer. She was born in Stockholm in 1955 and graduated from the Gerlesborgsskolan Fine Art School in 1973 and the National College of Art, Craft and Design in 1978. She has exhibited widely in Sweden and abroad, and won the Swedish design award in 1989. 4.15–17

ALAIN CARRÉ was born in 1945 and trained at the Art School of Design and the National School of Applied Art in Tours. In 1970 he founded the Alain Carré Design Studio while working for Pierre Cardin as chief of construction design. In 1984 he became the director of the French Designers Industry Union (UFDI). 3.33

ACHILLE CASTIGLIONI was born in Milan in 1918. He began his work as a designer in partnership with his brothers, Livio and Pier Giacomo, specializing in interiors, furniture and in lights, for which he is particularly well known. Castiglioni is one of the foremost talents in Italian design, and has been honoured seven times with the Compasso d'Oro, as well as having six of his pieces selected for exhibition at the Museum of Modern Art, New York. He is currently professor of Industrial Design and Decoration at the University of Milan. 1.126–131

PAUL CHAMBERLAIN AND PETER CHRISTIAN are British furniture designers currently working freelance. 1.6

JOAN CIRANNY is an American designer born in 1960. She graduated in 1984 in Industrial Design from California State University, Long Beach. She has contributed to many national and international award-winning projects in the areas of computers, consumer electronics, medical equipment and furniture. She currently works for Patton Design, Costa Mesa, California. 5.81

ANTONIO CITTERIO was born in Italy in 1950. He studied at Milan Polytechnic, and has been involved in industrial and furniture design since 1967. In 1973, he opened a studio with Paolo Nava and the two have worked jointly and individually for B & B Italia, Flexform and others. In 1979 they were awarded the Compasso d'Oro. 1.50–52, 54–56.

LLUÍS CLOTET was born in Barcelona in 1941 and studied at the Escuela Técnica Superior de Arquitectura from which he graduated in 1965. In 1964 he founded Studio Per with architects Pep Bonet, Cristian Cirici and OSCAR TUSQUETS BLANCA. He collaborated in numerous projects with Oscar Tusquets Blanca until 1983. He is a founder-member of Bd Ediciones de diseño, for which he has designed furniture and other objects. He has received many major design awards and has exhibited widely. 1.49

NIGEL COATES was born in 1949 in Malvern, England. He studied at the University of Nottingham and at the Architectural Association where he has lectured since his graduation in 1974. In 1985 he co-founded Branson Coates with Douglas Branson. He is known for his belief that architecture can be odd and amusing as well as extremely well built and durable, and his projects include work for Jasper Conran and Katherine Hamnett. He has also designed restaurants in Japan and his present plans include the Nishi Acabu Wall in Tokyo and the Sea Hotel in Otaru, Japan. 1.90–93, 3.20

COOP HIMMELBLAU was founded in Vienna in 1968 by architects Wolf Prix (born 1942, in Vienna) and Helmut Swiczinsky (born 1944, in Poland) and the practice now has offices in Vienna and Los Angeles. The earlier work consisted of installations, speculative projects and conversions in Vienna such as the Baumann Studio (1985), the Iso-Holding offices (1986), Passage Wahliss (1986), Rooftop Remodelling (1988) and the Funder Factory 1&3 (1988). They have recently graduated to larger-scale industrial projects in Austria, France, Germany, California and Japan. In 1987 they won two major competitions: the Ronacher Theatre, Vienna, and the Melun-Senart city planning project near Paris. Both partners lecture and exhibit internationally; Prix is currently Adjunct Professor at SCIARC, Los Angeles. 5.37, 38

NICK CROWE trained in Fine Art at the Cheltenham School of Art and worked as a graphic designer before becoming a partner of The Control Room. He has exhibited his clock designs in the UK. 5.24

RICCARDO DALISI was born in Potenza, Italy, in 1931. Since 1962 he has been conducting experiments in architectural form using light and geometry, and taking part in competitions connected with building construction at an academic level. He has written a number of books and teaches at the University of Naples. He is credited with revitalizing research into design in southern Italy and has been described by Alessandro Mendini as 'the brains behind design in the South'. 2.18

DAVID DANIELSON is a member of Henry Dreyfuss Associates. He joined the firm in 1986 as a senior project supervisor and is at present managing design for their client A T & T in the telephones and printers section. He graduated from the University of Illinois in industrial design in 1965 and is a member of the Industrial Designers' Society of America. 5.29

DAL MONDO is the design team for Mondo Srl, an Italian company set up in 1987 by Giulio Cappellini, Paola Navone and Rodolfo Dordoni. 2.16, 3.37

TOM DEACON graduated in architecture from the University of Toronto in 1982, winning the RAIC medal. In 1984 he established the firm AREA to manufacture his designs for seating and tables. He is currently developing furniture projects for several American and Canadian companies. 1.28

JEAN-CHARLES DE CASTELBAJAC trained as a fashion designer and is now involved in interior, furniture and object design. His main emphasis is on elegance and individualism. 1.7, 4.11

JAN-KEES DE JAGER was born in Holland in 1962 and trained as an industrial furniture maker. He is as present working as a product and furniture designer, specializing in small decorative objects. 5.10–13

MICHELE DE LUCCHI was born in Ferrara, Italy, in 1951. He studied first in Padua and then at Florence University, graduating in 1975 and subsequently teaching there. In 1978 he began a close collaboration with ETTORE SOTTSASS. He worked and designed for Alchimia until the establishment of Memphis in 1981. He created some of Memphis' best-known products. In 1979 he became a consultant for Olivetti in Ivrea and, under the supervision of Sottsass, he designed their *Icarus* office furniture. Currently he is designing for a wide range of furniture manufacturers. 1.121, 122

PUCCI DE ROSSI was born in Verona in 1947. He studied sculpture with the American H. B. Walker and in 1973 had his first exhibition of works in metal in Paris. He worked for Alchimia in Milan and in 1977 moved to Paris. He has exhibited in Paris (Galerie Néotù 1987 and 1989), Los Angeles, Tokyo, Milan, Nice and Cologne. 2.12

SERGI AND OSCAR DEVESA were born in 1961 and 1963 respectively in Barcelona. They both studied design and in 1987 founded the D & D Society with the purpose of collaborating in product design for national and international markets. They have exhibited widely and have worked with Metalarte, Disform, Blauet and Supergrif-Damixa. 2.21

ANNABELLE D'HUART was born in 1952 in France. In the 1970s she travelled widely in Africa and Asia and the culture of the nomadic tribes has directed much of her design, particularly her carpets, jewellery and tiles. She returned to Europe in the 1980s and worked with many of the major Italian design companies. In 1991 she became the artistic director of Tallu Design. 4.9, 10

FABIO DI BARTOLOMEI was born in 1954 in Udine, and trained at the Architectural University in Venice. He has received international recognition as an artist, and has exhibited at the Venice Biennale. He has planned and executed many public and private commissions in the fields of architecture and design, and has collaborated with major Italian furniture and lighting manufacturers. 1.32

TOM DIXON was born in Tunisia in 1959. He became a freelance graphic designer in 1979 and an independent designer in 1983. His furniture is characterized by his need 'to let processes be seen, to leave each machining stage—joints, fillets, and weldings—clearly visible in the finished product'. He is at present concerned with producing one-off pieces of furniture and has collaborated with Cappellini on their 'International Interiors Collection'. He has exhibited his work in the USA, Germany, London and Japan, and examples of it can be found in the permanent collections of the Victoria and Albert Museum, London, the Musée des Art Décoratifs and the Centre Georges Pompidou, Paris and the Vitra Chair Museum, Weil am Rhein. 1.98–100, 5.62.

SYLVAIN DUBUISSON, a French designer, began his career in the architectural practice of Ove Arup in London in 1973. After 1980 he worked independently on a wide range of projects. His work has been included in various exhibitions, notably 'Art et Industrie' at the Musée National des Monuments Français in 1986 and an exhibition at the Musée des Arts Décoratifs, Paris in 1989. He was named Designer of the Year for 1990 at the Salon International du Meuble, Paris. 1.65, 66, 3.21, 5.47

RENA DUMAS, on graduation from the Ecole Supérieure des Métiers d'Art in 1961, was part of the Warner, Burns, Toan and Lunde architectural and design team, and worked on the Four Seasons restaurant at La Guardia Airport, Chicago and the Hilton Hotel in Athens. After freelancing in Paris, she became manager of the Robert Anxionnat interior architectural firm, responsible for the Time Life Building, Paris, and the Police Headquarters of Seine Saint Denis, Paris. In 1971 she created her own design firm Rena Dumas Architecture Intérieure (RDAI). 3.30

CHARLES EAMES (1907–1979), the American designer and architect, was born in St Louis, Missouri. He studied architecture at Washington University from 1924 to 1926, before setting up his own practice in 1930. In 1941 he married Ray Kaiser and collaborated with her on a number of design projects, experimenting with new techniques and materials. Their work brought numerous awards, including the President's Medal of Honour from the Art Directors' Club, New York, in 1965 and the Architectural Award Grand Prix from the American Institute of Architects, Los Angeles, in 1967, as well as several honorary doctorates. Charles Eames was also noted as a director of documentary films on a variety of subjects, including his own work. 1.132

THOMAS EISL is an Austrian designer, who has lived and worked in England since 1969. 2.13

FUMIO ENOMOTO was born in Tokyo in 1957 and graduated from Tokyo University of Art and Design in 1979. Between 1980 and 1986 he worked for the Kuramata Design Office, before setting up his own studio, Fumio Enomoto Atelier. In 1988 his work was exhibited in a one-man show for Axis, Tokyo. 1.11, 12

HARTMUT ESSLINGER, a German product designer, was born in 1944 in Beuren, Simmersfield. He is the founder-member and chairman of Frogdesign, responsible for the Apple Macintosh family and Yamaha synthesizer designs, among others. 1.71, 72

ESTUDI BLANC is a leading Spanish design firm which has produced work for, among others, Metalarte, Disform and Grupo T. 1.48

AGENORE FABBRI, an Italian furniture designer, was born in Barba, Tuscany in 1911 and today lives and works in Milan. He has won awards for his work and has exhibited widely in Europe. His works are in the collections of various museums in Germany, Japan and Brazil. 1.37

DALE FAHNSTROM is an American designer who co-founded Fahnstrom/McCoy in 1984. He was formerly the director of the Institute of Design at Illinois Institute of Technology and is currently Professor of Design there. 5.88

MICHEL FEITH (born in 1949 in Winsen) and Claudia Schneider-Esleben (born in 1949 in Düsseldorf) first met in 1978 while studying at the Hamburg School of Applied Arts. In 1983, they formed LUX, which created neon-light designs for the film and theatre industries; they worked on Fassbinder's 1981 film *Death on the 33rd Floor*. In 1983 they founded the architectural and furniture design group Möbel Perdu, which functions both as workshop and gallery. As well as twice-yearly exhibitions at the gallery itself, they have exhibited their designs throughout Europe, and have worked on numerous commissions both public and private in Germany and, more recently, in the USA. 1.114, 115

TRISTRAM FETHERSTONHAUGH was born in London in 1965 and studied at the Royal College of Art and Imperial College, London University. In 1988 he joined LOVEGROVE AND BROWN and is at present working for Ross LOVEGROVE. He has exhibited at the Ideal Home Exhibition, London, in 1988 and at SAD 90, Paris. 5.44

MARIA GRAZIA FIOCCO was born in Verona in 1956 and graduated from the Verona Art Institute. She went on to take the Industrial Design Diploma at Milan Polytechnic in 1978, and in 1981 opened her own studio. She has designed sanitary ware for Ideal Standard and Pozzi Ginori and accessories for Gedi and Regis, perfume bottles for Yves Saint Laurent and Oscar de la Renta, and kitchenware for Biesse. She has received many awards for her work, including in 1989 the United States Packaging Prize and the Golden Compass Award. 3.41, 42

DIANA FIRTH is a New Zealand furniture designer. She was educated at the Wellington Polytechnic School of Design and the Elam School of Fine Arts. In 1986 she co-formed the furniture group Artiture. 1.38

SIGGI FISCHER was born in Cologne in 1954 and studied industrial design at Wuppertal University. Since 1990 he has worked freelance, with clients including Thomas Schulte Design. He has exhibited in both Germany and Japan. 2.39

ROY FLEETWOOD was born in 1946 in London and studied at the School of Architecture in Liverpool, England, and the British School in Rome. He worked as project director for Foster Associates from 1973 until 1986 when he left to establish Frontier Technology Consultants. He has since expanded to form an office for design strategy, as well as Sugimura Fleetwood Architects and Engineers in Tokyo. He has an extensive client list including Erco Leuchten GmbH in Germany and Vitra International in Switzerland. He has received several lighting awards, most recently the Emanon Lighting System Award for Industrial Design. 1.74, 2.45

TOM FRONING graduated from the University of Cincinnati's industrial design course and is at present working for Ziba Design. He has won recognition for his work within the United States. 5.52, 78

OLIVIER GAGNÈRE was born in 1952 in Paris where he continues to live and work. His furniture designs and his work in glass and terracotta have been widely exhibited, and he has received several awards, most notably from the Centre VIA in 1982. 3.25, 26

JORGE GARCIA GARAY was born in Buenos Aires, Argentina, and since 1979 has been working in Barcelona where he heads Garcia Garay Design. He now works almost exclusively on lighting. In 1989 his ceiling lamp *Fenix* and floor lamp *Enterprise* were chosen for exhibition in the London Design Museum. He has also exhibited in Spain and the USA. 2.19

ELISABETH GAROUSTE AND MATTIA BONETTI were born in Paris and Lugano in 1949 and 1952 respectively, and have worked together since 1980. Their designs have been exhibited in Europe, Japan and New York, and examples can be seen in the permanent collections of the Musées des Arts Décoratifs in Paris and Bordeaux. They have designed sets and costumes for the theatre, and have worked on prestigious interior design projects, notably the conversion of the Château de Boisdeloup for the Picasso family. 1.103, 104

KRISTIAN GAVOILLE was born in Brazzaville, France, in 1956 and studied architecture in Toulouse. He was employed by the City of Paris until 1986. He subsequently collaborated with PHILIPPE STARCK on many of his interior design projects, notably the Royalton Hotel, New York and the Teatriz Restaurant, Madrid. With the aid of VIA and Néotù he exhibited at the Milan Furniture Fair in 1989 and in 1990 became the artistic director of the ARDI Society (manufacturers of small domestic items). In 1991 he created a line for Sèvres Crystal and continues his interest in exhibition design. 1.101, 102

BRUNO GECCHELIN was born in 1939 in Milan where he currently lives and works. He studied architecture at Milan Polytechnic and has worked for various companies including Olivetti, Fiat, Venini, Guzzini and Arteluce Flos. He has won prizes and recognition for his designs both in Italy and internationally. 5.43

KENNETH GRANGE was born in London and educated at the Willesden School of Art. In 1959 he established his own design consultancy specializing in interior design, and in 1972 co-founded Pentagram, his work ranging from furniture and domestic appliances to military equipment and the exterior of the Intercity 125 train for British Rail. He continues to offer a consultancy service, and his clients include Thorn EMI and Wilkinson Sword. He is the industrial design advisor for the Design Council and lectures widely both in Britain and abroad. He has won international acclaim, culminating in a one-man show at the Boilerhouse Gallery at the Victoria and Albert Museum, an Honorary Doctorate from the Royal College of Art in London in 1984 and a CBE in the same year. In 1987 he was elected president of the Chartered Society of Designers. 2.11, 5.17, 42, 53, 75

TOBIAS GRAU was born in 1957 in Hamburg where he now works. He studied business administration in Germany, and design at the New York University, graduating in 1984 and forming Tobias Grau GmbH. 2.41, 42

MICHAEL GRAVES, the Princetown architect famed for his Post-Modern classicism, was born in 1934. His work, which has received numerous awards, includes the Newark Museum, the Whitney Museum, a library in San Jaun Capistrano, the Humana Headquarters in Louisville and a winery in California's Napa Valley. His paintings and murals are in several major museums and he has designed furniture for Memphis and Sawaya & Moroni, and products for Alessi and Swid Powell. 3.40

KONSTANTIN GRCIC is a German furniture designer who is at present working freelance in London and Munich. He was born in 1965 and trained as a cabinet-maker, continuing his education at the John Makepeace School for Craftsmen and the Royal College of Art, London. 1.94

DENNIS GRUDT is an American designer, born in 1950. He received a Bachelor of Science degree in Industrial Design from California State University, Long Beach in 1974. He worked for Design West, specializing in design engineering, and since joining Patton Design in 1989 has worked on computer, medical and consumer products. 5.54, 77, 79

MONICA GUGGISBERG AND PHILIP BALDWIN established their studio and design office outside Lausanne, Switzerland in 1982, producing one-off and production glass. Since 1985 they have worked with Rosenthal in Germany and since 1989 with Steuben in the USA. Their work is exhibited regularly in the USA, Japan and Europe, and has received recognition awards in Germany, France and the USA. 3.1–3

RICHARD HEATLY was born in India in 1950 and educated in England. He is mainly a furniture designer concerned with limited batch editions. 5.50, 51

MATTHEW HILTON was born in 1957 and graduated from the Kingston School of Art, England, in 1979. He worked as a designer and model-maker from 1980–84 when SCP launched his first commercial furniture collection at the Milan Furniture Fair. He has exhibited in Europe and Japan. 1.95

YOSHIKI HISHINUMA is a fashion and textile designer, born in Sendai, Japan in 1958. He has presented collections from 1984 onwards, showing both in Japan and Europe. He also designs theatrical costume and in 1990 he created the uniform and monument for the Friendship Pavilion in the International Green and Greenery exhibition in Osaka, Japan. 4.26, 27

JOSEF HOFFMANN (1870–1956) was an Austrian architect and designer. He co-founded the Wiener Sezession and the Wiener Werkstätte in 1903 with KOLOMAN MOSER and Fritz Waerndorfer. One of his most spectacular commissions was the Palais Stoclet in Brussels, planned in co-operation with Czeschka and Klimt in 1905–11. In 1920 he was appointed director of building for the City of Vienna, at which time he designed the residential development for Laxenburgerstrasse. In addition to numerous architectural works, Hoffmann also created art and craft objects of all kinds. 4.29

HANS HOLLEIN was born in Vienna, Austria in 1934. He received his diploma from the Academy of Figurative Arts in Vienna, attended the Illinois Institute of Technology in Chicago and obtained a Master's degree in architecture from Berkeley University. He has received numerous awards and has undertaken design projects for companies such as Herman Miller, Cleto Munari, Alessi, Memphis, Poltronova, Knoll International, Baleri and Swid Powell. Since 1978 he has been the Austrian Commissar for the Venice Biennale. 1.63

TAKENOBU IGARASHI was born in 1944 in Hokkaido, Japan. He graduated from Tama Art University in 1968 and went on to obtain a Master's degree in art from the University of California, Los Angeles in 1969. He is now professor and guest lecturer respectively at the above universities and set up his own company, Takenobu Igarashi Studio, in 1985. He is acclaimed both nationally and internationally, and is vice-president of the Alliance Graphique International and a member of the Board of Directors of the Japan Graphic Designers Association. 1.13, 5.14, 16

MASSIMO IOSA GHINI is an Italian designer working in the areas of furniture, textiles, fashion and advertising. Born in 1959 in Borgo Tossignano, he studied in Florence and graduated in architecture from Milan Polytechnic. In 1981 he joined the group Zak-Ark, and from 1984 has collaborated with the firm AGO. Since 1982 he has worked on a number of discothèques, video projects and magazines. In 1986 he took part in the Memphis group's '12 New' collection. 1.57–59, 5.1–4

DAKOTA JACKSON was, in his early twenties, a professional magician. His sense of mystery and illusion was invested in early pieces of one-off furniture, expressed in moving parts and hidden compartments. He works in his own studio in New York and is the recipient of a National Endowment for the Arts Design Fellowship. He has lectured at universities and industry events. 1.53

CARSTEN JØRGENSEN was born in 1948 and was educated at the Copenhagen School of Art, where he later taught. From 1969 to 1970 he was a designer at Royal Copenhagen and in 1972 co-founded and lectured at the experimental school of art 'Atelier 12'. In 1974 he started work for Bodum, establishing their design department. He has been a member of the Danish Design Board since 1968. 3.43–46.

RICHARD JUNG is an American designer, born in 1960. He graduated in 1984 in industrial design from California State University, Long Beach. He is currently vice-president of Patton Design. He has contributed to many national and international award-winning projects in the areas of computers, consumer electronics, medical equipment and furniture. 5.54, 77, 79, 86, 87

TIBOR KALMAN was born in Budapest in 1949 and studied journalism at New York University. In the early 1970s he worked for Barnes & Noble Bookstores, eventually becoming their design director. In 1979 he founded the multi-disciplinary design firm M & Co. His watch collection is on permanent display in the Museum of Modern Art, New York. 5.20–23

MIKIO KAMEGI was born in 1961 and graduated in architecture from the Musashino Art University in 1984. He has since worked for Toshiba Corporation's Design Center in Tokyo where he is responsible for the product design of electrical home appliances. 5.58

JEFFREY KAPEC graduated with honours from the Pratt Institute, receiving a Bachelor of Industrial Design degree. He is an active member of the Industrial Design Society of America and the Human Factors Society. In 1972 he began his career with A. P. Montalbano Associates where he developed a reputation as an accomplished product designer. In 1976 he worked for Human Factors Industrial Design, subsequently being promoted to project manager. He formed the Tanaka Kapec Design Group along with KAZUNA TANAKA in 1980. 5.49

HIJUNG KASUYA was born in Tokyo and graduated from Musashino College of Art in 1974. She worked as an interior designer with Arflex, Japan, until she launched her own company, Contemporary Market, specializing in stationery design. She has many clients, including Sanyo electronics. She is a frequent contributor to many industry publications and periodicals, and since 1990 has lectured at Tokyo Modo Gakuen. 5.19

KAZUO KAWASAKI was born in Fukui City, Japan, in 1949. After graduating from Kanazawa University of Arts, he joined Toshiba and worked on the development of hi-fi audio products. Since then he has worked independently as an industrial designer, moving his studio back to Fukui in 1980. He has won several awards for his work, including the Design Forum Silver Prize and the Small and Medium Enterprise Agency Prize. He currently teaches part-time at Kanazawa and Fukui Universities. 5.15

MILES KELLER AND HELEN KERR were both born in 1959 and graduated together from the Ontario College of Art in Toronto, Canada, in 1988. Helen Kerr is also a graduate in environmental studies from the University of Waterloo, and the activities covered by Kerr Keller Design include environmental design as well as product, furniture and graphic design. 5.18

PERRY A. KING AND SANTIAGO MIRANDA founded King and Miranda Associati in 1976. King was born in London in 1938 and Miranda in Seville, Spain, in 1947. They now work in Milan, and are active in the fields of interior, graphic and product design. Both their award-winning work in furniture and lighting, and their work in the design of computer equipment interface, has received much attention. 1.30, 31, 2.8, 9

TOSHIYUKI KITA was born in 1942 in Osaka, Japan, and graduated in industrial design in 1964. Since 1969 he has divided his time between Osaka and Milan where he has worked on furniture and accessories for many major manufacturers. He has received the Japan Interior Design Award, the Kitaro Kunii Industrial Design Award and the Mainichi Design Award. The *Wink* armchair and *Kick* table which he designed for Cassina are in the permanent collection of the Museum of Modern Art, New York. 1.64

JUNKO KONRAI was born in Japan in 1956 and graduated in product design from the Tama Art University in 1981. She is currently employed by the Design Department of the Matsushita Electric Industrial Company. 5.40

HARRI KORHONEN is a Finnish furniture designer who founded and still owns Inno, being responsible for production from the end of 1970 to the beginning of 1980. His most recent design is the *Oscar* family of chairs. Many of his creations have been awarded prizes from the Museum of Applied Arts in Finland. 1.68

JOSEPH KOSUTH, an American artist, was born in Toledo, Ohio. His work represents the analytical stream-of-consciousness movement in art, using the printed word and textual quotations and consolidating these ideas with numerous writings. He is represented in many of the world's galleries and museums. Recent exhibitions include Leo Castelli, New York, in 1988 and the Museo de Capodimonte, Naples, in 1989. 5.55

AXEL KUFUS was born in Essen in 1958. He served a carpentry and joinery apprenticeship in Kempen, Niederrhein and founded the Wood and Bronze workshop along with the sculptor Richard Mühlemeier. In 1985 he studied industrial design at the HDK Berlin, and since 1986 has been a partner in the Crelle-Workshop in Berlin. He has worked with JASPER MORRISON and ANDREAS BRANDOLINI for Utilism International, and since 1989 has collaborated with Jonas Milder in New York. 1.86

SHIRO KURAMATA (1934–1991) was born in Tokyo and trained at the Tokyo Technical High School of Art and the Kuwasawa Institute of Design. In 1965 he created his own design office. As well as his celebrated glass armchair of 1976, and a number of other equally elegant but innovative pieces of furniture, Kuramata has designed interiors, notably for Issey Miyake and Esprit. He participated in the first three Memphis shows, and has also had various private exhibitions in Japan and London. In 1981 he received the Japan Cultural Design Prize. 1.1, 2

MASAYUKI KUROKAWA was born in Nagoya, Japan, in 1937. He graduated in architecture from the Nagoya Institute of Technology in 1961 and completed his training at the Graduate School of Architecture, Waseda University, in 1967. In the same year he established Masayuki Kurokawa Architects and Associates. He has been awarded numerous prizes for his work, including six IF prizes for designs of tables and lighting fixtures. 2.3

MARIE-CLAUDE LALIQUE, granddaughter of Réné Lalique, was born in Paris at the end of the 1930s and studied at L'École Nationale des Arts Décoratifs, graduating in theatre design. She trained at the crystal factory of Wingen-sur-Moder and collaborated with her father Marc Lalique from this time until his death in 1977. She is now chairman of Lalique, and designs 30 to 40 new pieces each year. 3.23, 24.

PIERRE LALLEMAND was born in Belgium in 1959 and graduated in architecture from the Académie des Beaux-Arts, Brussels, in 1983. From 1985 onwards he co-founded and became a partner in several companies: Consulting Office 'A2Z' (1985); LTZ Architects (1988); Moonlight (1988); and Art and Build, Architects and Engineers Partners (1989). He is also an assistant lecturer in sculpture at the ENSAV La Cambre, Brussels. 2.36

VOLKER LAPRELL was born in 1939 in Hann, Düsseldorf. After studying Technical Furniture Design, he attended the Academy of architecture in Wuppertal. In 1961 he not only gained his degree, but also won two prizes in the International Furniture Competition in Cantù. In 1962 he designed a range of upholstered furniture for Walter Knoll, after which he decided to diversify, becoming involved in domestic architecture, and interior and exhibition design. In the 1970s he returned to furniture design, collaborating with many major German manufacturing companies. He has received awards from the Design Centre in Stuttgart and has won the Dupont Prize. 1.18

TILL LEESER was born in 1949 and studied at the Folkwangschule in Essen, Germany. He began his career as a photographer before becoming involved in design in 1985 when he co-founded the company Bilderberg. He has exhibited in Germany, France, the USA and Japan, and an example of his design work can be seen in the permanent collection of the Deutsches Architekturmuseum in Frankfurt. 2.30

DAVID LEWIS, an industrial and product designer, was born in London in 1939 and educated at the Central School of Art in the Department of Industrial Design. He moved to Denmark in the early 1960s, designing television sets for Bang & Olufsen and also working for two of the company's former designers. He started his own studio in the early 1970s and is now the main designer for Bang & Olufsen, responsible for all their television set product design. 5.92

SOL LEWITT is one of the 11 European artists commissioned by Meta Memphis to create a range of furniture designed from the standpoint of art rather than design. 1.125

JOSEP LLUSCÀ was born in Barcelona in 1948. He studied industrial design at the Escola Eina where he is now professor, and at the École des Arts et Métiers, Montreal. He was vice-president of ADI-FAD (Industrial Designers' Association) from 1985 to 1987, and was one of the founder members of the ADP (Association of Professional Designers). He is a member of the Design Council of the Catalonian government, and has been the recipient of several major awards such as the 1990 National Design Award. Lluscà frequently attends international exhibitions and conferences, most recently 'Catalonia 90's' in New York and 'International Design' at the Design Museum, London. 2.31–34, 5.35

CHRISTOPHER LOEW was educated at the Institute of Design, Illinois Institute of Technology, Chicago, where he graduated with a Bachelor of Science in Design. He then joined the IBM Corporation. In 1987 he moved to ID Two as an industrial designer and is at present heading design on projects for Nynex. He has also participated in several of ID Two's interaction design schemes, including a design strategy programme for Philips. He has won acclaim in the USA, being chosen for three years for inclusion in ID magazine's Annual Design Review. 5.30

GLEN OLIVER LOEW was born in Leverkusen, Germany, in 1959. He graduated from the University of Wuppertal with a degree in industrial design, then moved to Milan where he received a Master's degree in design from the Domus Academy. Since 1987 he has collaborated with ANTONIO CITTERIO, designing products for companies such as Vitra, Kartell, Olivetti Synthesis, Biesse and others.

JOHN LONCZAK graduated from Syracuse University, and began his career at Pulos Design Associates and Cousins Design, later becoming a partner at Stowell/Smart Design. In 1985 he established his own company, working on cosmetics, household goods, electronic and personal care products. He has received recognition from several major museums, including the Museum of Modern Art, New York, as well as from a number of design publications. 5.27

ROSS LOVEGROVE was born in Wales in 1958 and studied at Manchester Polytechnic and the Royal College of Art, London, from which he graduated in 1983. He worked for several design consultancies, including Allied International Designers and the German group Frogdesign. In 1984 he was a member of the Atelier de Nîmes with JEAN NOUVEL and PHILIPPE STARCK, and in 1986 he co-formed LOVEGROVE AND BROWN in London. This was dissolved in 1990 when he set up his own studio, Lovegrove Design. 3.38

LOVEGROVE AND BROWN was a British product design company founded by ROSS LOVEGROVE and Julian Brown in 1986 and dissolved in 1990. Among others, their clients featured Knoll International, Metalarte, Wedgwood and British Airways. 2.20

VICO MAGISTRETTI was born in Milan in 1920. He took a degree in architecture in 1945 and subsequently joined his father's studio. Until 1960 he was mainly concerned with architecture, town planning and interiors. He began designing furniture and household articles for his buildings in the 1960s and now collaborates closely with a number of manufacturers who produce his designs. He has participated in nearly all the Milan Triennali since 1948 and has won numerous awards. Fifteen of his pieces are in the permanent collection of the Museum of Modern Art in New York. 1.110

PATRICK MAGNIN, an architect and furniture and lighting designer, was born in Geneva in 1957, and trained in engineering and architecture. Since 1968 he has worked widely on projects ranging from domestic commissions to university complexes. 2.7

ERIK MAGNUSSEN studied at the Danish School of Arts and Crafts and Industrial Design, where his main interest was sculpture. He designed his first porcelain range in 1965, its puritanical and functional emphasis an example of his need to reduce his designs to their basic practical value. In 1977 his vacuum jug was awarded the Danish Industrial Design Prize and in 1983 he was chosen as Danish Designer of the Year by the Danish Design Council. 3.31

PETER MALY, a furniture, textile and interior designer, trained at the Detmold School of Architecture, after which he became an editorial adviser to the German magazine *Schöner Wohnen*. In 1970 he set up his own studios in Hamburg and designed products that have been manufactured by some of the best-known German furniture manufacturers, including Reim Interline and Walter Knoll. He began his colloboration with Ligne Roset in 1983. 1.62

ENZO MARI is an Italian designer, born in 1932. He studied at the Brera Academy of Fine Art in Milan and taught design methods at Milan Polytechnic. In 1972 he participated in 'Italy: The New Domestic Landscape' at the Museum of Modern Art, New York. Since the 1950s he has worked on the design of glass for Danese as well as on furniture for Driade and Gabbianelli. He has been awarded the Compasso d'Oro twice: in 1967 for his research, and in 1979 for his *Delfina* chair, manufactured by Driade. 1.60

JAVIER MARISCAL, a Spanish designer, was born in 1950. He trained as an artist and graphic designer and collaborated on the Memphis collection of 1981. He has designed lights with Pepe Cortès for the Barcelona firm Bd Ediciones de diseño, textiles for Marieta and carpets for Nani Marquina. His most recent projects are a cartoon series on Cobi, the mascot for the Barcelona '92 Olympic Games, which he designed in 1988, and work with Alfredo Arribas on the interior of the Torres de Avila bar, Barcelona. 4.19

ELIO MARTINELLI was born in 1922. He studied scenography at the University of Florence, then worked on a number of interior design projects, both public and private. In 1960 he began the transformation of his father's commercial business into a company producing lighting apparatus. This was to become Martinelli Luce. Martinelli has been designing new products and models every year since then. He has shown his work at all the major exhibitions and fairs, including the first Eurodomus in 1966 and the 14th and 15th Triennale. In 1979 he participated in the selection for the Compasso d'Oro. He was awarded the Premio Segnalazione AIPI in 1990 for his *Sistema* of that year. 2.4

JOSEP MASSANA AND JOSEP TREMOLEDA were born in Barcelona in 1947 and 1946 respectively. They are both industrial designers and members of ADI-FAD (Industrial Designers' Association), ADP and BEDA. In 1973 they founded Mobles 114; initially a retail outlet, by 1981 it had developed into a manufacturing enterprise dealing with contemporary furniture and lighting. In 1978 they won international acclaim with their lamp *Gira* and have been the recipients of several design awards and selections of the ADI-FAD and SIDI. From 1989–1990 Josep Tremoleda was President of the ADI-FAD. 2.38

PAUL MATHIEU AND MICHAEL RAY were born in France in 1960 and America in 1963 respectively, and are involved in object, furniture and porcelain design, as well as painting. They have also worked on television advertisements and in magazine and book graphics. They have exhibited their work in both Paris and the USA. 1.75–78

INGO MAURER was born in Germany in 1932. After training as a typographer and graphic artist, he emigrated to the USA in 1960. He moved back to Europe in 1963 and started his own lighting design firm in 1966. He now designs furniture, and his work has been collected by the Museum of Modern Art, New York and Neue Sammlung, Munich. He has also exhibited in Germany, Italy, France and Russia. 1.47, 2.1, 2

SIGI MAYER was born in 1950 and studied at the Academy of Arts in Vienna. He specializes in architecture, and interior, graphic and packaging design. 5.7

HILTON MCCONNICO was born in Memphis, Tennessee and worked initially in film and show-business design, being responsible for the decor in the 1981 Jean-Jacques Beinex film *Diva*. In 1988 he expanded his interest to cover textile, lighting and tableware design. He lives and works in Paris. 4.1

MICHAEL MCCOY is co-chair of the Design Department at Cranbrook Academy of Art, and is partner, with his wife Katherine, in the design firm McCoy and McCoy. In 1984 he formed Fahnstrom/McCoy with DALE FAHNSTROM. 5.88

ANNETTE MEECH trained in industrial design (ceramics) at Leicester Polytechnic, England, and the Royal College of Art, London. From 1972–83 she was the design consultant for Ravenhead Glass and is currently director of The Glasshouse. She also teaches part-time at the West Surrey College of Art and Design. She has exhibited widely and her work appears in permanent collections at the Crafts Council, London and the Musée des Arts Décoratifs, Paris. 3.36

DAVIDE MERCATALI, an Italian architect and designer, was born in Milan in 1948. He established the Zeus group in association with Noto in 1984, and Metals in 1989. 3.28

CARLO MOLLINO (1905–1973) was a nonconformist Italian architect and furniture and interior designer, whose work reflected influences ranging from Gaudì and Mendelsohn to Aalto and Le Corbusier. Mollino's buildings include the Faculty of Architecture in Turin, where he was the Chairman of Architechtonic Composition and Decoration for 18 years. None of his interior designs survives. 1.133, 134

JOSEP MORA was born in Barcelona in 1949. He is a lecturer in Aerodynamics at the Engineering School of Barcelona and Escola Elisava. He has collaborated with industrial designers on many occasions and is a specialized designer in his own right of light vehicles and complex mechanical objects. 2.38

CARLO MORETTI was born into a traditional glass-making family in Murano in 1934. He has spent his life combining skills learned from an early age with new technological developments and influences taken from the study of design and avant-garde architecture. He seeks to creat light, airy glasswork rather than traditional heavy glass processed at the grindstone. 3.39

JASPER MORRISON is a British furniture designer, educated in New York, Frankfurt and England. He graduated from the Royal College of Art, London, in 1985 and since then has designed and made limited batch production pieces. In 1986 he started in private practice and took part in Zeus' exhibition in Milan. He has also produced a number of projects for Sheridan Coakley (SCP), London, Idée, Japan, and Cappellini, Italy. His prototypes have been donated to the Vitra Museum, Germany. 1.87–89

KOLOMAN MOSER (1868–1918) was a Viennese graphic artist, painter and designer. He studied painting at the Kunstakademie in Vienna where he later became professor. He was one of the founders of the Wiener Sezession, and in 1903 he co-founded the Wiener Werkstätte, along with JOSEF HOFFMANN and Fritz Waerndorfer, which produced quality craft products designed by leading artists and conceived complete interiors. In 1904 he designed the windows for the Am Steinhof church in Vienna and, after breaking from the Werkstätte, concentrated on painting and stage design. 4.28

PASCAL MOURGUE began working as an interior designer at the end of the 1960s. Since 1982 he has been concentrating on furniture and carpet design, tableware and even trimarans. He was named French Designer of the Year in 1984, and in 1986 won the Grand Prix de la Critique de Meuble Contemporain. His work can be seen in the permanent collection of the Musée des Arts Décoratifs, Paris. 1.112, 113

FORREST MYERS, a sculptor and furniture designer, works exclusively in metal. He was born in 1941 in Long Beach, California and educated at the California School of Fine Arts, San Francisco. He has exhibited widely in the USA. 1.43

PATRICK NAGGAR was born in 1946 in Cairo, Egypt, and graduated in architecture from the École Nationale Supérieure des Beaux Arts, Paris. He continued his training by completing a Master's degree in urban studies at the University of Paris VIII, City Planning and Sociology Department. From 1971–1983 he completed numerous residential and commercial architecture and interior design projects, and in 1987 co-formed the company Nile Inc. Naggar has received several awards and has exhibited both in Paris and the USA. Current work includes a new collection of furniture and objects being shown at the Galerie Néotù in Paris, offices for Yves Saint Laurent in New York and several art galleries in Paris and London. He is a frequent guest lecturer in America. 1.118, 119, 5.45

RICHARD J. NEUTRA (1892–1970) was born in Vienna and belongs, together with Le Corbusier, Gropius, Alvar Aalto, Mies van der Rohe and others, to the generation of the great pioneers of modern architecture. He graduated in 1918 from the Technischen Hochschule in Vienna and moved to the USA in 1923 where he worked with Frank Lloyd Wright. In 1926 he opened his own office in Los Angeles and from 1928–29 taught architecture at the Academy of Modern Art. His best-known projects include the Lovell House and the VDL Research House, both in Los Angeles. In 1977 he was awarded a posthumous gold medal from the American Institute of Architecture. In 1989 a retrospective exhibition was organized at the Museum of Modern Art in New York. 1.135–138

MARC NEWSON is an Australian designer, born in 1962 in Sydney where he took a diploma in jewellery design at the College of Art. He has worked with RON ARAD in London, and in Japan where he spends long periods. He has built up a large collection of furniture designs which have the love of detail and emphasis on manual craftsmanship acquired from his original concern with jewellery. 1.96, 97, 5.26

GUIDO NIEST was born in 1958 in Venezuela. He came to Europe in 1979 and from 1982 studied industrial design at the Fachhochschule, Munich where he specialized in product design. Since 1986 he has worked for Sabattini Argenteria and has also founded his own design studio, Atelier Canaima, in Como, where he produces silver jewellery, tableware and household objects. 3.8

NINABER/PETERS/KROUWEL Industrial Design was established in 1985 by Bruno Ninaber van Eyben, Wolfram Peters and Peter Krouwel with the aim of producing a wide variety of line assembly and mass-produced products for the consumer and professional market. Ninaber graduated from Maastricht Art Academy in 1971, Peters and Krouwel from the Delft Technical University in 1978. Their work is characterized by a strong international orientation and covers all stages from design through development to pre-production management. They have won recognition both within The Netherlands and abroad, and their work can be seen in the permanent collections of the Museum of Modern Art, New York, the Stedlijk Museum, Amsterdam and the Design Museum, London, among others. In 1990 nine of their products received a Gute Industrieform recognition. 5.56

JEAN NOUVEL, one of France's best-known contemporary architects, was born in 1945. His most celebrated project is the Institut du Monde Arab, Paris, for which he won the Equerre d'Argent in 1987. In the same year the Salon International du Meuble nominated him Designer of the Year for his furniture. As well as architecture and furniture, Jean Nouvel has had a life-long interest in theatre and set design. 1.61

EMILY OBERMAN graduated from Cooper Union, USA in 1985. She has been a senior designer at M & Co. for four years. 5.21

KATSUHIKO OGINO was born in 1944 and graduated from the Musashino Art University in 1966. Until 1969 he lectured at the Japan Design School. He established Mono-Pro Kogei, Humpty-Dumpty Ltd, and Time Studio Ltd in 1975, 1976 and 1978, respectively. He has received design awards within Japan and in 1986 became a member of the G Mark selection committee. 5.61

ROBERTO PAMIO graduated in architecture in Venice in 1968. His projects include both domestic and industrial design, and he has worked in a number of countries as well as Italy, including the USA, Australia, Mexico and Japan. He has also judged several international competitions and has taken part in group exhibitions, as well as solo shows at the Palazzo Grassi in Venice and the Axis Design Center in Tokyo. 1.81

TIM PARSEY trained at the Central School of Art, London, graduating in 1982 with a Bachelor of Arts in industrial design. In the same year he moved to the USA where he later joined Human Factors Industrial Design, New York, designing an award-winning child's corrective foot-brace. In 1988 he joined ID Two where he has designed and managed a broad range of projects, winning a Recognition of Design Achievement award from the ID Society of America for a non-invasive blood pressure measurement system. 5.30

DOUG PATTON is an American designer, born in 1953, who graduated in industrial design from California State University, Long Beach, in 1980. After working for a firm of consultants, he established Patton Design Enterprises in 1983, in order to specialize in furniture, audio, medical, computer and consumer projects. 5.54, 79, 80, 86, 87, 99

RICHARD PEDUZZI was born in Argentan, France, in 1943 and studied at the Académie de Dessin in Paris under the sculptor Charles Auffret, specializing in fine art and theatre scenography. In 1967 he started his collaboration with Patrice Chereau, designing sets including those used in Wagner's *Ring* cycle for the 100th anniversary of the Bayreuth Festival. This partnership culminated in their joint artistic direction of the Théâtre des Amandiers at Nanterre from 1981–89. In 1979 he met Michel Laclotte, the director of the Louvre, and became interested in interior and exhibition design. He has worked on many major shows such as the Degas retrospective in Paris in 1988. Since 1988 he has also designed furniture for Mobilier National. Today he is the Director of the École Nationale Supérieure des Arts Décoratifs in Paris. 1.26, 27

JIŘÍ PELCL was born in Sumperk, Czechoslovakia, in 1950, and trained at the Art School in Brno, the Academy of Applied Art in Prague and the Royal College of Art in London. He now works as a freelance interior and furniture designer, and in 1990 was responsible for giving a new look to President Vaclav Havel's study and meeting room in Prague Castle. He has exhibited in Czechoslovakia, Germany, Austria and France. 1.36

JORGE PENSI is a Spanish architect and industrial designer, born in 1946 in Buenos Aires, Argentina. In 1977 he formed Grupo Berenguer, Design, Form and Communication with Alberto Lievore, Norberto Chaves and Oriol Pibernat. Since 1979 he has been associated with Perobell, the SIDI group and the magazine *On Diseño*. His products have been shown in exhibitions in Barcelona, Valencia and Cataluna and he has been featured in many Spanish and international publications. 1.84, 85

ROBERTO PEZZETTA was born in Treviso, Italy, in 1946. He began his career as a product designer in 1969 and has been head of the Industrial Design Centre of Zanussi Elettrodomestici since 1982. His awards include the Compasso d'Oro in 1981 and the Sami du Design in Paris in 1990. His works can be seen in permanent collections in several European museums. 5.48

KUNO PREY was born in 1958 in San Candido in the Dolomites where he lives today. He has worked as research and design consultant for many international companies and has won recognition both in Italy and abroad. 5.41

ANDRÉE PUTMAN was born in Paris, and studied composition at the Paris Conservatoire. After several years as a journalist she began working as an industrial designer and was co-founder of Créateurs et Industriels in the 1970s, bringing together designers such as Issey Miyake and DE CASTELBAJAC to produce objects as well as fashion. In 1978 she founded Écart International, specializing in re-editions, and began her own career as an interior designer, working on schemes such as Morgan's Hotel in New York in 1987 and the Bordeaux Museum of Contemporary Art in 1990. 2.23, 24, 3.49

DOUGLAS RICCARDI became a senior designer for M & Co., New York, after graduating from Rhodes Island School of Design in 1984. He remained with M & Co. until 1989 when he was appointed art director of *Egg* magazine. He now lives in Treviso, Italy, and works as creative director of corporate communications for the Benetton fashion group. 5.20, 23

PAOLO RIZZATTO was born in Milan in 1941. He studied architecture at Milan Polytechnic and at the same time designed lamps for Arteluce. He graduated in 1976 and in 1978 founded Luceplan with Riccardo Sarfatti. As well as interior light design, Rizzatto is experienced in interior design, working mainly in the fields of exhibitions and private domestic commissions. He exhibits widely and has been awarded the Compasso d'Oro on two occasions in 1981 and, in 1989, for the series of *Lola* lamps which can be seen at the Museum of Modern Art, New York. 1.4

MICHAEL ROWE was born in 1948 in High Wycombe, England. He graduated from the Royal College of Art, London, in 1972 and set up his own metalworking studio the same year. He became head of the Department of Metalwork and Jewellery at the RCA in 1984. Rowe's work is in the British Crafts Council, the municipal galleries of Birmingham and Leeds, the Victoria and Albert Museum, London, the Karlsruhe Museum, Germany, and the Art Gallery of Western Australia. 3.22

LINO SABATTINI is an Italian silversmith, born in 1925. His metalwork first attracted international attention in 1956 when it was exhibited in Paris at a show organized by the architect Giò Ponti. Since then Sabattini has continued to be closely associated with a simple, sculptural approach to metal and glassware, working for companies such as Rosenthal and Zani. He exhibits at the Milan Triennale and other major venues. In 1979 he was awarded the Compasso d'Oro. His work is in the permanent collections of the Museum of Modern Art and the Cooper-Hewitt Museum, New York, as well as the British Museum, London. 3.4

MASATOSHI SAKAEGI was born in 1944 in Chiba-ken, Japan. In 1983 he founded the Masatoshi Sakaegi Design Studio which specializes in ceramic and melamine tableware. He has won many awards for his work, most recently at the Japanese Ceramic Sculpture Contest. In 1991 he became an assistant professor at the Art University of the Province of Aichi. 2.26, 3.5

JOHAN SANTER is a British product designer, born in 1949. He studied at the Central School of Art and Design, London, from 1968–71, and after a short period in teaching joined the Pentagram design consultancy in 1972. He was made an associate in 1989. He has worked on a wide range of consumer and industrial products for clients including Kenwood, Reuters and Thorn Lighting. Most recently he has been working with major Japanese companies in the development of a range of bathroom fittings for Inax and a child car safety seat for Takata. 2.11

AFRA AND TOBIA SCARPA are an Italian husband-and-wife team who have worked together for more than 25 years. Tobia, born in 1935 in Venice, spent some time working in the glass industry before their collaboration. Afra, born in Montebelluna in 1937, graduated from the Architectural Institute, Venice. In 1958 they began working in glass with Venini at Murano. They occasionally work as architects as well as designers. Examples of their work can be seen in major museums all over the world and many pieces have been chosen for international exhibitions. 2.6

ECKHARD SCHUSSLER graduated in design in 1986 after studying history of art, law and design. In 1986 he founded Studio Protos which acts as an industrial and furniture design consultancy. Also in that year he exhibited a hand-blown glass centrepiece, *Tasa*, at the Milan Furniture Fair for the Anthologie Quartett stand 'Old and new proposals for the revival of the rich table'. *Tasa*, the candleholder *Lux-or* and the drinking glasses *Amarna* form a series of tableware inspired by antique architecture. 3.32

MASAFUMI SEKINE was born in 1949 in Saitama Prefecture, Japan. He trained at the Tokyo National University of Fine Arts and Music where he continued his studies until 1973, specializing in crafts and metal carving. He has received recognition for his work within Japan, culminating in the Prize for Excellence from the Japan Crafts Design Association Exhibition in 1990. 5.8, 9

TADAO SHIMIZU trained at the Cranbrook Academy of Art, Michigan, after which he worked for the Burdock Group. From 1984–87 he taught industrial design at the University of Washington. He is at present Professor of Environmental Product Design at Chiba University in Japan. He has received many national and international awards, including the first prize at the ID Annual Design Review in 1987. 5.91

BOŘEK ŠÍPEK was born in Prague in 1949. He studied furniture design in Prague, architecture in Hamburg and philosophy at Stuttgart University. His works are included in the collections of the Museum of Modern Art, New York, the Museum of Decorative Arts, Prague, and museums in Düsseldorf and The Hague. He has a studio in Amsterdam, designing for Sawaya & Moroni, Driade, Vitra and Cleto Munari as well as for the Dutch company, Alterego. In 1990 he accepted the position of professor at the Academy of Decorative Arts in Prague. 1.14–17, 2.15, 3.14–19

FINN SKODT is a Danish painter, graphic artist and textile designer who lives and works in Aarhus. 4.5

ETTORE SOTTSASS was born in Innsbruck, Austria, in 1917. He graduated as an architect from Turin Polytechnic in 1939, and opened an office in Milan in 1946. Since 1958 he has been a design consultant for Olivetti but is also active in fields as various as ceramics, jewellery, decorations, lithographs and drawing. He has taught and exhibited widely. In 1980 he established Sottsass Associati with other architects, and in 1981 founded Memphis. He has received the Compasso d Oro on many occasions, and has lectured and exhibited all over the world. 5.46, 74

BRIGITTE STARCK trained as a lawyer. She is now one of the leading figures in the PHILIPPE STARCK design team and in 1982 was commissioned, along with her husband, by President Mitterrand to give a new look to part of the Elysée Palace. 4.2

PHILIPPE STARCK was born in Paris in 1949 and works as a product, furniture and interior designer. In Paris he was commissioned to refurbish part of the Elysée Palace, and designed the Café Costes, together with a number of fashion shops. In New York he remodelled the interior of the Royalton Hotel, and in Tokyo he has designed two restaurants. His recent projects include the Teatriz nightclub in Madrid and the Paramount Hotel in New York. His furniture design has been commissioned by companies such as Disform, Driade, Baleri and Idée. Among his industrial design projects are cutlery for Sasaki, clocks for Vittel and kitchen accessories for Alessi. 1.20–25, 5.31–34

DAVIN STOWELL graduated from Syracuse University in 1976 as a Bachelor of Industrial Design. He founded his first company, Davin Stowell Associates, in 1978 as a consultant to Corning Glass Works, designing consumer products. In 1985 he co-founded Smart Design along with TUCKER VIEMEISTER, Tom Dair and Tamara Thomsen. Stowell has been the recipient of numerous IDEA awards and three ID Designer's Choice awards. An active member of the Industrial Designers' Society of America, he also lectures for professional organizations and has served on juries for design competitions. 3.29

REIKO SUDO was born in 1953 in the Ibaragi Prefecture, Japan. He was educated at the Musashino Art College where, following graduation, he assisted the textile professor until 1977. In 1984, after working as a freelance textile designer, he helped found Nuno Corporation of which he is still director. He has exhibited widely in Japan and abroad, and has work in permanent collections in the Cooper-Hewitt Museum, New York, The Museum of Art, Rhodes Island School of Design, and the Museum of Applied Arts, Finland. 4.12–14

MARCO SUSANI was born in Milan in 1956. He graduated in architecture at Milan Polytechnic and in 1984 acquired a Master's in Industrial Design at the Domus Academy where he now teaches industrial technology. Since then he has worked as a product design consultant and is at present an associate of Sottsass Associati in charge of co-ordinating the industrial design department. He has received many awards for his achievements and frequently exhibits in Italy. 5.74

MARTIN SZEKELY, born in 1957, is a French furniture and interior designer who lives and works in Paris. He has exhibited widely in Europe, the USA, Japan and Israel, and his work can be seen in the permanent collections of the Musée des Arts Décoratifs, Paris, the Cooper-Hewitt Museum, New York and the Kunstgewerbe Museums in Berlin and Cologne. His interior designs include the Musée de Picardie, Amiens, France and the Reading Room for the 'Encyclopedia Universalis', Paris. In 1987 he was elected Designer of the Year by the Salon du Meuble, Paris. 1.106–108, 5.5, 6

REIKO TAKADA was born in 1961 and graduated from the School of Art and Design at the University of Tsukuba. He joined Toshiba Corporation in 1985. 5.90

SHIN TAKAMATSU was born in 1948 in Shimane Prefecture, Japan. In 1971 he graduated from the Architectural Faculty at Kyoto University and gained a doctorate from there in 1980. In the same year he opened his own architectural office in Kyoto and has since gained great acclaim for his designs. He has received several awards including a prize at the Venice Biennale in 1985. Takamatsu has lectured at the Fukui Institute of Technology, the Osaka College of Art and the Kyoto Institute of Technology. He is currently assistant professor at Seika University and lecturer at Kyoto University. 1.5

MASAHITO TAKASUNA was born in 1958 in Chiba Prefecture, Japan, and graduated from Tokyo University of Art and Design in 1982. He is currently working for the Design Centre of Toshiba Corporation. 5.39

MARIO TALLI NENCIONI, an Italian textile designer, studied at the Textile School of Bergamo, Italy, and at the Bocconi University, Milan. He has been art director of his own manufacturing company, Telene, for 20 years. 4.4

KAZUNA TANAKA attended the Ochanomizo Design School in Tokyo, before studying in America. In 1973 he received a Bachelor of Industrial Design degree from the Pratt Institute, Brooklyn, while at the same time being employed as a mechanical and industrial designer for Wahl Associates and Lanbsing Plumb. From 1976–1980 he worked as a freelance designer, then with JEFFREY KAPEC set up Tanaka and Kapec Design Group where today he is president. 5.49

GERARD TAYLOR was born in Glasgow, Scotland, in 1955. He studied design at Glasgow School of Art and then the Royal College of Art, London, from which he graduated in 1981. After working for BBC Television in London he moved to Milan, joining Sottsass Associati in 1982. As well as working on furniture and retail design projects, he has also exhibited with the Memphis design group in Europe and the USA. In 1985 he established a design partnership in London with DANIEL WEIL. 1.8

AJIN TOGASHI was born in 1960 in Tokyo, Japan, and graduated from the Crafts Division of Tokyo National University of Fine Arts and Music in 1983. After completing a Master's course in wrought metal he joined Sasaki Glass where he has been responsible for developing the design of the *Clearball* speaker systems. 5.89

OSCAR TUSQUETS BLANCA was born in Barcelona in 1941. He attended the Escuela Tecnica Superior de Arquitectura, Barcelona, and in 1964 established Studio PER with Lluis Clotet, collaborating on nearly all their projects until 1984. He has been a guest professor and lecturer at universities in Germany, France and the USA, and his work has been exhibited worldwide. Both his architecture and his design projects have received many awards. 1.33–35, 3.12, 13

CARLO URBINATI-RICCI is an Italian designer, born in 1955. He studied architecture in Rome and today lives and works in Venice. 2.25

DAVID VAN DEN BRANDEN is a graduate of the Institute of Design at Illinois Institute of Technology and at present manages the Chicago office of Fahnstrom/McCoy. 5.88

ALESSANDRO VECCHIATO is an Italian designer, born in 1959. He studied architecture in Venice where he now lives and works. 2.25

TUCKER VIEMEISTER graduated from the Pratt Institute, Brooklyn, in 1974. Six years after he began working for Davin Stowell Associates, he co-founded Smart Design with DAVIN STOWELL, Tom Dair and Tamara Thomsen. He has lectured around the world and his work has been selected for many design awards. His products are displayed at the Design Museum, London, the Cooper-Hewitt Museum, New York, and other museums. 3.29

KEVIN WALZ studied fine art at the Pratt Institute, Brooklyn and the New York Studio School, the influences of which are very much in evidence in his interior designs. He has worked for himself since 1976 and in 1982 established Walz Design Inc. He has received many awards and most recently was noted by the ID 1990 Annual Review for offices designed for the New York Midtown Electric Supply Co. 1.120

ANDREAS WEBER was born in Lörrach, Baden, Germany where he studied architecture and urban development. He practised as an architect until 1981 when he presented his first design objects. Since then he has been marketing his own collection, 'Andreas Weber Wohndesign and Artwork', while at the same time working on architectural and interior design projects. He has received awards for his work and participated in international exhibitions. 3.10

DANIEL WEIL was born in 1953 in Buenos Aires where he studied architecture at the university. In 1977 he began studies at the Royal College of Art, London, and later started his own manufacturing company, Parenthesis, to produce electronic products. From 1983–85 he was a unit master at the Architectural Association in London. He then set up a design partnership with GERARD TAYLOR to work on a variety of projects for companies such as Driade, French Connection, Alessi and Anthologie Quartett. 1.8

HERBERT WEINAND was born in Wittlich, Eifel, Germany in 1953. After an apprenticeship as a cabinet-maker, he studied interior, product and furniture design in Germany and Italy. He has worked in film design and in 1983 was involved with the interior design for the Villa Malaparte, Fondazione Ronchi, Capri for which he also created *objets d'art*. Since 1984 he has designed many interiors and has opened his own gallery. His work has been exhibited in Germany, Austria and Italy, and has featured at the German avant-garde shows. 2.43

FRANZ WEST was born in 1947 in Vienna where he attended the Academy of Fine Art, exhibiting in his first solo show in 1970. He works primarily as a sculptor, experimenting with ideas of mass and space as well as colour. 2.14

LYNNE WILSON was born in 1952 and studied at Kingston Polytechnic and the Royal College of Art. In 1979 she moved to Italy and worked for Cassina and for Mario Bellini. She then became a freelance designer and in 1983 presented the *Lotto* armchair at the Salone del Mobile for Mobilia Italia. In 1985 she exhibited her first textile collection for Assia and has since been involved mainly in this area of design. From November 1986 she has been working part-time for the Royal College of Art. She participated in the Milan Triennale in 1987. 4.20

TERENCE WOODGATE was born in London in 1953 and studied industrial design at Westminster and Middlesex Polytechnics. He continued his training by taking a higher diploma in furniture design at the London College of Furniture. Althouth qualified as an industrial designer, he has specialized more recently in lighting and furniture design. In March 1991 he set up a studio in Brussels where he now lives and works. 2.44

YAMADA DESIGN SUDIO is the in-house design group of Yamada Lighting, Japan. 2.40

KIYOSHI YAMAMOTO was born in 1949 in Beppu-City, Japan. He graduated in textile design from the Tokyo Zokei University in 1973, after which he was employed by HIROSHI AWATSUJI. Since 1976 he has worked freelance in textile design, using natural patterns and developing an interest in printed techniques. 4.25

YAMO graduated from the National Arts School of Algiers in 1982 and the École National des Arts Décoratifs (ENSAD), Paris in 1988, where he studied interior and industrial design respectively. Since 1988 he has been in charge of the prototype workshop of the furniture section of ENSAD and has received numerous French design awards. Since 1990 he has expanded his interests to cover exhibition design and is responsible for the conception and realization of the 'Tribute to Orpheus' space at the Decorative Arts Exhibition, Paris. 3.27

HELEN YARDLEY, a British textile designer, studied at Plymouth and Manchester Polytechnics and received a Master of Arts in textile design from the Royal College of Art, London, in 1978. Her work has been exhibited throughout the UK and in Germany and Czechoslovakia, and her first solo exhibition was held in 1989 at the New York Furniture Fair. 4.7, 8

MARCO ZANUSO was born in 1954 in Milan and studied architecture at the University of Florence. He became assistant to the Professor of Industrial Design at Milan Polytechnic in 1980, and in the same year set up his own practice which specializes in architectural, industrial and exhibition design. In 1981 he was one of the founder-members of the lighting trademark Oceano Oltreluce. 1.111, 3.9, 5.63, 65

ALESSANDRO ZULIANI was born in 1958 in Udine. He studied architecture in Venice and design at Milan Polytechnic. Under various collaborations he has produced many limited edition designs for the home, notably lighting with Giuseppe Rocco. He has had honourable mention at several national and international design exhibitions. 3.34, 35

HELLE ABILD
Ole Suhrs Gade 21, 1 TV 1354 K, Copenhagen, Denmark.

ALEPH
See *Driade*.

ALESSI SPA
Via Privata Alessi 6, 28023 Crusinallo, Novara, Italy. *Outlets* Denmark: Gense AS, 17 Maglebjergvej, 2800 Lyngby. Finland: Casabella OY, 24 Yliopistonakatu, 20100 Turku. France: Société Métallurgique Lagostina, 62 rue Blaise Pascal, 93600 Aulnay-sous-Bois. Germany: Van Der Borg GmbH, 6 Sandbahn, 4240 Emmerich. Japan: Italia Shoji Co. Ltd, 5-4 Kojimachi, 1-chome, Chiyoda-ku, Tokyo 102. The Netherlands: Interhal BV, 8 Zoutverkoperstraat, 3330 CA Zwijndrecht. Sweden: Espresso Import, 10E Furasen, 42177V, Frolunda. Switzerland: Guido Mayer SA, 9 rue du Port Franc, 1003 Lausanne. UK: Penhallow Marketing Ltd, 3 Vicarage Road, Sheffield S9 3RH. USA: The Markuse Corporation, 10 Wheeling Avenue, Woburn, MA 01801.

ALGORYTHME
79 rue Melingue, 75079 Paris, France. *Outlets* Austria: Officina, 18–20 Pangl Gasse, Vienna 1040. Germany: Best Form, 40 Weibelsheidestrasse, Arnsberg-1 5760. Japan: Eternal Inc., 3F Nakajima Building, 3-17-15 Nishiazabu, Minato-ku, Tokyo. The Netherlands: Wilhelm Broekelmann 23–35, Groot Nieuwland Et Alkmaar 1811. Spain: Bd Ediciones de diseño, 291 Mallorca, 08037 Barcelona. Sweden: Asplund, 26 Nybrogatan, Stockholm 11439.

ALIAS SRL
Via Respighi 2, 20122 Milan, Italy. *Outlets* France: Roger Von Bary, 18 rue Lafitte, 75009 Paris. Germany: Peter Pfeifer, Focus, 87 Leopoldstrasse, 40 Munich 8. Japan: Casatec Ltd, 2-9-6 Higashi, Shibuya-ku, Tokyo 150. The Netherlands: Kreymborg, 63 Minervaalan, 1077 Amsterdam. Sweden: Design Distribution, 38a/1 Dobelnstan, 11352 Stockholm. Switzerland: Renato Stauffacher, 2 Capelli, 6900 Lugano. UK: Artemide GB Ltd, 17–19 Neal Street, London WC2H 9PU. USA: International Contract Furniture, 305 East 63rd Street, New York, NY 10021.

ALTEREGO
3 Jennerstraat, Amsterdam 1016 UJ, The Netherlands. *Outlets* France: Néotù, 25 rue du Renard, F-75004 Paris. Hong Kong: Le Cadre Gallery, 10th floor, Bay Tower, 2–4 Sunning Road, Causeway Bay. Italy: Driade SpA, Via Padana Inferiore 12, 29012 Fossadello di Caorso, Piacenza. Japan: Chambres d'Amis, 3-18-20 Minami-Aoyama, Minato-Ku Tokyo 107. UK: The Ikon Corporation, B5L Metropolitan Wharf, Wapping Wall, London E1 9SS.

AMEDEI TRE SNC
Via Amedei 3, Milan, Italy.

ANDREU WORLD SA
Cno. de los Mojones, Km 2,5, 46970 Alaquas, Valencia, Spain. *Outlet* UK: Kesterport Limited, Kestrel House, 111 Heath Road, Twickenham, Middx TW1 4AH.

ANTHOLOGIE QUARTETT
Schloss Huennefeld, Haus Sorgenfrei, 4515 Bad Essen, Germany. *Outlets* Belgium: Surplus, 9 Zwarte Zusterstraat, 9000 Ghent. France: Altras, 24 rue Lafitte, 75009 Paris, Hong Kong: Le Cadre Gallery, 8 Sunning Road G/F, Causeway Bay. Italy: Via R. Drengot 36, 81031 Aversa. Lebanon: Intermeuble Sarl, Boite Postale 316, Beirut. The Netherlands: Binnen, 82 Kaisergracht, 1015 Amsterdam. Switzerland: Andome, 75 Schaffhauserstrasse, 8302 Kloten.

APPLE COMPUTER
3565 Monroe Street, Santa Clara, California, USA.

ARC INTERNATIONAL INC.
2345 Harper Street, Jacksonville, Florida 32204, USA.

ARREDAESSE
Via sm Maddalena 37, 22060 Arosio, Italy.

ART ET INDUSTRIE
106 Spring Street, New York, NY 10012, USA.

ARTELANO
150 boulevard du Montparnasse, 75014 Paris, France.

ARTELUCE FLOS
Via Angelo Faini 2, Bovezzo, Brescia 25073, Italy. *Outlets* France: Flos Sarl, 23 rue de Bourgogne, 75007 Paris. Germany: Flos GmbH, Probsthof 94, 5300 Bonn 1. Japan: Flos Co. Ltd, PMC Building 1-23-3 Higashiazabu, Minato-ku, Tokyo 106. The Netherlands: Flos SA, Gossetlaan 50, 1720 Groot-Bijgaarden, Belgium. Scandinavia: Flos SpA, Ludersvej 4 Frihavnen, 2100 Copenhagen, Denmark. Spain: Flos SA, C/Bovedillas 16, San Just Desvern, 08960 Barcelona. UK: Flos Ltd, The Studio, 120 High Street, South Milford, Yorks. LS25 5AQ. USA: Flos Inc., 200 McKay Road, Huntington Station, New York, NY 11746.

ARTIPRESENT GMBH
Rohrer Strasse 140, D-7022 Leinfelden-Echterdingen, Germany. *Outlets* Austria: Prodomo, Flachgasse 35–37, A-1152 Vienna. France: Jean-Marie Ritterbeck, 1 allée Taine, F-77340 Pontoult-Combault. Italy: Authentics Italia SRL, Via Del Borroccio 14/B, 1-40138 Bologna, Japan: Shimada Int. Ass. Inc., Canal Tower 10F, 9-3 Koamicho, J-103 Tokyo. The Netherlands: Cees Teulings BV, Postbus 116, NL-5258 ZI Berlicum; Artwork Collection ALM BV, PO Box 9, NL-4286 ZG Almkerk. Portugal: A Cunna & Neto LDA, Av. Boavista 1539, P-4100 Porto. Spain: Pilma, Valencia 1, E-08015 Barcelona; Fisura SA, Paseo Condesa de Sagasta, E-24001 Leon.

ATELIER INTERNATIONAL LTD
International Design Center, 30-20 Thomson Avenue, Long Island City, NY 11101, USA.

AT&T
5 Wood Hollow Road, Parsippany, NJ 07054, USA.

A/Z STUDIOS
3–5 Hardwidge Street, London SE1 3SY, UK.

BALDINGER ARCHITECTURAL LIGHTING INC.
19-02 Steinway Street, Astoria, New York 11105, USA. *Outlet* Canada: Primavera, 160 Pears Avenue, Suites 111 & 215, Toronto, Ontario, Canada M5R 1T2.

BALERI ITALIA
Via San Bernardino 39, Lallio 24040, Bergamo, Italy. *Outlets* Belgium: Kreymborg, 66 avenue Molière, Brussels 1180. Denmark: Lysign, Horseager 1, Greve 2670. France: Francis Helven, 21 Côte des Chapeliers, Valence 26000. Germany: (North) Walter Schiedermeier, Marienbergerweg 12, Cologne 71; (South) Giovanni Marelli, PO Box 148, Via Oberdan 5, 20036 Meda, Italy. Japan: Casatec Ltd, 9-6 Higashi, 2-chome Shibuya-ku, Tokyo 150. Scandinavia: Design Distribution, 38/A1 Dobelnsgatan, Stockholm 11352, Sweden. Spain: Josep Cunill Bonmati, San Juan Bautista de la Salle S/N Esc. A. III II, Premia de Mar 8330. UK: Viaduct Furniture Ltd, Spring House, 10 Spring Place, London NW5 3BH. USA: I.C.F. Inc., 305 East 63rd Street, New York, NY 10021.

BANG & OLUFSEN AS
15 Peter Bangsvej, Struer 7600, Denmark. *Outlets* Australia: Bang & Olufsen (Australia) Pty Ltd, 136 Camberwell Road, East Hawthorn, Victoria 3123. Austria: Bang & Olufsen GmbH, Hietzinger Kai 137a, 1130 Vienna. Belgium: SA Bang & Olufsen Belgium NV, Avenue Reine Astrid 53, 1780 Wemmel. Canada: Lenbrook Industries Ltd, 633 Granite Court, Pickering, Ontario L1W 3KI. Finland: OY Bang & Olufsen AB, Kuortaneenkatu 1, 00520 Helsinki. France: Bang & Olufsen France SA, 4 rue de Port, 92110 Clichy. Germany: Bang & Olufsen (Deutschland) GmbH, Rudolf-Diesel-Strasse 8, 8031 Gilching bei München. Greece: J. UI KyriaCo.poulos & Co., 19 Amerikis Street, 10671 Athens. Holland: Bang & Olufsen Nederland BV, PO Box 111, 1200 AC Hilverseum. Hong Kong: Bang & Olufsen (Hong Kong) Ltd, 10/F Block C, Sea View Estate, 2–8 Watson Road, North Point. Italy: DODI SpA, Via San Francesco d'Assisi 31, 20090 Opera, Milan. Japan: Bang & Olufsen of Japan Ltd, Kudan New Central Building, 1F, 4–5 Kudan-kita 1-chome, Chiyoda-ku, Tokyo 102. Korea: Daiyoung Industrial Co. Ltd, 1027-5, Bangbae Dong, Seocho-ku, Seoul (137-060). Mexico: Bang & Olufsen de Mexico, Ave. Periferico Sur 3343, 10200 Mexico, D.F. Norway: Bang & Olufsen AS, Ingvald Ludvigsens Gate 14, Box 7034, 2027 Drammen. Portugal: Antonio Churro Lda, Rua D Joao V, 6A, Porta 4 (Ao Rato), 1200 Lisbon. Saudi Arabia: Arabian Sounds and Lights, Osama Siraj Zahran Ests, PO Box 12-374, Jeddah 21473. Singapore: Bang & Olufsen (Singapore) Pte Ltd, 601 Sims Drive, 01-07 Pan. 1 Complex, Singapore 1438. Spain: Bang & Olufsen España SA, Ctra. Fuencarral – Alcobendas km 14,5, 28100 Alocobendas.

Sweden: Bang & Olufsen Svenska AB, Albygatan 1324, 17125 Solna. Switzerland: Bang & Olufsen AG, Grindelstrasse 15, 8303 Bassersdorf. UK: Bang & Olufsen UK Ltd, Eastbrook Road, Gloucester GL4 7DE. USA: Bang & Olufsen of America Inc., 1150 Feehanville Drive, Mt Prospect, Illinois 60056.

BD EDICIONES DE DISEÑO
291 Mallorca, 08037 Barcelona, Spain. *Outlets* Belgium: Quattro, Centre Le Bosquet, Jodoigne-Geldenaken 5900. Canada: Triedei, 460 McGill, Montreal, Quebec H2Y 2H2. France: Nestor Perkal, 8 rue des Quatre Fils, 75003 Paris. Germany: IMD Inter-Marketing Distribution AG, Flothbruchstrasse 11, 4156 Willich 2, Anrath. Hong Kong: Le Cadre Gallery, 8 Sunning Road G/F, Causeway Bay. Italy: Bd Italia, Piazza San Marco 1, 20100 Milan. Japan: Gendai Kikakushitsu, Koshin Building, 302 2-2-5 Sarugaku-cho, Chiyoda-ku, Tokyo. Switzerland: IMD Inter-Marketing Distribution AG, Eerburnestrasse 26, Hausen (AG) 5212. UK: The Ikon Corporation, B5L Metropolitan Wharf, Wapping Wall, London E1 9SS. USA: Manifesto, 200 West Superior Street, Chicago, Illinois; Lymnn, 457 Pacific Avenue, San Francisco 94133.

G. B. BERNINI SpA
Via Fiume 17, 20048 Carate Brianza, Milan, Italy. *Outlets* France: Sarl New Model, BP 48, La Fare Les Oliviers 13580. Japan: The Seibu Department Stores Ltd, 3-1-1 Higashi-Ikebukuro, Toshima-ku, Tokyo 170. Scandinavia: Lysign, 1 Horseager, Greve 2670, Denmark. Spain: Idea International, 12/18 Bajos C. Vico, Barcelona 08021. UK: Interior Marketing, 6 Newtown Road, Bishop's Stortford, Herts. CM23 3SD.

BIEFFEPLAST
PO Box 489, 1 35100 Padua, Italy.

BIESSE SpA
No. 2 Via de Gasperi, Collebeato, Brescia 25060, Italy. *Outlets* France: Fliba, 7 rue Taine, 75012 Paris, France. The Netherlands: Algemene Agenturen MiJ BV, Distelweg 88 10131 HH, Amsterdam. Portugal: Rivitex Ltda, Extrada Exterior Da Circunvalacao 12252, Aspartado 128, Senhora da Hora 4457 Matasinhos Codes-Portogallo. Spain: Pinti España, Av. Da De Barcelona 22/A, Sant Joan Despi. UK: Alpac UK Ltd, 130 Walham Green Court, Moore Park Road, Fulham, London SW6 2DG.

BLAUET
Santa Eulalia 36–40, Escal B Piso 1, Desp 1 08902, Barcelona, Spain. *Outlets* Australia: Tangents Imports Pty Ltd, 6–36 Boronia Street, Refdern, NSW 2016. Canada: Tendex Silko Inc., 264 The Esplanade, Toronto, Ontario M5A 4J6. Denmark: Vantage, Jyllingtevej 12–14, 2720 Vanlose; Pasta Lab International, Duevej 54, 2000 Copenhagen. France: S.I.C.A., 225 avenue d'Argenteuil, 92270 Bois Colombes. Germany: King Kong, Am Wischdeich 25, 2209 Borsfleth. Holland: Indoor, Paulus Potterstraat 22–24, 1071 DA Amsterdam. Hong Kong: Executive Design, 14–16 Blue Pool Road G/F, Happy Valley; Leo's Collection Ltd, 37 Java Road, 1/F North Point. Japan: Akane Ing, 10–

15 Higashinakano 5-chome, Nakano-ku, Tokyo. UK: Lighthouse Interiors, 71 Richmond Avenue, London N1 OLX. USA: Hinkley Lighting, 12600 Berea Road, 44111 Cleveland, Ohio.

BODUM (SCHWEIZ) AG
Kantonsstrasse, Triengen 6234, Lucerne, Switzerland. *Outlets* France: Bodum (France) SA, Z.A. de Courtaboef, 18 avenue de Québec/Bât N3-B.P. 703, F-91961 Les Ulis, Cedex. Germany: Peter Bodum GmbH, Boschstrasse 6, D-2358 Kaltenkirchen. The Netherlands: Bodum (Nederland) BV, Satijnbloem 63, NL 3068 JP Rotterdam. Scandinavia: Peter Bodum AS, Nøglegårdsvej 18, 3540 Lynge, Denmark. UK: Bodum (UK) Ltd, Unit 1 Witan Park/Station Lane, Witney, Oxon. OX8 6FH. USA: Bodum Inc., 2920 Wolff Street, Racine, WI 53404.

FLORIAN BORKENHAGEN
39 Piazza Roma, Como 22100, Italy.

BOSSE TELEKOMSYSTEME GMBH
Reichenberger Strasse 80, 1000 Berlin 36, Germany.

MARYSE BOXER DESIGNS
Studio 15, Talina Centre, 23A Bagleys Lane, London SW6 2BW, UK. *Outlets* Germany: Kirschke, Tarpen 40, 2000 Hamburg 62. Japan: Barneys Japan Co. Ltd, 2-20-16 Kabukicho, Shinjuku-ku, Shinjuku, Tokyo 160. The Netherlands: Nicole Bossuroy, Style 2001, Rollebeekstraat, 24 rue de Rollebeek, Brussels 1000, Belgium. New Zealand: Maggie Bryson, 128 St Georges Bay Road, Parnell, Auckland. Spain: Domestica Sede, Hagsaba SA C/Maldonado 14, 28006 Madrid. USA: La Casa Di, 225 Fifth Avenue, Room 808, New York, NY 10010; Mottura California, LA Merchandise Mart, Los Angeles, California.

BRAVO-U SA
Poligono Eitua S/n, Berriz 48240, Vizcaya, Spain.

CADET MANUFACTURING CO.
PO Box 1675, Vancouver, Washington 98668, USA.

CANDLE
Via Salaino 7, Milan, Italy. *Outlet* UK: Lumino Ltd, Lumino House, Lovet Road, The Pinnacles, Harlow, Essex CM19 5TB.

CANON INC.
PO Box 5050, Shinjuku Dai-ichi Seimei Building, Tokyo 163, Japan. *Outlets* Austria: Canon, Modecenterstrasse 22 A-2, 1030 Vienna. Belgium: Canon Copiers Belgium NVISA, Luidlaam 33-Bus 6, 100 Brussels. Canada: Canon Canada Inc., 3245 American Drive, Mississauga, Ontario L4V 1N4. Denmark: Christian Bruhn AS, Vasekaer 12, 2729 Herlev. France: Canon France SA, PO Box 40, 93151 Le Blanc Mesnil. Germany: Canon Copylux GmbH, Leurriper Strasse 1–13, 4050 Mönchengladbach. Italy: Canon Italia SpA, Centro Direzionale, Palazzo Verocchio, 20090 Milan 2-Segrate MI. The Netherlands: Canon Verkooporganisatie Nederland BV, Cruquiusweg 29, 2102 LS Heemstede,

Amsterdam. Norway: Noiseless AS, Tventenveien 30B, Oslo 6. Spain: Canon Copiardoras de España SA, Avd. Menendez Pelayo, 57 Torre del Retiro, Madrid. Sweden: Canon Svenska AB, Box 2084, Stensatrava gen 13, 12702 Stockholm. Switzerland: Canon SA, 1 rue de Hesse, 1204 Geneva. UK: Canon (UK) Ltd, Canon House, Manor Road, Wallington, Surrey SM6 0AJ. USA: Canon USA Inc., One Canon Plaza, Lake Success, New York, NY 11042-9979.

CAPPELLINI ARTE
Via Marconi 35, 22060 Arosio, Italy. *Outlets* Austria: Wolfgang Bischof OHG, Judenplatz 6, 1010 Vienna. Belgium: Rika Andries, Turnhoutsebaab 144B, 2200 Borgerhout. France: Cerutti Giuseppe, Loc. Grand Chemin 1, 11020 Saint Christophe. Germany: Novus (Sig. Pfeiffer), Gartenstrasse 26, 7959 Achstetten Bronnen 3. The Netherlands: Hansje Kalff Meubelagenturen, Puttensestraat 8, 1181 Je Amstelveen. Sweden: Mobile Box AB, Nybrogatan 11, 11439 Stockholm. Switzerland: Yves Humbrecht Diffusion, Mon Repos 3, 1066 Epalinges. UK: SCP Ltd, 135–139 Curtain Road, London EC2. USA and Canada: Ivan Luini, 453 West 19th Street, App. 6A, New York, NY 10011.

CARLOS JANÉ CAMACHO SA
S/No Pol. Industrial 'Els Xops', Granollers 08400, Barcelona, Spain.

CASA COMUNITÀ, CIDUE SpA
Via San Lorenzo 32, 36010 Carre, Vicenza, Italy. *Outlets* France: Jacques Dollard, 32 bis rue des Jardiniers, Nancy 5400. Germany: Cidue Deutschland GmbH, Fliegenstrasse 8, 8000 Munich 2. Japan: Italcomm Ltd, Iikura Cmfy Building B101, 4-4 Azadubai 3-chome, Minato-ku, Tokyo. The Netherlands: Espaces et Lignes NU, Nassaulaan 2A, JS The Hague 2514. Scandinavia: Inside AB, PO Box 3310, Stockholm 10366, Sweden. Spain: Xarma SL, Euskadi Etorbidea 53-5⁰ dcha, Pasaia 20110. UK: Roger Mallins, 2 Davenport Close, Teddington, Middx TW11 9EF. USA: Cidue Off: M.I.E. Inc., 18910 Wentworth Drive, Miami, Florida 33015.

CASAS MOBILPLAST
Poligono Santa Rita, Castellbisbal 08755, Barcelona, Spain.

CASSINA SpA
Via Luigi Busnelli 1, Meda 20036, Milan, Italy. *Outlets* France: Sanda, 168 rue du Faubourg Saint Honoré, Paris 75008. Germany: Pesch, Kaiser Wilhelm Ring 22, Cologne. Japan: Cassina Japan Inc., 2-9-6 Higashi, Shibuya-ku, Tokyo 150. The Netherlands: Mobica, 31 Middenweg, 3401 Ijsselstein. Spain: Mobilplast, 40 calle Milagro, 08028 Barcelona. UK: Marcatré, 179 Shaftesbury Avenue, London WC2H 8AR. USA: Atelier International Inc., The International Design Center, 30-20 Thomson Avenue, Long Island City, NY 11101.

CATALANA DE GAS SA
Av. Portal del Angel 22, 08022 Barcelona, Spain.

CLASSICON
8 Perchtinger Strasse, D-8000 Munich 70, Germany. *Outlets* France: Claude Cenet, Hery sur Alby, Alby Sur Cheran F-74540. Japan: Yamada Shomei Lighting Co. Ltd, 3-16-12 Sotokanda, Chiyoda-ku, Tokyo 101. The Netherlands: Design for Living, Jasonstraat 52, Amsterdam KH NL-1007. Scandinavia: Finn Sloth, Heilsmindevej 1, Charlottenlund DK-2920, Denmark. UK: Aram Designs Ltd, 3 Kean Street, Covent Garden, London WC2B 4AT.

COMS CO. LTD
COMS No. 601, 2–3 Uguisudani-cho, Shibuya-ku, Tokyo 155, Japan.

CONCORD LIGHTING LTD
174 High Holborn, London WC1V 7AA, UK. *Outlets* Australia: Concord Lighting Pty Ltd, PO Box 18, Oakleigh South 3167. France: Jumo Concord, Tour Horizon, 52 Quai de Dion Bouton, 928000 Puteaux. Germany: Concord GTE Licht, Lichtarchitektur, Zeiss Strasse 2, 5000 Cologne 40. Italy: Tecnolyte SpA, Via Nazionale 193, 00184 Rome. The Netherlands: GTE Licht, PO Box 2039, 4800 CA Breda. Scandinavia: Hovik Lys, Postboks 100, N-1751 Halden, Norway. Spain: Dula Co.nCo.rd SA, calle Poniente 27, Madrid 28036.

COR WOHN- UND BÜROMÖBEL, HELMÜT LÜBKE GMBH & CO.
17 4840 Rheda-Wiedenbruck, Germany. *Outlets* Australia: Deutsches Möbel Studio, 38 River Crescent, AUS Cypress Gardens 4218. Austria: Höchsmann & Schiebel, Schüttelstrasse 75, A-1020 Vienna. Belgium: Lijn pvda, Frik Vandeput, O. L. Vrouwstraat 123, B-2800 Mochelen. France: Michel Bollinger, Kéréon-Vihon, F 20170 Fouesnant. The Netherlands: Hans Bom, Hoofdstraat 170, Postbus 1010, NL 2070 BA Santpoort-Noord. Scandinavia: UNICUM, Thorburnsgatan 5, S-40125 Göteborg. Switzerland: Handelsagentur René Wollschleger, Am Tych 7, CH-4665 Oftringen.

NICK CROWE
90–92 Highgate Road, Kentish Town, London NW5 1PB, UK. *Outlet* The Netherlands: Intermezzo, Voorstraat 178, 3311 ES Dordrecht.

DAKOTA JACKSON
306 East 61st Street, New York, NY 10021, USA.

JAN-KEES DE JAGER
30 Beatrixlaan, Vught 5261 VE, The Netherlands.

DESIGN STUDIO TAD
3-8-16-608 Nishiogi-Minami, Suginami-ku, Tokyo 167, Japan.

DRAENERT STUDIO GMBH
Steigwiesen 3, 7997 Immenstaad, Bodensee, Germany.

DRIADE SPA
Via Padane Inferiore 12, Fossadello di Caorso 29012, Piacenza, Italy. *Outlets* Belgium: Espace et Lignes, 55 rue Ulens, Brussels 1080. France:

Arturo del Punta, 7 rue Simon Lefranc, 75004 Paris. Germany: Stefan Müller, 18 Maximilianplatz, Munich 8000. Japan: Ambiente, Sumimoto Seimei Building 3-1-30, Minami-aoyama, Minato-ku, Tokyo. Spain: Sellex, 53A PCD de Mandas Torre Atocha 1, San Sebastian. Sweden: Design Distribution, Doebelnsg 38A1, Stockholm 11352. Switzerland: Peter Frischknecht, 31A Feldlistrasse, St Gallen 9000. UK: The Ikon Corporation, B5L Metropolitan Wharf, Wapping Wall, London E1 9SS. USA: Tonia Pozzoli, Primalinea, 30 Gustafson CT 94974, Novato CA.

ÉCART INTERNATIONAL SA
111 rue St Antoine, 75004 Paris, France. *Outlet* Japan: H A Deux Inc., Hiroo Garden Hills A-703, 4-1-6 Hiroo, Shibuya-ku, Tokyo 150.

EDEN GROUP
The Chapel, Rainow, Cheshire SK10 5XF, UK. *Outlet* UK: TriGem Computer (UK) Ltd, 69 Buckingham Avenue, Slough Trading Estate, Slough, Berks. SL1 4PN.

EDITION B-S
34 Waldstrasse, Kosslarn D-8399, Germany. *Outlet* Germany/Switzerland/Austria: Design Trade Management, 35 Von Richthofenstrasse, Regensburg 8400, Germany.

EDIZIONI DE PADOVA
Corso Venezia 14, Milan 20121, Italy. *Outlets* Denmark: Paustian, 2 Kalkbraenderjiloebskay, Copenhagen 2100. France: Galeries Agora, 16 rue de la Grange Batelière, Paris 75009. Germany: Habit, 44 Surderstrasse, 509 Leverkusen 22. Japan: Casatec Ltd, 9-6 Higashi Hsiboya-ku, Tokyo 150. The Netherlands: Koos Rijkse, Pr. Christinelaan, 7437 X2, Bathmen. Spain: Idea Mueble, 185 Via Augusta, Barcelona 08021. Switzerland: Formatera, 54 Stockerstrasse, 8002 Zurich. USA: ICF, 33 Kings Highway, Orangenburg, New York, NY 10962.

THOMAS EISL
3 Nimrod Passage, London N1 4BU, UK.

ERCO LEUCHTEN GMBH
Postfach 2460, D 5880, Lüdenscheid, Germany. *Outlet* UK: Erco Lighting Ltd, 38 Dover Street, London W1X 3RB.

ERCUIS
32 rue de Paradis, 75010 Paris, France. *Outlets* France: PETER, 191 Faubourg Saint Honoré, 75008 Paris; Georges Pelse, 18 rue de l'Arcade, 75008 Paris.

EUROLOUNGE
12 Dolland Street, London SE11 5LN, UK.

EWE-KÜCHEN GMBH
14 Dieselstrasse, Wels A-4601, Austria. *Outlets* Germany: Günter Machmerth, 3 Fliederweg, Neu Ulm, D-7910. Italy: Claudio Chiodo, 37b Via Trieste, Mestrino 35035. Japan: Sekisui House Ltd, 2-27 6-chome Nakanoshima, Kita-ku Osaka 530. Switzerland: Werner Spanring, 301 Zürcherstrasse, Frauenfeld CH 8500. USA: Coop Himmelblau, 2497 Armacost Avenue, West Los Angeles, CA 90064.

FAHNSTROM/McCOY
500 Lone Pine Road, Bloomfield Hills, Michigan 48303, USA.

MICHEL FEITH
Schulterblatt 58C, D-2000 Hamburg 36, Germany.

231

FERMOB
Zone Industrielle Saint-Didier, Thoissey 01140, France. *Outlets* Belgium; Tradix, avenue Louis Lepoutre 104, 1060 Brussels. Germany: D-Tec, Telleringstrasse 5, 4000 Düsseldorf 13. Japan: Ambiante International Inc., Sumitomo Seimei Building 3-1-30, Minami-aoyama, Minato-ku, Tokyo. The Netherlands: Van Ommen, Postbus 189, 8070 AD Nunspeet. Scandinavia: In-Art, Sveavagen 109, S 11350 Stockholm. UK: Viaduct Furniture Ltd, Spring House, 10 Spring Place, London NW5 3BH. USA: N.D.I., PO Box 812, Farmington, GA 30638.

TRISTRAM FETHERSTONHAUGH
35 Merthyr Terrace, London SW13 9DL, UK.

FIAM ITALIA SPA
Via Ancona 1/13, 61010 Tavullia, PS, Italy. *Outlet* UK: Casa Bianchi, Rosyln House, Sun Street, Hitchin, Herts. SG5 1AE.

FLEX SPA
Via Einaudi 23–25, Meda 20036, Milan, Italy. *Outlets* Germany: Designer's House, 17 Schonfeldstrasse, 22 Munich 8000. Japan: Joint Inc., Daikanjama, Parkside Village 207, 9-8 Sarugakucho, Shibuya-ku, Tokyo 150. The Netherlands: Smedicus Inter, 166 Willemsparkweg, Amsterdam 1071 HT. Scandinavia: AB Nordiska Galleriet, 11 Nybrogatan, Stockholm S 11439. Spain: Mosel Interiors, 53 Gran Via, Bilbao. USA: Frederic Williams, 200 Lexington Avenue, New York, NY 10015.

FLUOCARIL-GOUPIL
69-75 rue de Monthlery, Rungis 94152, France.

FORM FARM INC.
270 Lafayette Street, No. 1301, New York, NY 10012, USA.

FOSCARINI MURANO SPA
1 Fondamenta Manin, Murano, Venice 30141, Italy. *Outlets* France: Horas International, 150 rue Championnet, Paris. Germany: Alta Linea GmbH, 6 Sandhof, 4040 Neuss 21 Norff. The Netherlands: Horas International, Beemdstraat 25, Ruisbroek 1610. UK: Liaison, 917–919 Fulham Road, London SW6 5HU.

FOURNITURE ÉDITIONS
51 rue de Presles, 93531 Aubervillier Cedex, France.

FUJI EIGHT CO. LTD
Fuji-TV Building 1, 2–23 Nakano-cho, Ichigaya, Shinjuku-ku, Tokyo 162, Japan. *Outlets* Japan: Kiyoshi Yamamoto Design Studio Inc., 2-3-15-101 Jingumae, Shibuya-ku, Tokyo 150.

FUJIE TEXTILE CO. LTD
4-7-12 Sendagaya, Shibuya-ku, Tokyo 151, Japan.

OLIVIER GAGNÈRE
Galerie Maeght, 42 rue du Bac, Paris 75007, France.

GALERIE WEINAND
Wielandstrasse 37, D-1000 Berlin 12, Germany.

JORGE GARCIA GARAY SA
13 San Antonio, Sta Coloma de Gramanet 08923, Barcelona, Spain. *Outlets* Austria: Plan Licht, 187a Vomperbach, Schwaz A-6130. Germany: Mega Light, 4 Tilsiter Strasse, Frankfurt 6000. The Netherlands: GA GA Specialists, 12/14 Het Eilandhuis Galgenstraat, Amsterdam 1013 LT. UK: Opus Lighting, 58 Mount Ephrain, Tunbridge Wells, Kent TN4 8BB. USA: Illuminating Experiences Inc., 233 Cleveland Avenue, Highland Park, New Jersey 08904.

YVES GASTOU
12 ru Bonaparte, 75006 Paris, France.

GLACIER WATER CO.
16-16 Whitestone Expressway, Whitestone, NY 11337, USA.

GLASS DESIGN
Via Rivolta 6, 20050 Macheno, Milan 30, Italy.

KENNETH GRANGE
11 Needham Road, London W11 2RP, UK.

TOBIAS GRAU KG GMBH & CO.
Borselstrasse 18, 2000 Hamburg 50, Germany. *Outlets* Japan: Weinberger & Co. Ltd, Shinmachi Grace Building 2F, 20-6 Sinmach 2-chome, Nishi-ku, Osaka. The Netherlands: GI Design, Burgstraat 2, 4283 GG Giessen.

GRUPO T SA
Casanova Bo. 37, Barcelona 08011, Spain.

REDE GUZZINI SRL
Via le Grazie, 31 Recannati 62019, Italy. *Outlets* Belgium: Comeximma, rue de Wautiers Straat 121, 1020 Brussels. Germany: Mercantile GmbH, Robert Koch Strasse 4, 8033 Planegg, Munich. Japan: Nakayamafuku Co. Ltd, Shimanouchi Chuo-ky, Osaka 542. The Netherlands: Termaat BV, PO Box 2271, Zilvorenberg 3, 5202 C G'Hertogenbosch, Holland. Spain: Nimbex SA Intern. Avda de Tarragona S/N, Apart 295, Vilafranca del Penedes, Barcelona. Sweden: Frieline AB, Box 1087, 26901 Bastad. USA S. P. Cassina Inc., 9936 Foxborough Circle, Rockville, MD 20850.

HARMAN GAS CORPORATION
6-2-35 Iwatacho, Higashi, Osaka 578, Japan.

RICHARD HEATLY
Hill Oak, Bishop's Frome, Worcs. WR6 5BH, UK.

BRYAN HEIGHTON
91a Westend Road, Westmere, Auckland, New Zealand.

HIGH VISBILITY
Via Rita Tonoli 5, 20145 Milan, Italy.

HISHINUMA ASSOCIATES
5-41-2 Jingumae, Shibuya-ku, Tokyo 150, Japan.

ICF/UNIKA VAEV USA
305 63rd Street, New York, NY 10021, USA.

IDÉE
5-4-44 Minami-aoyama, Minato-ku, Tokyo 107, Japan. *Outlet* France: Idée Europe, 21 rue Danielle Casanova, Paris 75001.

INCOM BV
PO Box 302, 2160 AH Lisse, The Netherlands.

INDY SpA
Via XX Settembre 180, 28025 Gravellona Toce, Novara, Italy. *Outlets* Canada: Regalart Import Limited, 6 Avenue Montreal, Quebec H2A 3E4; Gisesco NV Ltee, 169 Est Rue Beaubien, Montreal, Quebec. France: Cristel D.J.A.S.A., 25490 Feches Le Chatel. Germany: D. S. Produkte, Dieter Schwarz GmbH, Stormarnring 14, Stapefeld Amburgo 73D. UK: P.M. Imports, 11 Periwinkle Close, Sittingbourne, Kent.

INNO INTERIOR OY
Merikatu 1, 00140 Helsinki, Finland.

ISHIMARU CO. LTD
7-3-24 Roppongi, Minato-ku, Tokyo, Japan.

ITALO BOSA
Via Molini 44, 31030 Borso de Grappa, Italy.

KAI INTERNATIONAL CO. LTD
3-9-7 Iwamoto-cho, Chiyoda-ku, Tokyo 101, Japan. *Outlets* Japan: Yamada Shomei Lighting Co. Ltd, 6-7-5 Minami-aoyama, Minato-ku, Tokyo 107. USA: Gallery of Modern Art, 310 Washington Street, Plaza Level, Suite 1, Marina del Rey, California.

KÄLLEMO AB
Box 605, 33126 Varnamo, Sweden. *Outlets* France: Nobilis, 40 rue Bonaparte, F-75006, Paris. Switzerland: PUR Sitzmöbel/Martin Stegemann, Postfach 486, Gaswerkstrasse 33, CH-4900 Langenthal.

KARTELL SpA
Viale delle Industrie 1, 20082 Noviglio, Milan, Italy. *Outlets* Australia: Plastex, 85 Fairbank Road, 3168 Clayton, Victoria. Austria: Eugen Leopold, 19 Grunauerstrasse, 4020 Linz. Belgium: Tradix SA, 104 Avenue Louis Lepoutre, 1060 Brussels. Denmark: John Anker, 6 Esplanaden, 1263 Copenhagen. France: Marais International Group, 5 rue de Faubourg St Antoine, 75011 Paris. Japan: Kartell Japan Co. Ltd, Dowa Building 4F, 18-18 Roppongi, 5-chome, Minato-ku, Tokyo 106. The Netherlands: Modular Systems, Assumburg 73-1, 1081 GB Amsterdam. Spain: Grupo T SA, 37 Casanova, Barcelona 08011. Switzerland: Piermilio Gatto, 3 Ch. des Graviers, 2016 Cortaillod. UK: Ideas For Living, Lin Pac Mouldings, 5 Kensington High Street, London, W8 5NP. USA: Kartell USA, PO Box 1000, Easley SC 29640.

KEILHAUER INDUSTRIES LTD
946 Warden Avenue, Toronto, Canada M1L 4C9.

KENWOOD LTD
New Lane, Havant, Hants. PO9 2NH.

KLAESSON INTERNATIONAL
Box 18, S-716 21 Fjugesta, Sweden. *Outlets* Denmark: Scandinavian Trade Mart, Bella Center, Center Boulevard, DK-2300 Kopenhamn S. Finland: Nomart OY, Merikasarminkatu 6, SF-00160 Helsinki. Norway: Klaessons Möbler AB, Vidar Ottesen, Postboks 94, N-1930 Aurskog.

KURAMATA DESIGN OFFICE
3-24 Roppongi, 7-chome, Minato-ku, Tokyo, Japan.

KVADRAT
8400 Ebeltoft, Denmark. *Outlets* Australia: Woven Image Pty Ltd, 666 Willoughby Street, Willoughby, NSW 2068. Germany, postal codes 1–3: Søren Kragelund, Bahnhofstrasse 24, D-W-2165 Bargstedt; postal codes 4–5: Heinz Linz, Bedburger Strasse 45, D-W-4040 Neuss 21; postal codes 7–8: Detlef Jung, Jägerhausstrasse 70, D-W-7100 Heilbronn. Holland: Danskina, Postbus 22620, Hettenheuvelweg 14, NL-1101 BN Amsterdam ZO. Iceland: Epal HF, Faxafen 7, 108 Reykjavik. Italy: Rapsel SpA, Via Alessandro Volta 13, I-20019 Settimo Milanese, Milan. Japan: Euro Design Ltd, 6F Matsukl Building, 3–8 Shiba Park 1-chome, Minato-ku, Tokyo 105. Norway: Gudbrandsdalens, Uldvarefabrik AS, Postboks 38, N-2601 Lillehammer. Switzerland and Austria: Kvadrat AG, Postfach 87, CH-8370 Sirnach. UK: Kvadrat Ltd, 62 Princedale Road, London W11 4NL.

LALIQUE
11 rue Royale, 75008 Paris, France. *Outlets* Japan: Lalique Japan Co. Ltd, 7 Ginza Daini Toshiba Bld., 6-4-4 Ginza, Chou-ku, Tokyo 104. UK: Lalique Limited, 162 New Bond Street, London W1Y 9PA. USA: Jacques Jugeat Inc., 400 Veterans Bld., Karlstadt NJ 07072.

LAMMHULTS MÖBEL AB
Böx 26, S-360 30 Lammhult, Sweden. *Outlets* Belgium and Holland: Design Mart Hofstraat 269, B-9000 Ghent. Denmark: Collection Creative, Danas Plads 15, PO Box 113, DK-2000 Frederiksberg. Finland: Nomart OY, Merikasarminkatu 6, SF-00160 Helsinki. France: Lammhults France, Jacques Cabantous 10, rue Renault, F-94160 Saint Mande. Germany: SDC GmbH, Kaiser-Wilhelm-Ring 43, W-4000 Düsseldorf 11; Albrecht Kohler Laustrasse 85, Stuttgart 70; Lammhults Werksvertretung, Anzingerstrasse 1, W-8000 Munich 80. Iceland: Stalhusgögn, PO Box 9005, Is-129 Reykjavik. Italy: Rapsel SpA, Via Volta 13, I-20019 Settimo Milanese, Milan. Norway: Tor Torp Holte AS, Sagvejen 28, PO Box 2683, St Hanshaugen, N-0131 Oslo 1. Switzerland and Austria: Collection Elley, Vejlesöparken 1-617, DK-2840 Holte. UK: TUA Ltd, Unit 2, Shipton Way, Express Park, Rushden, Northants. NN10 9GL.

TILL LEESER DESIGN
Eppendorger Weg 87a, 2000 Hamburg 20,
Germany.

L.I.D.O
Via Verdi 7, Lomagna 22050, Como, Italy.

LIGNE ROSET
BP 09 Briord, Serrières de Briord 01470,
France. *Outlets* Germany: Roset Möbel GmbH,
Industriestrasse 51, Gundelfingen 7803. Italy:
Roset Italia SRL, Via Manzoni 45, Milan 20121.
Scandinavia: K. J. Partners, Osterled 17,
Copenhagen. UK: J. Joshi, 38 Tuffley Road,
Westbury, Bristol BS10 5EG. USA: Roset USA
Corp 1305, 200 Lexington Avenue, New York,
NY 10016.

LISAR
Via Boccacio 78/72, Carbonate, Como, Italy.

**CHRISTOPHER LOEW AND TIM
PARSEY**
IDTWC, 1527 Stockton Street, San Francisco
94133, California, USA.

ROSS LOVEGROVE (STUDIO X)
81 Southern Row, London W10 5AL, UK.

LUMEX INC.
100 Spence Street, Bayshore, NY 11807, USA.

LUXO ITALIANA SpA
Via delle More 1, Presezzo, Bergamo 24030,
Italy. *Outlets* France: Luxo France, 11 rue
Auguste Lacroix, Lyon F-69003. Germany:
Mazda Licht, Postfach 1405, Limburg, Lahn
6250. The Netherlands: Ansems Industrial
Design, 10A Dorpsstraat, Ledeacker 5846 AA.
Scandinavia: Luxo Lamper, 27–29 Tempovej,
Ballerup 2750. Spain: Luxo Espanola, 39–41
Sugranyes, Barcelona 08028. Sweden: Luxo
Sweden, 10A Krakaterpsgatan, Molndal S-431
33. UK: Thousand and One Lamps Ltd, 4
Barmeston Road, London SE6 3BN.

MARCATRÉ SpA
Via Sant'Andrea 3, Misinto 20020, Milan, Italy.
Outlets France: Marcatré Sarl, 32 avenue Hoche,
Paris 75008. Italy: Marcatré SpA, Via Manzoni
12, Milan 20121. Japan: CASATEC Inc., 2-9-6
Higashi, Shibuya-ku, Tokyo 150. The
Netherlands: Casala Meubelen Nederland BV,
10 Rolweg, Culemborg 4100 AD. Spain:
Marcatré España SA, 22 calle Claudio Coello,
Madrid 28001. Switzerland: Wohnshop Projecto
SA, 8 rue Neuve, Lausanne 1000. UK:
Marcatré Ltd, 179–199 Shaftesbury Avenue,
London WC2H 8AR. USA: Atelier
International Ltd, 30-20 Thomson Avenue,
Long Island City 11101, New York.

MARTINELLI LUCE SpA
Via T. Bandettini Lucca, I-55100 Lucca, Italy.
Outlets Austria: Ambiente Licht Design,
Ziehrerplatz 4–5, A-1030 Vienna. France.
Lumières International, avenue de la
Bourdonnais 67, Paris. Germany: Novus,
Gartenstrasse 26, D-7959 Achstetten 3. Japan:
Atic Alive Trading Ltd, 2-9-8 Higashi,
Shibuya-ku, J-150 Tokyo. The Netherlands:
Kreymborg BV, Minervalaan 63, NL-01077
Amsterdam. Spain: IDEA International SA,

Figueras 55, E-Prat de Llobregat, Barcelona.
UK: Atrium Ltd, 22–24 St Giles High Street,
London WC2H 8LW.

**MATSUSHITA ELECTRIC INDUSTRIAL
CO. LTD**
Kitchen Appliance Division 3-8-3 Himezato
Nishiyodogawa, Osaka City, Osaka 555, Japan;
Office Equipment Division 247 Fukutake,
Saijo, Ehime 793, Japan; **Communication
Division** 600 Saedo-cho, Midori-ku,
Yokohama 226, Japan; **Television Sector** 1–1
Matsushita-cho, Ibaraki, Osaka 567, Japan;
Audio Division 1–4 Matsuo-cho, Kadoma
City, Osaka 571, Japan. *Outlets* Australia:
Panasonic (Australia) Pty Ltd, PO Box 319,
95–99 Epping Road, North Ryde, NSW 2113.
Germany: Panasonic Deutschland GmbH,
Winsbergring 15, D-2000 Hamburg 54. Italy:
Fratelli Milani Srl, Via Valsolda 20143, Milan
13. The Netherlands: Haagtechno BV,
Rietveldenweg 60, Postbus 236, Den Bosch.
Scandinavia: Panasonic Svenska AB,
Instrumentagen 29–31, PO Box 47327, 10074
Stockholm, Sweden. UK: Panasonic Business
Systems UK, Panasonic House, Willoughby
Road, Bracknell, Berks. RG12 4FP. USA:
Panasonic Communication & Systems
Company, Communication Systems Division, 2
Panasonic Way, Secaucus, New Jersey 07094.

MATTEO GRASSI SpA
Via Sta Caterina de Siena 26, 22066 Mariano
C.se, Como, Italy.

INGO MAURER
47 Kaiserstrasse, Munich 40 8000, Germany.
Outlets France: Altras Sarl, 24 rue Lafitte, Paris
75009. Italy: Pierre Daverio & C. SAS, Via del
Colle 3, Casciago 21020. The Netherlands:
Peter A. Hesselmans, 284 P. J. Oudstraat,
Papendrecht 3354 VJ. Scandinavia (except
Sweden): Finn Sloth, 2 Heilsmindevej,
Charlottenlund, Denmark 2920. Switzerland:
Domani AG, 231 Seefeldstrasse, Zurich 8008.
USA: Ivan Luini, 453 West 19th Street, Apt.
6a, New York, NY 10011.

M & CO. LABS
50 West 17th Street, 12th Floor, New York,
NY 10011, USA.

ANNETTE MEECH
65 Long Acre, London WC2E 9JH, UK.

METALARTE SA
Avda de Barcelona 4, 08970 Saint Joan Despi,
Barcelona, Spain. *Outlets* France: Electoama, 11
boulevard Saint Germain, 75006 Paris.
Germany: Alta Linea, 6 Sandhof, 4040 Neuss 21
Norff. The Netherlands: Hooge Products, 12
Bebers Pijken, 5221 ED Hertogenbosch. UK:
Direct Light Ltd, 275 Fulham Road, London
SW10 9PZ. USA: California Artup
Corporation, 3000 Shanon, Santa Ana,
California 92704; Hansen Lamps Inc., 121 East
24th Street, New York, NY 10010.

**META MEMPHIS
(MEMPHIS MILANO SRL)**
Via Olivetti 9, Pregnana Milanese 20010, Italy.
Outlets Australia: Artemide Pty Ltd, 69 Edward
Street, Pyrmont, NSW 2009. Austria:
Prodomo, 35–7 Flachgasse, 1150 Vienna.

Belgium: Horas SA, 25 Beemstraat, 1610
Ruisbroek. Canada: Artemide Ltd, 354
Davenport Road, Designers Walk, 3rd Floor,
Toronto M15 RK5. Denmark: Renzo d'Este,
1A Brodrevej, 2860 Soborg, Copenhagen.
France: Roger Von Bary, 18 rue Lafitte, 75009
Paris. Germany: Agentur Brunnbauer, 51
Ehmckstrasse, 2800 Bremen 33. Hong Kong:
Le Cadre Gallery, 8 Sunning Road G/F,
Causeway Bay. The Netherlands: Copi, 90A
Prinsestraat, 2513 CG, The Hague. Switzerland:
Bell'Arte C. Arquint, 13 Loostrasse, 6430
Schwyz. UK: Artemide GB Ltd, 17–19 Neal
Street, London WC2H 9PU. USA: Memphis
Milano, International Design Center, Center
One, Space 525, 20–30 Thomson Avenue, Long
Island City, NY 111001.

MITSUBISHI
5757 Plaza Drive, Cypress, California 90630,
USA.

MÖBEL PERDU
Fettstrasse 7a, W-2000 Hamburg 36, Germany.

MOBLES 114
114 Enric Granados, Barcelona 08008, Spain.
Outlets France: Protis, 135 avenue Louis Roche,
92230 Gennevilliers, France. Germany: Elmar
Flototto, Ringstrasse 38–40, D-4835 Rietberg-2.
The Netherlands: Quattro Benelux, Chausée de
Melin 19BP 29, B-5905, Saint Remy, Geest,
Belgium. Portugal: Altamira, Ave. Vizconde
Valmor 35, 1000 Lisbon. Scandinavia: Casa
Lab, Dvevej 5Y, 2000 Copenhagen, Denmark.
UK: Conran Shop, 81 Fulham Road, London
SW3 6RD.

MOONLIGHT DESIGN SA
53 rue des Carburants, 1190 Brussels, Belgium.
Outlets Belgium: Ardeco International, avenue
du Général de Gaulle 39, B-1050, Brussels.
France: Artelux, rue de l'Abreuvoir 4, F-92415
Courbevoie Cedex. Germany: Arte Lumen
GmbH, Postfach 52, D-8501 Untermichelbach.
The Netherlands: Interlite Lichtontwerpen, 40
Larenweg, NL-2234 Ka's Hertogenbosch.
Sweden: Annell International, Surbrunnsgatan
14, S-11421 Stockholm. Switzerland: Neuco
AG, 5 Würzgrabenstrasse, CH-8048 Zurich.
UK: Lumino Ltd, Lovet Road, The Pinnacles,
Harlow, Essex CM19 5TB. USA: Lumen Inc.,
8845 Beverly Boulevard, Los Angeles, 90048
California.

NILS HOLGER MOORMAN
22 Hauptstrasse, Frasdorf 8201, Germany.
Outlet Switzerland: Andome Engros, 75
Pfungener Strasse, Oberembrach 8425.

CARLO MORETTI SRL
3/13 Fondamenta Manin, Murano, Venice
30141, Italy.

MOROSO
Via Nazionale 60, Cavalicco di Tavagnacco,
33010 Udine, Italy. *Outlets* Australia: Canberra
Flair Pty Ltd, 8 Ipswick Street, Fyshwick Act.
2609. Austria: Michel Pilte, Via dei Colli 24,
33019 Tricesimo, Udine, Italy. Belgium:
Interdiff SPRL, rue de la Sablonnière 21, 1000
Brussels. Denmark and Sweden: Swedia
Moebel AB, PO Box 138, 36030 Lammhult.
Finland: Stanza OY, Annankatu 24, 00100

Helsinki. France (Paris): Signature's, avenue de l'Observatoire 34, 75015 Paris; (regions) Francois Carlier, avenue Jean Jaurès 113, 92120 Montrouge. Germany, postal codes 1–3: Thomas Graeper, Enzianstrasse 8, 4902 Bad Salzuflen; postal codes 4–5: Walter J. Schiedermeier, Marienbergerweg 12, 5000 Cologne 71; postal codes 6–8: Hubert Essenko, Maxim-Wetzgerstrasse 6, 8000 Munich 19. Hong Kong: Le Cadre Gallery Ltd, 4B Sunning Road G/F, Causeway Bay. Japan: Corrente Corporation, 3-2-chome, Kanda-Isukasa-cho, Chiyoda-ku, Tokyo. The Netherlands: Ivo Verbeek Meubelimport, Johan Huizinhgalaan 288, 1065 JN Amsterdam. Singapore: Abraxas Design Pte Ltd, 4 Shenton Way, 01-01 Shing Kwan House, Singapore 0106. Spain: Roger Sin Roca, Ronda Gral. Mitre 174–176, 08006 Barcelona. Switzerland: Oliver Ike, Kroenleinstrasse 31/a, 8044 Zurich. UK: Orchard Associates, 2 Davenport Close, Teddington, Middx TW11 9EF.

NÉOTÙ
25 rue du Renard, 75004 Paris, France. *Outlet* USA: 133 Greene Street, New York, NY 10012.

NEW TONE, DANIEL MENU
2 rue de la Roquette, 75011 Paris, France.

GUIDO NIEST (ATELIER CANAIMA)
Via Resistenza 16, Bregnano 22070, Como, Italy.

NIPPON TELPHONE AND TELEGRAPH
1–6 Uchisaiwai-cho-1-chome, Chiyoda-ku, Tokyo 100, Japan.

NUNO CORPORATION
Axis B1, 5-17-1 Roppongi, Minato-ku, Tokyo 106, Japan.

OCEAN MICRO SYSTEMS
246 Hacienda Avenue, Cambell, California 95008, USA.

OHYAMA B. IND.
C/o 3-2-2 Shinyuku-ku, Shinyuku, Tokyo, Japan.

OKAMURA CORPORATION
Sanno Grand Building, 2-14-2 Nagata-cho, Chiyoda-ku, Tokyo 100, Japan.

OLUCE
Via Cavour 52, San Giuliano Milanese, Milan 20098, Italy. *Outlets* Belgium: Kreymborg, 66 avenue Molière, Brussels 1180. France: Devoto, 11 rue Azais Barthes, Beziers 34500. Finland: Funkiio, 7 Loennrotinkatu, Helsinki 12. Germany: Floetotto Handelsagentur, 38–40 Ringstrasse, 4835 Rietberg 2. Greece: Deloudis, 3–5 Spefsippou, Kolonaki, Athens. Japan: Flos Japan Co. Ltd, 1-23-5 Higashi-Azabu J., Minato-ku, Tokyo 106. The Netherlands: Carlo Wanna, PO Box 1035, Zwijndrecht 3330. Scandinavia: Inside, PO Box 3310, Stockholm, Sweden. Spain: Idea International, 12–18 Vico, Barcelona 21. UK: Flos Ltd, The Studio, 120 High Street, South Milford, Yorks. LS25 5AQ.

OXO INTERNATIONAL
230 Fifth Avenue, New York, NY 10001, USA. *Outlet* UK: JLR Sales and Marketing Co. Ltd, The Mill, Hatfield Heath, Bishop's Stortford, Herts. CM22 7DL.

PAF SRL
Via Edison 118, Settimo Milanese, Milan 20019, Italy. *Outlets* Austria: Die Kommode, 12 Lerchenfelderstrasse, Vienna 1080. France: Pierre Nourissat Sarl, 2 Burospace, Bievres Cedex 91571. Germany: Interprofil GmbH, 9 Ruhberg, 6301 Fernwald 1. Japan: Matsushita Electric Works, Viale Elvezia 18, Milan 20154. The Netherlands: Kreymborg BV, 63 Minervalaan 63, Amsterdam 1077. Scandinavia: Atelje Lyktan Ab, Box No. 3, Ahus 29600, Sweden. Spain: Carpyen SA Illuminacion, 29 Duran i Borrel, Barcelona 08023. UK: Ambience, 273 Brighton Road, Sutton, Surrey SM2 5S4. USA: PAF USA, 400 Long Beach Boulevard, Stratford, CT 06497.

RICHARD PEDUZZI
18 rue Notre Dame de Lorette, Paris 75009, France.

ATELIER PELCL
3 Melnicka, Prague 150 00, Czechoslovakia.

JORGE PENSI
1–4° Pl. Ramon Berenguer Gran, Barcelona 08002, Spain.

PHILIPS CORPORATE INDUSTRIAL DESIGN, JAPAN
35-1 Sagamiohono 7-chome, Sagamihara City, Kanagawa 228, Japan.

PHILIPS ELECTRONICS NV
Building SX, PO Box 218, 5600 MD Eindhoven, The Netherlands. *Outlets* Austria: Österreichische Philips Industrie GmbH, 64 Triester Strasse, 1100 Vienna. Belgium: NV Philips, 2 De Brouckereplein, PO Box 218, 1000 Brussels. Denmark: Philips Elapparat AS, 80 Pragsboulevard, 2300 Copenhagen. Finland: OY Philips AB, 8 Kaivokatu, Helsinki. France: SA Philips Industriale et Commerciale, 50 avenue Montaigne, 75380 Paris. Germany: Philips GmbH, Unternehmensbereich Haustechnik, 19 Kilanstrasse, 8500 Nuremberg; Allgemeine Deutsche Philips Ind. GmbH, 94 Steindamm, 2000 Hamburg. Italy: Philips Italia SA, Piazza IV Novembre 3, 20100 Milan. Japan: Philips Industrial Development and Consultants Co. Ltd, Shuwa, Shinagawa Building, 26–33 Takanawa 3-chome, Minato-ku, Tokyo 108. Norway: Norsk AS Philips, PO Box 5040, 6 Soerkedaksveien, Oslo 3. Spain: Philips Iberica SAE, 2 Martinez Villergas, Apartado 2065, 28027 Madrid. Sweden: Philips Norden AB, 11584 Stockholm. UK: Philips Electrical and Associated Industries Ltd, Arundel Great Court, 8 Arundel Street, London WC2 3DT. USA: North American Philips Corporation, 100 East 42nd Street, New York, NY 10017.

PLUS DEVELOPMENT/LACIE LTD
19552 SW 90th Court, Tualatin, Oregon 97062, USA.

POLTRONOVA DESIGN SRL
Via Prov. Pratese 23, Montale, 51037 Pistoia, Italy. *Outlets* Belgium: C.V. Novalis G., Gallery 'Bourdon Arcade', Emile Braunplein 45, 9000 Ghent. France: Paul-Patrice Vischel, 43 bld. Alfred Wallach, F-68100 Mulhouse. Japan: Ambech Co. Ltd, Sumimoto Seimei Building 3-1-30, Minami-aoyama, Minato-ku, Tokyo 107. Spain: Via Agents Asociados scp, Av. del Enlace 2, 08190 Sant Cuga T Del Vallès, Barcelona. Switzerland: Guido Mayer SA, Z.I. Portettes, CH-1312 Eclepens Gare VA.

PRIMO FURNITURE PLC
Baird Road, Enfield, Middx EN1 1SJ, UK.

PROSPETTIVE SRL
Via Emila 363, Ospedaletto 56014, Pisa, Italy. *Outlets* Germany: Ulrich Lodholz GmbH, 47 IM Hederichsfeld, Łeverkusen 3 5090. Japan: Italcomm Ltd, Likura Comfy Building, B-101 4-4 Aza Budai 3-chome, Tokyo 106. Switzerland: Pra-Mobil AG, 37 Chilesteig, Wuerenlos 8116. USA: Archetype Associates, 452 Eighth Street, Brooklyn, New York, NY 11215.

RESOUND CORPORATION
220 Saginaw Drive, Redwood City, California 94063, USA.

ROSTI HOUSEWARES AS
Sdr. Mellemvej 4, Roskilde DK-4000, Denmark.

MICHAEL ROWE
401½ Workshops, 401½ Wandsworth Road, London SW8, UK. *Outlet* USA: Rezac Gallery, 301 West Superior, 2nd Floor, Chicago, Illinois 60610.

SABATTINI ARGENTERIA SpA
Via Don Capiaghi 2, Bregnano 22070, Como, Italy. *Outlets* Germany: Sabattini Deutschland, 50 Kennedyallee, Frankfurt 6000. Japan: Studio De. Co. Inc., 604-2-14-7 Mita, Minato-ku, Tokyo 108. The Netherlands: Mobica NV, 50 Gossetlaan, Groot-Bijgaarden 1720, Belgium. Scandinavia: Linea Domani, 159 Smakkegardsvej, Gentofte 2820, Denmark.

SAKAEGI DESIGN SUDIO
1–74 Nakamizuno-cho, Seto-shi Aichi 489, Japan.

SASAKI CRYSTAL INC.
41 Madison Avenue, New York, NY 10010.

SASAKI GLASS CO., LTD
2-2-6 Nihonbashi-Bakuro-cho, Chuo-ku, Tokyo, Japan.

FRANZ SCHATZL, DESIGN WERKSTÄTTE
A-4801 Traunkirchen, Austria. *Outlets* Belgium: Creadis Design Distribution, Obterrestraat 67, B-8972 Proven, Poperinge. The Netherlands: Bibird, Valkenstraat 16, NL-4847 Teteringen.

THOMAS SCHULTE DESIGNMANUFAKTUR
2 Bruckenstrasse, 5090 Leverkusen 3, Germany.

SCP LTD
135–139 Curtain Road, London EC2A 3BX,
UK. *Outlets* Germany: Teunen & Teunen,
Postfach 36, 6222 Geisenheim 2. Japan: Kiya
Gallery, Office 9-2 Sarugaku-cho, Shibuya-ku,
Tokyo. The Netherlands: Jones Import, Ch de
Ruisbroek 290, 1620 Drogenbos, Belgium.
Scandinavia: C & B1 Interior, Birgerjarlsg 34,
Box 26126 Stockholm, Sweden. Spain: Pilma,
Llanca 33, Barcelona 08015. Taiwan: Vivo 107-
1, Section 4, Hsin Yi Road 10657, Taipei,
USA: Palazzetti Inc., 515 Madison Avenue,
New York, NY 10022.

MASAFUMI SEKINE
2-490-2 Kushibikicho, Omiya-shi Saitama-ken
331, Japan.

SHARP CORPORATION
22-22 Nagaike-cho, Abeno-ku, Osaka 545,
Japan.

SKIPPER SPA
Via Serbelloni 1, Milan 20122, Italy. *Outlets*
France: Gennaro Dellisanti, 17 rue des
Closeaux, 77240 Vert St Denis. Germany: E.
Rohoff, 6–8 Reinhard-Hoppe Strasse, 6900
Heidelberg 25. The Netherlands: Ludo K.
Kokken, 124 Antwerpsesteenweg, 2630
Aartseaar, Antwerp. Switzerland: Gianni
Fedrigo, Via Washington 102, 20100 Milan,
Italy.

SILHOUETTE INTERNATIONAL GMBH
Linz A-4021, Austria.

**SOCIÉTÉ DES AMIS DU MUSÉE
NATIONAL D'ART MODERNE**
Centre Georges Pompidou, 75191 Paris, Cedex
04, France.

SONY CORPORATION
6-7-35 Kitashinagawa, Shinagawa-ku, Tokyo
141, Japan.

STELTMAN EDITIONS
Spulstraat 330, 1012 VX, Amsterdam, Holland.

A/S STELTON
1 Gl. Vartov Vej, Hellerup 2900, Denmark.
Outlets Australia: Stelton, 57 Donald Street,
Prahran, Victoria 3181. Austria: O and S
Dunkelblum, Herrengasse 6-7-3, 1010 Vienna.
Belgium: Tradix SA, 104 avenue Louis
Lepoutre, 1060 Brussels. France: Anc. Ets.
Martin SA, 49 rue Ernest Renan, BP 13, 94201
Ivry-sur-Seine. Germany: Stelton, Verkaufsbüro
Deutschland, Musterhaus am Messekreisel 30,
Deutz-Mulheimerstrasse 30, D-5000 Cologne
21. Italy: SIMAS sas di Alberto Sancio & C.,
Casella Postalle 46, Via XXIV Magio 8, 28041
Arona, Novara. Japan: J. Osawa & Co. Ltd, 2–
8 Shibaura, 4-chome, Minato-ku, Tokyo 108.
The Netherlands: Mobach BV, Portengen 5,
3628 EB Kockengen. Norway: Royal
Copenhagen Norge AS, Pilestedet 15, 0164
Oslo 1. Spain: Lidia Roqueta Soriano, Pasaje
Gayola 24 bajos, 08013 Barcelona. Sweden:
Royal Copenhagen Svenska AB, Västra
Hamngatan 12, 41117 Göteborg. Switzerland:
Leutwiler AG, Buttenhalde 38, 6006 Lucerne.
UK: Storrington Trading, PO Box 32,
Chichester, West Sussex PO19 4FD. USA:
Stelton USA, 23 East 78th Street, New York,
NY 10021-1224.

STILDOMUS SPA
Via Laurentina 27, Pomezia 00040, Rome, Italy.
Outlets Spain: Kaes SA, 24 Avenida de Navarra,
Bajo-Zarautz 20800.

SWID POWELL
213 East 49th Street, New York, NY 10017,
USA.

TAKEFU KNIFE VILLAGE
Hamono-Kogyodanchi, Ikenokami, Takefu-
Fukui 915, Japan.

TATUNG
2850 El Presidio Street, Long Beach, California,
USA.

TECHNILAND
15 rue Gassendi, Paris 75014, France. *Outlets*
Germany: Restform, Wiedelsheidestrasse 40,
Arnsberg 1, D5760.

TECNO SPA
Vigli 22, Milan, Italy. *Outlets* Austria: Tecno
SpA, Waehringstrasse 2–4, Vienna. France:
Tecno SpA, 242 bd. St Germain, Paris.
Germany: Tecno SpA, Friedrich-Ebert-Strasse
9, Düsseldorf; Tecno SpA, Lenbachplatz 5,
Munich. Greece: Tecno SpA, 2 od Vas
Alesandrou, Athens. Italy: Tecno SpA, Via del
Babuino 155a, Rome. The Netherlands: Tecno
SpA, Buitenveldertselaan 158, Amsterdam;
Tecno SpA, 60 Avenue Louise, Brussels,
Belgium. Spain: Tecno SpA, Gran Via de les
Corts Catalanes 642, Barcelona; Tecno SpA,
calle Nunez de Balboa 12, Madrid. Switzerland:
Tecno SpA, 9 Place Bourg de Four, Geneva.
UK: Tecno SpA, 19 New Bond Street, London
W1Y 9HF.

TELENE SPA
Via Vincenzo Monti 79, Milan 20145, Italy.
Outlets France: Claude Blanc, 14 rue
d'Hauteville, Paris 75010. Germany: Philmond
Handelsagentur GmbH, 10 Kreutz Hof Strasse,
Munich 71 D8000. Italy: Telene SpA, Strada
Padana Superiore 56, Cernusco S/Naviglio
20063. Japan: The New Thema Co. Ltd, Yuki
Building 6F, 3–9, 3-chome Hiranomachi,
Chuo-ku, Osaka. Spain: Codintex SA, calle
Consell de Cent 80, 4° 3a Y 3° 4a, Barcelona
08015. UK: David Misan Agencies, 2 Stanhope
Mews West, London SW7 5RB. USA: Roger
Laviale Ltd, 135 West 50th Street, New York,
NY 10020.

TEMPI DI CARTA
Via Cosimo Del Fante 4/A, Milan 20100, Italy.

**THAILAND CARPET
MANUFACTURING**
Srivikorn Building, 18/8 Sukhumun 21,
Bangkok 10110, Thailand. *Outlet* Scandinavia:
Carouschka Design, 23 Nybrogatan, Stockholm
11439, Sweden.

THORN LIGHTING LTD
Lincoln Road, Enfield, Middx EN1 1SB, UK.

TOKYO GAS
16–25, Shibaura 1-chome, Minato-ku, Tokyo
105, Japan.

TOSHIBA CORPORATION
1-1, Shibaura 1-chome, Minato-ku, Tokyo 105-
01, Japan.

TOULEMONDE BOCHART
BP18 Wissous 91320, France. *Outlets* Belgium:
Vanhee Agencies, Leffingestraat 60, 8400
Ostend. Germany: Design Focus, 1 Adenauer
Strasse, 5042 Erftstadt. Italy: Tisca, Via
Donizetti 6, Murano 24053. Japan: Nest
(Seibu), 1-18-4 Minami Ikebukuro, Toshima-
ku, Tokyo 171. The Netherlands: B & G
Collection, Havikskgruit 25, Zeewolde 3892.
Portugal: Parisete, Av. de Paris 7a, 1000
Lisbon. Spain: Bedre, Paseo Colon 102–104,
08430 Cardebeu, Barcelona.

TRÁFICO DE MODAS
27 Marino Albesa, Valencia 46002, Spain.

UMBRA
2358 Midland Avenue, Scarborough, Ontario,
Canada M1S 1P8.

VERRERIE DE NONFOUX
1417 Nonfoux, Switzerland. *Outlets* France:
Quart Diffusion, 12 rue des Quatre Vents, Paris
75006. Germany: Lichtenberg Studio Glass,
Chrustel Schmidt-Allee 25, 2070 Ahrensburg.
Switzerland: Rennweggalerie, Rennweg 4, 8011
Zurich. USA: New Gladd, 345 West
Broadway, New York, NY 10013.

VITRA
9 Feverbachstrasse, Weil-am-Rhein, D-7858
Germany. *Outlets* France: Vitra Sarl, 59 avenue
D'Iena, Paris F-75116. Italy: Decor Design Srl,
6 Corso di Porta Romana, Milan. The
Netherlands: Vitra Nederland BV, 152
Assumburg, Amsterdam, NL-1081 GC.
Switzerland: Vitra (International) AG, 20
Klunenfeldstrasse, Birsfelden CH-4127. UK:
Vitra Ltd, 13 Grosvenor Street, London W1X
9FB.

VORWERK & CO. TEPPICHWERKE KG
Kuhlmannstrasse 11, 3250 Hameln, Germany.

WITTMANN DESIGN LTD
Suite 104, 1 Northumberland Avenue, London
WC2N 5BW, UK.

WOKA LAMPS VIENNA
16 Singerstrasse, Vienna A-1010, Austria.
Outlets Australia: Lightmakers Pty Ltd, 384
Elisabeth Street, Melbourne, Victoria. France:
Altras, 24 rue Lafitte, F-75009 Paris. Germany:
H.H. Bunnagel, 2A Robert Koch Strasse, D-
5000 Cologne 41. Italy: Galimberti, Via
Ponchielli 44, I-20052 Monza. Japan: Aidec, 28
Mori Building 6F 16–13, Tokyo 106, Minato-
ku, Nishiazabu 4. The Netherlands: Art
Collection, 63 Weijland, NL-2415 bd
Nieuwerbrug. Scandinavia: IDE Individuell, 6
Basargatan, S-41117 Göteborg, Sweden. Spain:
Bd Ediciones de diseño, 291 Mallorca, 08037
Barcelona. UK: M.W. United Ltd, 19 Dacre
Street, London SW1H 0DJ. USA: George
Kovacs Inc., 24 West 40th Street, New York,
NY 10018.

YAMAGIWA CORPORATION
4-1-1 Sotokanda, Chiyoda-ku, Tokyo, Japan.

ZANOTTA SpA
Via Vittorio Veneto 57, 20054 Nova Milanese,
Italy. *Outlets* Australia: Arredorama
International Pty Ltd, 1 Ross Street, Glebe,
NSW No. 2037. Austria: Prodomo, 35–37
Flachgasse, 1060 Vienna. Belgium: Zaira Mis,
35 boulevard Saint Michel, 1040 Brussels.
Denmark: Paustian, 2 Kalkbraendrilbskaj, 2100
Copenhagen. France: Giuseppe Cerutti, 1
Località Grand Chemin, Saint Christophe
11020, Italy. Germany: Fulvio Folci, 14
Dahlienweg, 4000 Düsseldorf 30. Japan: Nova
Oshima Co. Ltd, Sakakura Building, Akasaka,
Minato-ku, Tokyo. The Netherlands: Hansje
Kalff, 8 Puttensestraat, 1181 Je Amstelveen.
Norway: Bente Holm, 64 Parkveien, Oslo 2.
Spain: Bd Ediciones de diseño, 291 Mallorca,
08037 Barcelona. Sweden: Inside, 37
Hamngatan, 11147 Stockholm. Switzerland:
Peter Kaufmann, 123 Rychenbergstrasse, 8400
Winterhur. UK: The Architectural Trading Co.
Ltd, 219–29 Shaftesbury Avenue, London
WC2H 8AR. USA: International Contract
Furnishings, 305 East 63rd Street, New York,
NY 10021.

ZANUSSI ELETTRODOMESTICI SpA
Via Giardini Cattaneo 3, Pordenone 33170,
Italy. *Outlets* Austria: IAZ Elektrogeräte
GmbH, Markhofgasse 19, A-1034 Vienna.
Belgium: Electrolux Belgium NV,
Bergensesteenweg 719, B-1520 Halle, Lembeek.
Denmark: Zanussi Danmark AS, Lino
Zanussivej, DK-6360 Tinglev. France: IAZ
International France SA, 52 ru Emile Zola, F-
93107 Montreuil Cedex. Germany: Zanussi
Elektrogeräte GmbH, Rennbahnstrasse 72–74,
D-6000 Frankfurt 73. Holland: Electrolux
Netherland BV, Postbus 120, 2400 AC Alphen
A/D Rijn. Norway: Zanussi AS, Spireavn 14,
Okern 0511, Oslo 5. Portugal: Electrolux Lda,
Rua Palmira 23, 1196 Lisbon Codex. Spain:
Albilux SA, Augustin de Foxà 25, 28036
Madrid. Sweden: Electrolux Mayor and Floor
Care Appliances, Luxbacken 1, Lilla Essingen,
S-105 45 Stockholm. UK: Zanussi Ltd,
Hambridge Road, Newbury, Berks. RG14 5EP.

PUBLICATIONS

AUSTRALIA
Australian Design Series (14 issues a year, ten
titles) Australia's leading niche-market
publication on domestic and commercial design,
each looking at a specific subject.

Belle (bi-monthly) Showcase for contemporary
Australian architecture and interior design, with
a round-up that includes many imported
influences.

Design World (quarterly) Technical and
educational articles covering the design world in
the Antipodes.

Interiors (bi-monthly) Comprehensive analysis
of latest upmarket trends in fabrics, textiles and
designs.

Interior Design (bi-monthly) Dedicated to
decoration, with a mixture of articles on avant-
garde designs and traditional interiors.

Vogue Living (ten issues a year) Lively, glossy
lifestyle magazine on decoration and design.

CANADA
Canadian Interiors (eight issues a year)
Quality magazine targeted at professionals with
an interest in architecture and their
environment. English text.

Contract Magazine (bi-monthly) Geared
towards qualified designers, it deals with the
planning and management of interiors for
commercial establishments and public
institutions. English text.

Décormag (monthly) Deals with interior
decoration, offering articles on different styles
and editorials on specific rooms. French text.

Designs (quarterly) With a text in French and
English this is the first and only bilingual trade
magazine in Quebec. It deals with residential
and commercial furniture, lighting, materials
and interior decoration.

DENMARK
Arkitekten (23 issues a year) and **Arkitektur**
(eight issues a year). Edited by the Danish
Architectural Press for the professional
federations of architects and building
contractors.

Bo Bedre (monthly) Translates into English as
'Live Better', precisely the editorial policy
behind this consumer home-interest magazine.

Design from Scandinavia (annual) For the
past 18 years a useful index of designers and
manufacturers against a background of
illustrated stories of architectural interest.

Fair Facts (quarterly) Published in Danish and
English, the magazine deals with the major
European furniture fairs and exhibitions.

Living Architecture (bi-annual) Scandinavia's
best-looking glossy magazine on buildings and
their interiors, by the celebrated photographer
and architect Per Nagel. English text.

Rum og Form (annual) 'Space and Form',
edited by the Danish Association of Furniture
Designers and Interior Designers.

FINLAND
Design in Finland (annual) Published by the
Finnish Foreign Trade Association to promote
the year's products abroad, with good-quality
illustrations and an index of manufacturers and
designers.

Form Function, Finland (quarterly) A magazine concerned with mass production and functional design in Finland, aimed at the export market, published by the Finnish Society of Craft and Design.

Muoto (monthly) Magazine on interior and industrial design, with articles on individual designers.

Space & Place (annual) Contract furniture collections presented by the Furniture Exporters' Association.

FRANCE

Architectural Digest (monthly) French version of the American magazine; see under USA.

Architecture Intérieure Créé (bi-monthly) Leading professional design magazine with an architectural background.

Art et Décoration (eight issues a year) Concerned primarily with the plastic arts and interior decoration.

L'Atelier (ten issues a year) Specializes in objects, gadgets and daring designs.

BAT (monthly) Excellent coverage of design and advertising in fields as diverse as graphic design, videos and interiors.

Beaux Arts (monthly) This celebrated art and architectural magazine has recently included contemporary design articles.

Les Carnets du Design (irregular) Thematic presentation of various subjects concerned with design and interior decoration, such as chairs, tableware, sofas etc.

City Magazine International (ten issues a year) Lifestyle magazine dealing with design, interiors and fashion for the upwardly mobile.

Décoration Internationale (monthly, but erratic) Eclectic publication in its eleventh year, covering houses, objects and painters in exotic locations.

Elle-Décoration (eight issues a year) Fashion-based design magazine aimed at the younger market.

Intramuros (monthly) Large-format design and interiors magazine with in-depth interviews with people ahead of the pack. Technical information, freshly presented, is aimed at professionals, but the layout makes it generally appealing.

La Maison de Marie Claire (monthly) 'Le style français' in a glossy magazine in which everything from plates to pastries is chic.

Maison et Jardin (monthly) High-life review of famous interiors and gardens with specific design articles included in most issues.

Maison Française (monthly) Covers furniture, interiors and architecture with special regional bias and promotional features.

Show Room (bi-monthly) Started in 1990, contains useful information on design exhibitions and fairs for the professional market. Sold by subscription only.

Vogue Décoration (quarterly) Weighty and opulent interiors magazine with beautiful presentation and in-depth interviews.

GERMANY

Ambiente (bi-monthly) A consumer magazine on interior design.

Architektur und Wohnen (monthly) Interviews with the architects and owners of remarkable homes. It links professional and consumer interests, and contains exhaustively researched product reports.

Art Aurea (quarterly) Theme-related articles on art, design and fashion, with text in German and English.

Design Report (bi-monthly) Factual magazine on the state of design in Germany, with reports, commentaries and interviews.

Form (quarterly) Living articles discussing international design and the market-place.

Häuser (monthly) House case-histories, architectural portraits, design product round-ups and extensive floor plans. There is an English-language supplement.

MD Möbel Interior Design (monthly) Modest (black-and-white), interesting publication on furniture, with bold graphic covers.

Schöner Wohnen (monthly) The world of architecture and design in Germany, with reports from correspondents in all other major countries. Popular, informative and technical.

Terrazzo (twice a year) German version of the Italian/US magazine.

Wolkenkratzer Art Journal (bi-monthly) Art, design, image, architecture and music.

ISRAEL

Architecture of Israel (quarterly) Publicizes the interiors and exteriors of many of Israel's new and more interesting buildings.

Binyan Diur (three issues a year) Design and interior architecture articles with interviews and special projects, aimed at the domestic market.

ITALY

Abitare (ten issues a year) English text published alongside the Italian in a heavily merchandized, up-to-the-minute round-up of new designs. Architects and interior designers look to its photographic stories for an international perspective. Some issues are devoted to a single country.

L'Arca (ten issues a year) Recently launched publication, dedicated to architecture, design and visual communication, with technical monographs.

AReA (bi-monthly) Design-as-art magazine concentrating on objects and decoration for the interior. Interviews with designers, artists, architects and students.

Casa Vogue (eleven issues a year) Definitive listing of new trends-in-the-making around the world in interiors, decoration, houses and furniture. An invaluable talent-spotters' magazine, famous for the inspired art direction of its merchandizing stories.

Disegno (quarterly) Technical, covering the tools, instruments and software needed for graphic and industrial design.

Domus (monthly) Giò Ponti founded this authoritative magazine on architecture, interiors, furniture and art; now Mario Bellini is its outspoken, informed editor. More textual than visual, it is consulted by architects and designers who submit schemes.

Gap Casa (monthly) Trade figures and commercial marketing strategies sit alongside the product lines in this stylish magazine aimed at retailers.

In Design (bi-monthly) Bi-lingual (English/Italian) review of architectural projects, designs and interior design, aimed at a specialist market.

Interni (monthly) More than its name suggests, a round-up of products relating to external, as well as interior, design. Has interesting supplements, catalogues of addresses and international editions.

Modo (monthly) articles and opinions on design in depth, with a directory of products and producers, created by the omnipresent Alessandro Mendini. Regarded as the magazine of the avant garde in Italian design.

Ottagono (quarterly) A review of architecture, interior design, furniture and industrial design worldwide, published in Italian and English editions by eight Italian manufacturers – Arflex, Artemide, Bernini, Boffi, Cassina, Flos, ICF and Tecno. Leading writers contribute to this small-format publication.

JAPAN

AXIS (bi-monthly) First-rate international publication with coverage of a wide variety of furniture, product and interior design projects, with a special interest in Italy. Some English summaries.

Design News (eight issues a year) Aimed at professionals and sold on subscription, this has a good coverage of Japanese design projects with an emphasis on industrial and product design.

FP: Fusion Planning (bi-monthly) Emphasis leans towards architecture and interior design in this well-produced and edited magazine with a good selection of international design projects.

GA: Global Architecture (irregular) Editor Yukio Futagawa established this as the première photo-essay magazine of architecture worldwide.

Icon (monthly) Targeted at architects and designers in Japanese and English, an iconoclastic review of architecture, design, interiors and art.

Japan Architect (monthly) Architectural and interior design magazine aimed at the professional market, featuring exclusively Japanese designs.

Portfolio (bi-monthly) A less glossy, slightly down-market version of *AXIS* with more emphasis on quirky urban interiors and architecture.

SD: Space Design (monthly) Interior space – a thoroughly Japanese magazine concept – with a broad international coverage of projects which fits into theme-edited issues.

W.IN.D (quarterly) International coverage of interior design – shops, restaurants and commercial space – with frequent special issues on non-superstar designers. Japanese only.

MEXICO

Magenta (quarterly) Produced by a private foundation to promote design, this is proof of the need for private initiative.

THE NETHERLANDS

Avenue (monthly) Stylish photo-reportage of design products (including lighting and furniture), travel, interviews, avant-garde fashion and art festivals.

Industrieel Ontwerpen (bi-monthly) Eminently technical and professional publication covering industrial design and product development.

Textiel-Visie (quarterly) Predominantly fabrics for home furnishing with styling forecasts and articles on lifestyles and consumer psychology.

NEW ZEALAND

New Zealand Home Journal (monthly) A home-interest magazine with interior design coverage.

NORWAY

Byggekunst (eight issues a year) Covers building, landscape architecture and interior design.

Hjem & Fritid/Bonytt (monthly) A consumer magazine on interior design, aimed primarily at the wealthy connoisseur rather than the professional.

Hus og Hem (quarterly) Glossy magazine on decoration and interiors.

Skala (monthly) Architecture and design from around the world.

POLAND

Design – Wiadomości Instytutu Wzornictwa Przemyslowego (bi-monthly) Aimed at the professional market, this magazine, produced by the Institute of Industrial Design in Poland, covers national and international history and theory of design, plus new design solutions and events.

SPAIN

Ardi (bi-monthly) Brilliantly art-directed publication introduces the best Spanish designers, architects, cartoonists and graphic artists to the world, alongside special reports on the international avant garde.

La Casa 16 de Marie Claire (monthly) Spanish edition of the French magazine, edited by Group 16.

De Diseño (monthly) Brainchild of Quim Larrea and Juli Capella, currently directors of *Ardi*. After a rigorous, risk-taking start, it later changed direction.

Diseño Interior (eleven issues a year) Professional magazine dealing with architecture and interior design worldwide, intended to act as a forum between architects and designers and manufacturers.

Futura (bi-annual) Covers art and design and is excellently printed in northern Spain.

Hogares (monthly) 'Homes' is published in colour with photographic spreads on Spanish houses and interviews with Spanish designers.

I La Nave Va (fortnightly) Internationally published booklet in which the well-known Valencia group La Nave puts forth its latest multi-disciplinary ideas. Private circulation only.

Nuevo Estilo (monthly) Major publication on design and furniture, aimed at a wide public; not avant garde, but the editing is exemplary.

ON Diseño (monthly) Pioneer in design, with articles on home-grown talent, and an international round-up of graphics and architecture.

SWEDEN

Arkitekten (monthly) A small, in-house official publication for the Federation of Architects and allied building trades in Sweden.

Arkitektur (ten issues a year) A round-up of architects' projects in Sweden, with plans and pictures.

Form (eight issues a year) The professional magazine for interior, graphic and industrial designers. Text in Swedish and English.

Möbler and Miljö (ten issues a year) This specialist magazine, 'Furniture and Environment', is read by the decision-makers who buy and make furnishings for interior designers.

Sköna Hem (quarterly) Sweden's showcase home-interest magazine with colourful photographic coverage of architecture and interior design.

SWITZERLAND

Textile Suisse (quarterly) Published by the Swiss Office for the Development of Trade, a review of the state of the textile business.

Innendekorateur (monthly) Professional, black-and-white magazine dealing with interior design.

Schöner Wohnen Schweiz (monthly) Swiss supplement of the German magazine *Schöner Wohnen*; gives information solely on the Swiss architectural and interior design scene.

Werk, Bauen und Wohnen (monthly) Austere, sober publication on architecture and industrial design.

UK

Architects' Journal (weekly) The professional, opinionated and sometimes controversial magazine for British architects.

Architectural Review (monthly) A well-written and informed magazine which examines projects, with plans, worldwide.

Art and Design (bi-monthly) Art, architecture, design, fashion, music, photography, news.

Blueprint (10 issues a year) Fast-forward into what's being planned, built, assembled, launched or revived. Racy layouts in a large format, mostly black-and-white, with informed, hard-hitting comment.

Creative Review (monthly) Well-presented review of mainly graphic design, whether applied to computers, textiles or advertising.

Design (monthly) The official publication of the British Design Council, parochial and sometimes carping.

Design Week (weekly) Energetic design publication, highly agile in image and content with news and views on the industry.

Designers' Journal (monthly) The enlightened companion to the *Architects' Journal*, aimed at a predominantly contract market with interviews covering all aspects of design from theatre to products.

Homes & Gardens (monthly) The home-interest magazine equivalent to the high-street design shop, seen as inspirational by those who buy it.

House & Garden (monthly) Condé Nast's biggest-selling design and decoration magazine in the UK. Although the emphasis of the editorial is on interior decoration, the design and architectural information is strongly merchandized and it sponsors the annual competition 'The New Designers'.

Metropolitan Home (bi-monthly) Glossy, contemporary design and homestyle magazine for the younger, urban reader.

Review (annual) The exhibition catalogue for the new additions to the permanent collection of the Design Museum, London, aimed at a professional market and serving as an industrial products design handbook.

World of Interiors (eleven issues a year) The interiors magazine to be seen in, offering a voyeuristic tour around some of the world's most lavishly decorated homes, with international gallery listings that are wide-ranging and talent-spotting.

USA

Architectural Digest (six issues a year) An authoritative celebrity round-up of the lavish homes of the rich and famous, presented in a highly successful coffee-table format.

Architectural Record (monthly) A professional and trade-orientated architectural magazine.

ID (bi-monthly) The industrial designers' product guide, with some coverage of the design industry, graphics and fashion.

Interiors (monthly) Rigorous and professional coverage of decoration for interior designers.

Metropolis (ten issues a year) The blueprint for *Blueprint* (UK), this large-format tabloid with spirited news, views and ideas in the design world is creatively edited with a strong New York bias.

Metropolitan Home (monthly) An energetic trend-spotting magazine for the upwardly mobile, with fashions in furnishings and furniture presented by a young editorial team with a strong sense of direction. Plenty of consumer information.

Progressive Architecture (monthly) One of America's two heavyweight architectural journals, a forum for spirited debate.

Terrazzo (twice a year) Magazine dealing with architecture and design. Interviews and in-depth articles.

Acquisitions by design collections in 1990. Dates given in parentheses refer to the dates of the designs (from 1960 to the present day).

AUSTRIA

Austrian Museum of Applied Arts, Vienna
Milan Knizak: chair, *Soft-Hard* (1974)
Gaetano Pesce: seat, *Feltri* (1978), manufactured by Cassina
Petra Schubert: rug, *Zig-Zag* (1989)
Bořek Šípek: seat, *Helena* (1988), manufactured by Driade
Helmut Swiczinsky/Wolf D. Prix (Coop Himmelblau): chair, *Vodöl* (1989), manufactured by Vitra

DENMARK

Museum of Decorative Art, Copenhagen
James Bohlin: lamp, *Larv* (1986), manufactured by Sweden
Norman Foster: Desk, *Nomos* (1988)
Jørgen and Karin Gammelgaard: chair (1990)
Gaetano Pesce: armchair, *Feltri* (1987), manufactured by Cassina
Rud Thygesen and Johnny Sørensen: chair (1988), manufactured by Botium
Jan Tragardh: teapot with brazier (1987), manufactured by A/S Søholm
Hans J. Wegner: armchair, *JH 701* (1965), manufactured by Johannes Hansens Møbelsnedkeri A/S (1990)

FRANCE

Musée des Arts Décoratifs, Paris
Avant-Première: chair (1988)
Franqis Bauchet: chair (1982)
Arlon Bayliss: decanter, manufactured by Rosenthal
Mario Bellini: tea set, *Cupola*, manufactured by Rosenthal
Ann-Marie Beretta: plates from the *Asiette Brisée* collection (1990), manufactured by Haviland
Réné-Jean Cailette: chair, *RJC* (1986)
Joe Colombo: two chairs (1965), manufactured by Kartell
Christian Duc: armchair, *Croixement* (1988)
Olivier Gagnère: pedestal table and chair (1982)
Paolini and Teodoro Gatti: seat, *Sacco* (1969), manufactured by Zanotta
Kristian Gavoille: pedestal table (1987)
Yves Gradelet: chair (1980)
Monica Guggisberg & Philip Baldwin: decanter, manufactured by Rosenthal
M. Harrison McIntosh: sandstone pot (1990)
Ronald E. Kent: wooden dish (1990)
Enzo Mari: ashtray, *Madagascar*, manufactured by Danese
Pascal Mourgue: chaise longue, *Arc* and chair, *Tipi* (1983); chair, *Lune d'Argent* (1985), manufactured by Fermob
Régis Protière: five-drawer chest (1980)
Eric Raffy: chair (1989)
Lino Sabattini: tea set, *Hommage à Darmstadt* (1989); place setting, *Sculptura*, manufactured by Rosenthal
Pierre Sala: chair (1981-82)
Richard Sapper: lamp, *Tizio* (1972), manufactured by Artemide
Timo Sarpavena: tea set, *Suomi* (1974), manufactured by Rosenthal
Eric Schmitt: chair, *Haricot* (1987)
Ronald Cecil Sportes: armchair from the Elysée Palace (1982)
Philippe Starck: chair, *Costes* (1982); stool, *Arc* (1986); toothbrush and stand (1990), manufactured by Fluocaril, France
Jean-Michel Wilmotte: chair, *Palmer* and console, *Washington* (1983)
Zanine: table (1988)

GERMANY

Kunstmuseum Düsseldorf
Joe Colombo: bar stool (1970), manufactured by Zanotta
Enzo Mari: calendar, *Formosa* (1963); set of instruments, *Kurili* (1970-73), both manufactured by Danese Milano
Kuno Prey: table clock (1986)
Ettore Sottsass: lamp, *Madison* (1970s), manufactured by Tronconi
Matteo Thun: various tableware designs (1989); watering can (1989), both manufactured by WMF Geislingen
Marco Zanuso: chair (1962), manufactured by Garina

Vitra Design Museum, Weil am Rhein
Over 1,200 designs have been collected to form this museum, devoted primarily to the development of the chair over the last 140 years. It was opened in November 1989 and is intended to serve as an exhibition space as well as a permanent collection. Some major acquisitions of last year are:
Shiro Kuramata: *Miss Blanche*, plus all important models
Frank O. Gehry: all his important cardboard furniture pieces
Alessandro Mendini: all important models, including the *Proust* and *Kandissi* chairs
Verner Panton: his whole collection
Gaetano Pesce: all important models, including four *Pratt* chairs, the *Croce* chair, *Golgotha* chair, *Il Pugno*, *Dalila* chairs, *Sansone*, *Carenza*, *Tramonto à New York* and the *UP* series
Ettore Sottsass: all important models, including the *Carlton*, *Beverley*, *Tartar* and *Tapeto Volante* chairs
Helmut Swiczinsky/Wolf D. Prix (Coop Himmelblau): chair, *Vodöl* (1989), manufactured by Vitra

JAPAN

There is no permanent design collection in Japan at the present time, although there are a few private collections. Several museums of modern art do have good examples of contemporary, international design, but these almost always have a practical purpose and are not part of their displays. Temporary design exhibitions have been increasing dramatically, however, and there is a very strong possibility of a permanent design collection being formed.

THE NETHERLANDS

Museum Boymans-van Beuningen, Rotterdam
Mario Bellini: copier (1977), manufactured by Olivetti, Italy
Joe Colombo: glasses, *Smoke* (1964), manufactured by Arnolfo di Cambio, Italy
M. van Lelyveld and N. Nyland: set of storage boxes (1967), manufactured by Mepal BV, Holland
Dieter Lubs and Dieter Rams: alarm clock (1978), manufactured by Braun, Germany
Floris Meydam: jug, *Partymix* (1969), manufactured by Glasfabriek Leerdam, Holland
Bruno Ninaber van Eijben: watch (1976), manufactured by Bruno Ninaber, Holland
Heron Parigi: chair, *Canasta* (1990)
Giancarlo Piretti: chair, *106* (1967); chair, *Plia* (1968); folding table, *Plano* (1970); all manufactured by Anonima Castelli, Italy
Dieter Rams: radio, *Tischsuper RT 20* (1961), manufactured by Braun, Germany
Florian Seiffert: coffee machine, *KF 20* (1972), manufactured by Braun, Gemany
Matteo Thun: teapot, *Tea for One*, manufactured by Arzberg, Germany
Bob Verheyden: chair, *Number One* (1989), manufactured by Verheyden Studio, Holland
Martin Visser and Joke van der Heyden: table, *Petalo* (1987-89)
Hannes Wettstein: chair, *Juliette* (1990), manufactured by Baleri, Italy
Tapio Wirkkala: vase (1961), manufactured by Kultakeskus, Finland

239

SWEDEN

Nationalmuseum, Stockholm
Bjorn Alskog: wall clock (1967), manufactured by AB Gustavsburg, Sweden
Jonas Bohlin: chair, *Point* (1985), manufactured by Källemo, Sweden
Britt-Marie Christoffersson: tapestry, *Nutida musik och ur tonsattaren Allen Pettersons tankar* (1981)
Marten Cyren and Jonas Osslund: chair, *Klykan* (1990), manufactured by Miljo Expo Scandinavia, Sweden
Helen Gibson: dish in 'fusing and slumping' technique (1990), manufactured by Goteburg, Sweden
Ian Godfrey: stoneware dish, open-work border (1970)
Knud Kristensen: glazed earthenware pot with lid (1990), manufactured by Viby, Denmark
Gunilla Lagerhem-Ullberg: carpets, *Hagga 981* and *Arkad 922* (1989), manufactured by Kasthall, Sweden
Borge Lindau and Bo Lindecrantz: collapsible chair from the *Bygg* collection (1967), manufactured by Lammhults Mekaniska, Sweden
Mikael Lofstrom: cupboard (1989)
Marie Norell: armchair, *Aten* (1990), manufactured by Skandi-Form, Sweden
Viveka Nygren: tapestry, *Vit vav* (1982); tapestry, *28.2 Morgon* (1986)
Gunvor Olin-Gronqvist: onion-shaped porcelain/stoneware (1988), manufactured by Arabia, Finland
Eva Rodenius: tapestry, *Speldosen* (1989)
Frederick Scott: chair, model *LWB ASC* from the *Supporto* series (1979), manufactured by Hille Ergonom, London
Max Walter Svanberg: tapestry, *Hjulspar. Hommage à Rimbaud* (1976), manufactured by Handarvetets Vanner, Sweden
Mats Theselius: armchair (1990), manufactured by Källemo, Sweden

Röhsska Konstslöjdmuseet, Göteborg
Åke Axelsson: chair, *Hellas* (1978), manufactured by Åke Axelsson, Sweden; chair, *Vaxholmaren* (1978), manufactured by Garsnas, Sweden; chair, *Plywood* (1990), manufactured by Proform Möbel, Sweden
Ulla Bodin: textile/fabric (1990), manufactured by Almedahls, Sweden
Thomas Brolin: textile/fabric (1990), manufactured by Kinnasand, Sweden
Wanja Djanajeff: textile/fabric (1990), manufactured by Almedahls, Sweden
Lena Fransson: textile/fabric (1988–89), manufactured by Kinnasand, Sweden
Shihoko Fukumoto: wall-hanging, *Shibori* (1980s)
Birgitta Hahn: textile/fabric (1989), manufactured by Ljungbergs Textiltryk, Sweden
Hertha Hillfon: cupboard (1990)
Fujiwo Ishimoto: textile/fabric (1986–88), manufactured by Marimekko Oy, Finland
Leo Johannsson: chair, *Diabas* (1988), manufactured by Eje Ström, Sweden
Christopher Jonsson: bowl (1988)
Mikael Löfström: cupboard (1989)
Staffan Nilsson: plate (1989)
Barbro Peterson: textile/fabric (1990), manufactured by Kinnasand, Sweden
Ritva Puotila: rug, *Autumn* (1980s); rug, *Woodnotes* (1980s)
Glenn Roll: bowl with cover (1989)
Sandin & Bülow Design: trolley, *Supporter*, manufactured by Akuma, Sweden
Philippe Starck: chair, *Café Costers MAH* (1982), manufactured by Driade, Italy
Mats Theselius: easy chair (1990), manufactured by Källemo, Sweden

UK

The Design Museum, London
James Dyson: vacuum cleaner, *G Force Cyclonic* (1986), manufactured by Alco International, Japan
Canon: still video camera, *Q-Pic RC-250* (1989); lap-top computer, *A1 Note IN 300* (1990)
Ninaber, Peters & Krouwel: child's car seat, *Bobob*

(1983); child's car seat, *Baby Bob* (1990), both manufactured by Dremefa
Nissan: van, *S-Cargo* (1988)
Olympus: camera, *Q-product* (1989)
Porsche Design: washing machine, *Supernova* (1989), manufactured by Eummenia Eudorawerke
Praktica: camera, *BMS* (1990)
Paul Priestman: Belling cooker, *series 325* (1990)
Sanyo: washing machine, *Singles* (1989)
Yamaha: Astarte/Tiffany stereo system *AST-C30* (1990)

Victoria and Albert Museum, London
No acquisitions were made by the furniture department during the last year. The ceramic and glass department acquired a large range of commemorative and topical mugs, and works including the following:
Maryse Boxer: tableware items from the *Dorado* range (1988); earthenware plate, *Rainbow Heart* (1989), both manufactured by Honiton Pottery; tableware items from the *Nautilus* range (1989), manufactured by Fez Cocema
Michael Casson: vase, *Swimmers*
Ken Eastman: pot (1989)
Gutte Eriksen: stoneware vase (1981)
Colin Gory: stoneware jug (1990)
T. G. Green: TV cup and plate, *Safari* (1960s)
Henry Hammond: stoneware bowl (1980)
Queensbury Hunt: earthenware bread bin and cover (1984), manufactured by Henry Watson Potteries (1990)
Danny Lane: glass chair (1986)
John Maltby: earthenware tankard (1990)
William Marshall: stoneware jug (1985)
Sarah McDonald: glass bowl (1990)
Simon Moore: vase (1987); two branch glass candelabra (1990–91)
Ridgway Pottery: tableware from the *Homemaker* range (1991)
Bernard Rooke: stoneware vase (1965–70)
Timo Sarpaneva: candle, *Timotei* (1967), manufactured by Juhava Oy; candles, *Temple, Ball, Raita* and *Baroque* (1963–1980)
Laurence Simon: candlestick, *Goat* (1991)
Peter Starkey: stoneware jar and cover (1970)
Angus Suttie: vase, *Large Blue Form no. 23* (1989)
Jaroslav Svoboda: medallion and box (1989), manufactured by Skrdlovice Glassworks
Susan Williams Ellis: cheese cover, *Talisman* (1960s), manufactured by Portmeirion

USA

The Art Institute of Chicago
Michael Banner: teapot and tea caddy (1989)
Wendell Castle: chest of drawers (1980)
Robert Davis: salt and pepper set, *Symetra* (1989)
Michele Oka Doner: chair, *Dialogic: Silver* (1991)
David Ebner: bench (1990)
Gregg Fleishmann: chairs, *Surround* and *Raleigh Side Chair* (both 1990)
Frank Gehry: chair, *Easy Edges* (1972 and 1982)
Curtis Lafollette: box with cover (1987)
Randy Long: *Hsing Teapot* (1986)
Richard Meier: armchair (1982)
Howard Meister: bench, *The Kata* (1989)
Brian Murphy: picket fence table (1990)
Henry Petzal: salver (1973)
Richard Snyder: chest of drawers, *Cabinet of Four Wishes* (1990)
Leonard Urso: goblet (1988)
Robert Wilson: chair, *Parzival, a Chair with a Shadow* (1987)

Cooper-Hewitt Museum, New York
Hiroshi Awatsuji: three plates (1988), manufactured by Nikko Company, Japan
Mario Barbaglia and Marco Colombo: lamp, *Edipo* (1990), manufactured by PAF, Italy
Michele Oka Doner: *Oka Chair* (1989)
Bibs Hosak-Robb: set of cutlery, *Edo*, manufactured by Robbe and Berking, Germany
Takenobu Igarashi: stool (1989), manufactured by Yamada Shomei Lighting Co., Japan
Lisa Krohn: wrist computer (1988)

Franz Lipp: set of cutlery (1989), manufactured by WMF, Germany
Carlo Moretti Studio: six stemmed glasses from the *Calici Natale 1990* series
Ferdinand Alexander Porsche: desk lamp, *Jazz*, manufactured by PAF, Italy
Philippe Starck: toothbrush and holder (1990), manufactured by Fluocaril, France
Matteo Thun: set of cutlery, *Park Avenue* (1990), manufactured by WMF, Germany

Denver Art Museum, Colorado
Gijs Bakker: chair, *Strip* (1974), manufactured by Castelijn
Michele De Lucchi: armchair, *First* (1983), manufactured by Memphis Milano
Daniel T. Ebihara: Lamp, *Maya* (1984), manufactured by Gallery 91
Eli Elysée: armchair (1990)
Rudolf Staffel: vessel, *Light Gatherer* (1986–88)
Shozo Toyohisa: cutlery, *Nóbile* (1987)
Masanori Umeda: cup and saucer, *Cerenova* (1983), manufactured by Yamaka International
Massimo and Lella Vignelli: tumblers and stemware (1979), manufactured by Venini

Metropolitan Museum of Art, New York
Concetta Mason: vessel, *Tribal Passage* (1985)
George Ranalli: side chair, *Valentine No. 2* (1988)
Jane Reumert: vessel, *No. 5 Feather Pattern* (1989), manufactured by Schlumberger
Ettore Sottsass: dinnerware, *Renaissance* (1986), manufactured by Swid Powell
Lella and Massimo Vignelli: decanter, *Brocchetta Rigata* (1971), manufactured by San Lorenzo

Museum of Art, Los Angeles
Charles Eames: sofa no. 3473 (1869), manufactured by Herman Miller Inc.
Quincy Jones: custom sofa for Spencer House, Los Angeles (1960)

Museum of Modern Art, New York
Olga de Amaral: wall hanging, *Rios 5* (1990)
Maria Benktzon, Hakan Bergkvist and Sven-Eric Juhlin: feeding utensils (1988), manufactured by RFSU Rehab, Sweden
Susan Berger: *Soft Chair* (1967), manufactured by Victoria-Werke, Switzerland
David Bush, Brain Lepine and Michael Zimmerman: electric violin, *Amazing*, manufactured by Bridges Musical Instruments, Canada
Canon Company Design: camera, *Photura* (1989), manufactured by Canon Inc., Japan
Robin Chu, Jack Daly and Christopher Loew: portable computer, *Gridpad* (1988), manufactured by Grid Systems Corp., California
Jim Gentes: bicycle racing helmets, *Aerohead* and *Air Attack* (1988), manufactured by Giro, USA
Bo Hansen: wrist-watch (1990), manufactured by Piquot-Meridian (International), Switzerland
IBM Company Design: solid logic technology module (1964); monolithic systems technology module (1969–70); large scale integration module, *Duchess Module* (1973); 33 sheets of ceramic substrate, unfixed (1981); two ceramic substrates, in fixed state (1981), manufactured by IBM, New York
Arne Jacobsen: sugar bowl and creamer (1964–67), manufactured by Stelton, Denmark
Hiroaki Kozu: speaker system (1989), manufactured by Yamaha Corp., Japan
David Lewis: video cassette recorder (1989), manufactured by Bang & Olufsen, Denmark
Steve McGugan: headphones (1984), manufactured by Bang & Olufsen, Denmark

Philadelphia Museum of Art
David Pye: bowl (1975–87)

The adult language learner

A guide to good teaching practice

edited by

Lore Arthur and Stella Hurd

Illustrations by Caroline Mortlock

C*i*LT

The views expressed in this book are those of the editors and contributors and do not necessarily reflect the views of CILT.

Acknowledgements

Photographs on the cover and in the book with kind permission of the Brasshouse Centre, Birmingham.

It has not been possible in all cases to trace copyright-holders; the publishers would be glad to hear from any such unacknowledged copyright-holder.

First published 1992
Reprinted 1993
Copyright © 1992 Centre for Information on Language Teaching and Research
ISBN 1 874016 30 5

Cover by Logos Design Associates
Printed in Great Britain by The Alden Press

Published by Centre for Information on Language Teaching and Research, 20 Bedfordbury, Covent Garden, London WC2N 4LB.

Contents